UNICORN DREAMS

AMBER STRYKER

Copyright © 2023 Amber Stryker
All rights reserved
First Edition

PAGE PUBLISHING
Conneaut Lake, PA

First originally published by Page Publishing 2023

ISBN 979-8-88654-991-1 (pbk)
ISBN 979-8-88654-990-4 (digital)

Printed in the United States of America

To Opsie,

A wonderful mechanic + friend

Thank you for your kindness over the years.

Gratefully,
Arlene Sptikas a.k.a Amber Stryker

To my husband, Bill, and my parents, Josephine and Al. Although you are no longer in this world, you live on in my heart. And to my uncle Skip, whose unflagging kindness and wisdom are so important to this grateful niece.

Contents

Acknowledgments vii
Introduction ix
Prologue xi

Chapter 1:   A Deathbed Reconciliation 1
Chapter 2:   A Match Made in England, Not Heaven 7
Chapter 3:   A Very Strange Greek Wake 14
Chapter 4:   Big Al's Little Girl 24
Chapter 5:   A Match Made in Queenstown, Still Not Heaven 35
Chapter 6:   Christmas in Camelot 45
Chapter 7:   Family Relationships Strengthened 55
Chapter 8:   Rum-Running in Suffolk County 64
Chapter 9:   An Alien Invasion 73
Chapter 10: Teddy Busby, Bon Vivant 81
Chapter 11: Pygmalion 89
Chapter 12: New York! New York! 98
Chapter 13: An Elizabethan Costume Party 109
Chapter 14: Goodbye, Dear Friends, Goodbye 119
Chapter 15: Uncle Theo's Den of Delights 128
Chapter 16: Touring Suffolk County 135
Chapter 17: The Stock Market Crash 143
Chapter 18: Depression in the Nation and at Home 151
Chapter 19: Family Upheaval 159
Chapter 20: Hell Hath No Fury 168
Chapter 21: Nuptials at Joyeuse Garde 176
Chapter 22: Medical School 184
Chapter 23: Bearding the Lion in Her Den 193
Chapter 24: From Criminal to Hero 202
Chapter 25: An Unexpected Visitor 211
Chapter 26: The British Isles 220

Chapter 27: There's No Place like Home! 232
Chapter 28: The Circle of Life 242
Chapter 29: Reminiscences 251
Chapter 30: Better Times 260
Chapter 31: Unicorn Dreams..268

Epilogue 281

Acknowledgments

In 1994, a very brave lady, Lissa Shaw, who wrote a column, A Word of Advice, for *This Week Publications* asked her readers to send in any unpublished manuscripts and said she would critique them free of charge. She had no idea that she would receive hundreds of manuscripts. Weeks later, she sent me a very complimentary letter praising *Unicorn Dreams* as the best of the manuscripts that she had received and urging me to publish it. True to her word, she went into detail in her praise of the manuscript, which she critiqued. I have tried to track her down but have been unsuccessful. Ms. Shaw, I thanked you forty years ago and want to do so again.

I want to thank my literary development agent from Page Publishing. He was presented with a torn cardboard box containing a yellowing manuscript that was liberally sprinkled with Wite-Out, which he had to present to his vetting team for publication consideration.

Mostly, I want to thank my publication coordinator for her patience and sweet disposition even when the arduous editing process strained my tolerance and made me want to throw in the towel.

Introduction

The manuscript for *Unicorn Dreams* was written forty years ago. It was a laborious task. It was typed on a manual typewriter, and the research was precomputer, which meant going to the library and actually reading books and taking copious notes by hand. There was no autocorrect, and the editors had their work cut out for them.

Of course, forty years later, my writing style has changed; and I would have eliminated so many quotes. I remember the challenge of finding a pertinent quote for each chapter. I considered making those changes but decided to leave things as I originally wrote them out of respect for my younger enthusiastic self. Being an English literature major, I had an idea that there was a quote that I had in the back of my mind but had to pore through numerous poetry books until I found it. Now I am too lazy for so much hard work. The research was extensive, and I tried very hard to find facts that would interest my readers. I attempted to encapsulate each decade with information that was glossed over in school and was relevant to the lives of the characters.

The title, *Unicorn Dreams,* refers to any goal that we set for ourselves that seems to be out of reach. Most of the characters in the book, like most of us in real life, have these goals. Some of these people are able to achieve their goals on their own or with the help of others, but for some, these goals or dreams remain as elusive as the capture of a unicorn.

To my readers, as you journey through life, I hope that you are all able to achieve your unicorn dreams.

Please look for my second novel, *Catherine, Child of the Night.* It is an adventurous, titillating historic romance set in the time of King Edward II of England.

Prologue

> We caught the beast called Unicorn,
> Who knows and loves a maiden best,
> And falls asleep upon her breast.
> —von Eschenbach, 1980

The older I become, the more convinced I am that the passage of time tends to transform the rare and extraordinary into the commonplace.

While I have managed to adapt myself to rocket ships and moonwalks, the sight of so many unicorns on the shelves of department stores and in the pages of numerous catalogs fills me with amazement. Yes, unicorns! Those mysterious creatures, whom only the pure of heart could hope to capture, are now being clutched between the grubby paws of my two-year-old granddaughter in the form of something called soft sculpture. Another unfortunate beast is owned by her not-so-virginal seventeen-year-old cousin in the form of a china music box that plays, appropriately, "The Impossible Dream."

However, if one really reflects on this phenomenon (and at seventy years of age, what else have I to do?), perhaps it really isn't so extraordinary after all. In a time of double-digit inflation, Son of Sam, and the Ayatollah Khomeini, it certainly is a pleasant change of pace to contemplate those delightfully innocent and carefree creatures known as unicorns.

Actually, unicorns are not something new to my family. My own introduction to those fabulous creatures goes back over fifty years and calls to mind memories that have long lain dormant—memories of another creature equally delightful but as to carefree or innocent...well, that's something I've never really decided.

CHAPTER 1

A Deathbed Reconciliation

> I met a lady in the meads,
>   Full beautiful—a fairy's child,
> Her hair was long, her foot was light,
>   And her eyes were wild.
> —Keats, 1926

"Do you really think that she'll come?" Marcie asked in wide-eyed astonishment and then proceeded to answer her own question (a habit that even after over thirty years of marriage, she would never overcome). "Yes, I'm sure she will. She probably hopes to plead a deathbed reconciliation with your father and be remembered in his will. I can just see her now, kneeling at his bedside, tears rolling down her cheeks as she confesses her guilt in causing the rift between your father and brother for the past thirteen years," she continued in her best dramatic fashion.

"Well, Arthur did say that he was probably bringing her today. Although if her motives are what you suggest, it won't do her any good now that Father's in a semicoma. I doubt if he'll even know she's there. As for the will, there's not going to be any large estate, and it's bound to all be left to Mother anyway," I confidently stated.

"How can you say that, Edward? Everyone knows that Andros's Emporium is a legend in Queenstown. She probably can't wait to try and get her greedy little hands on the store. She sounds just awful!"

"Who told you that she's awful? The family never even mentions her name. Don't tell me that Mother actually discussed Alissa with you!"

"Well, not really, but everyone in town talks about how awful she's been to your family. Why I'm surprised that she even has the nerve to show her face here! By the way, talking about faces, what does she look like?"

"How should I know? The last time I'm supposed to have seen her was when I was three years old. That was right before she and Arthur left Queenstown. Mother's description of Alissa wasn't too encouraging, but remember, that was thirteen years ago when Alissa was only fifteen years of age and Mother's not exactly unprejudiced."

"Well, what was your mother's description?"

"She said that Alissa was rather short, with what Mother describes as 'a stocky peasant's build.' She also was supposed to have a bad complexion and unstylishly long and tightly curled hair."

"In other words, your mother feels that she's short, fat, pimply, frizzy-haired, and with a barracuda's personality to boot. What a mess! What in the world did your brother Arthur ever see in her?"

What indeed did Arthur ever see in Alissa? A question that had haunted my family for thirteen long years. Why would a seemingly normal young man of almost nineteen years of age, the eldest son and heir to a successful family business, choose to alienate himself from his family for all those years? Thirteen years of absolutely no communication. Was it really, as everyone suspects, Alissa's instigation that led to the rift, or was it, in fact, Arthur's own decision? I wonder if I'd ever know the whole story.

Marcie couldn't understand why I'd never insisted that Mother or Father should answer my questions. In truth, I'd never given it much thought. I didn't remember my brother Arthur from when I was three years old, except as a vague memory of a kinder, gentler presence than my brothers Richard and John. Someone younger and more tolerant than my father. Someone who picked me up and comforted me when John, four years my senior, knocked me down or when Richard, twelve years my senior, had no time for my incessant questions. I did remember a sort of void in my young life that could have taken place when he left home, but the ensuing thirteen years made a stranger of him.

introduced to Alissa, Marcie was to race back to Father's room and sound the warning, enabling Mother and company to shore up all possible defenses against the advancing enemy. Needless to say, like all carefully formulated plans, it was a total flop.

I could not, in good conscience, really blame Marcie for failing to implement her part of the plan. Arthur and Alissa had already left the crowded elevator and advanced halfway down the corridor before I realized that they had passed by me. Finally recognizing the back of my dark, slender, debonair brother, from among the various posteriors facing me, I grabbed Marcie's hand and very unceremoniously ran after them. For the gamin-faced, sylphlike Marcie, this was no problem, but trying to propel inconspicuously and, above all, quietly my six-foot rather overweight self with all possible speed and decorum was another story.

The surprise on the faces of Arthur and Alissa as they turned to investigate the thudding sounds behind them could never compare with the totally thunderstruck faces of Marcie and myself when we saw Alissa. Instead of the gorgon that we were expecting, a very attractive, slender, poised young woman with long reddish brown hair and the biggest green eyes I had ever seen turned a startled and somewhat amused expression on the pair of red-faced hoydens advancing on them.

Graciously acknowledging Arthur's introductions to us, Alissa expressed sincere sorrow over my father's illness while I stood tongue-tied and gauche. She then complimented me on my pretty girlfriend, thereby winning Marcie's eternal gratitude and devotion. (It didn't take much with Marcie.)

The crowd of morbidly curious spectators, who couldn't all fit into Father's small room, parted like the Red Sea before Moses, creating a direct path to Father's bed beside which Mother was seated. Needless to say, never having received her promised warning, Mother was quite dumbfounded when Arthur and Alissa walked in. Keeping her eyes riveted to Father, Alissa took his hand and spoke to him in a voice so low that even Mother, to her great consternation, couldn't hear what was said.

While Alissa and Mother avoided each other's eyes, Mother shot venomous accusatory looks at her two delinquent advance scouts, who had left only minutes before overflowing with hatred and vengeance for that bane of her existence, only to return looking guilty and abashed. Marcie, whose big brown eyes stared at Alissa with slobbering devotion, especially incensed Mother. While I was, at worst, an abject failure, Marcie—poor, perfidious fool—was Judas Iscariot personified.

Having arrived late, the bell signaling the end of visiting hours soon rang. Alissa, probably hoping for a quick retreat, said goodbye to Father, promising to return soon; smiled at the family and spectators; avoided looking at Mother; and started to leave only to be held up by my dense brother Arthur, who was politely waiting for Mother to precede him from the room.

As the tension built between the two antagonists, side bets were being placed on which one would finally break the silence. It was ultimately Mother, otherwise known as Eleanor Etiquette to her family that model of British dignity and "good form," who grandly walked up to Alissa, looked her straight in the eye, and said, "Well, I'm glad to see that you've finally lost some weight!"

Chapter 2

A Match Made in England, Not Heaven

And o'er the hills, and far away,
Beyond their utmost purple rim,
Beyond the night, across the day,
Through all the world she followed him.
—Tennyson

Father's death two days later prevented Alissa from keeping her promise to see him again, and to do her justice, this was the only promise I would ever know her to break.

No matter how we try to prepare ourselves, death, when it strikes, was always devastating. It must be true that hope springs eternal in man, or why would the loved ones of the suffering mourn when the pain was finally ended? Many times during the final stages of Father's illness, when he would drift in and out of a coma, we would find ourselves desperately listening for a heartbeat. We would all wait with bated breath, each of us feeling the actual physical pain of tight chests and sinking stomachs that accompany such great apprehension. When the person seeking this very faint life sign finally discovered it, we would all breathe a collective sigh of relief.

I believe the person whom we actually mourn for was ourselves. Could we, in all honesty, say that we were selflessly thinking of the person who died? Did we cry by proxy, so to speak, because the deceased couldn't cry for the cessation of his life, the loss of all his unfulfilled hopes and aspirations? Well, perhaps to some degree, we did, but the person we were most concerned with when we mourn was ourselves. Death was so powerful that it could penetrate the protective armor of proper social conduct that we would usually don. Instead of putting the other person first, in our weakened state, we thought only of the great "I"—"I will miss him," "What will I do without him?" or the totally absurd "How could he leave me all alone?" implying some choice or the fulfillment of a spiteful vendetta on the part of the deceased.

Guilt also reared its ugly head during these times. The occasions when we were unjust, impatient, or caused pain or disappointment would suddenly color our entire relationship with the departed. These were the things in the forefront of our minds and memories as we recited our mea culpas, whether justified or not.

As was to be expected, Mother was devastated by Father's death. She was literally prostrate with grief and couldn't rouse herself to take care of any of the arrangements. Although they had not lived in connubial bliss, a partnership of almost thirty years was not easily dissolved.

Father had been born sixty-two years ago on the island of Somos, off the coast of Greece. Growing up in abject poverty gave him the incentive to seek new horizons. At the age of thirteen, he started his first business by selling sponges to the tourists who disembarked in Athens. Since the sponges were free to anyone who bothered to gather them, he earned a 100 percent profit. Having a good head for business, he soon hired his brother and some local boys to widen his trade to include the larger Athenian agoras or marketplaces. By careful observation, he soon learned what goods and assorted handicrafts were most in demand. He continued with his enterprise until he was twenty years old.

In 1884, one of the numerous wars broke out between the Greek and Turkish factions on Somos. Being good patriots, he and his brother Theo were soon involved in arms smuggling to help the badly outnumbered Greeks. During one of their forays, a very important Turkish official was killed. When the Turks discovered who was responsible, the small farm owned by the Andros family was razed, and the parents and sisters of Demetrius and Theo were publicly executed. With a price on their heads and their family dead, the two brothers fled back to Athens where they decided to put their pasts behind them and try their luck in England where several friends of theirs had disembarked some years before.

By the time he reached England, Demetrius was twenty-three and his brother was two years his junior. When after a long and extremely uncomfortable voyage, they landed in Blackpool; problems immediately beset them. Demetrius, who was of medium height and a slight build with wavy black hair and dark eyes, wanted to open some sort of shop. Theo, six feet tall and of a very large build, was not only a voracious eater; he was also an extremely good cook. Since Blackpool was a seaside resort, Theo rightly believed that a Greek restaurant would do very well since the town attracted many foreign sailors. Even the staid British might like to try something different in the way of culinary pleasures when they were on holiday. While Demetrius had little doubt of his brother's eventual success, he refused to get involved in a business where his role would be a little better than a waiter or busboy. Thus, the brothers shook hands and went their separate ways.

In 1893, twenty-two-year-old Eleanor Busby—accompanied by her father, stepmother, and seven-year-old half brother—was vacationing in Blackpool. Being a headstrong and impetuous girl, she received very little chaperonage from her stepmother, Emma, who was only ten years her senior. In truth, Emma had secret nightmares about being saddled with a spinster stepdaughter. Eleanor was really getting on in years and showing no interest in her suitors. Indeed, the foolish girl was actually openly hostile to them! As is too often the case, the relationship between the stepmother and stepdaughter was a very uneasy one. Emma only tolerated Eleanor's presence on their vacations so she could serve as a babysitter for her half brother, Teddy, for whom she showed genuine affection.

It was, in fact, Teddy who would be instrumental in bringing together Demetrius and Eleanor. Being attracted by a handsome marine window display in Demetrius's shop, Teddy dragged Eleanor in to purchase a souvenir for their father. The effect of the ruggedly good-looking Demetrius on that fair English rose Eleanor was tremendous.

Having decided long ago that British men were "weak milk and water," Eleanor had always, to her father's consternation, been attracted to foreigners and even more so to those of Mediterranean descent. The two young lovers soon began arranging secret assignations, which young Teddy was only too happy to facilitate since he saw the whole thing as "jolly good fun."

Like most secrets, this affair was soon unearthed by Eleanor's outraged father. Being a successful London banker, Danial Busby was appalled by the unsuitability of his prospective son-in-law, who was not only a shopkeeper but a foreigner as well! Knowing his chances of changing his daughter's mind about the match were hopeless and since she was well past legal age, as his wife was only too eager to point out, he agreed to help them if they would leave England and emigrate to America so that his London associates wouldn't discover the mésalliance.

Demetrius, who was never loathed to embark on a new adventure, agreed and, except for the sorrow of parting with Theo, was glad to put England behind him. He had never really liked the English whom he felt to be cold, conceited people who looked down their long noses at foreigners. America, with its melting pot, had always intrigued the warmhearted Demetrius. The few Americans, whom he had come in contact with, had greatly appealed to his democratic senses. He admired their hearty friendliness and felt them to be quite a cut above their British cousins. Thus, the Androses arrived in America where they were put in contact with business associates of Danial's who lived in Queenstown, New York.

Andros's Emporium was soon established and flourished under Demetrius's shrewd management. Again, using his instincts for market research, he discovered exactly what was needed by that little community and provided it at a fair price. When people left Demetrius's store, they felt good. His natural amiability and compassion along with a very good memory served to ingratiate him to his customers. He never failed to inquire after an ailing family member and often added, free of charge, some special treat for the invalid. If a farmer needed a special piece of equipment in a hurry, he could depend on Demetrius not only finding the equipment but also often delivering it gratis during sowing or harvesting season. Demetrius had long ago discovered the secret that if you care about people, they would, in turn, care about you—if only for what they consider your good taste in liking them.

Eleanor was not quite the social success that Demetrius was. Being a very private person, she kept to herself and had as little as possible to do with her neighbors whose egalitarian beliefs shocked her. In England, everyone knew his place, but in America, ideas were very different, and so she determined to make the store, her home, and her family a complete enough world in themselves. Declaring American household help to be "incompetent snoops" with ideas above themselves, Eleanor did most of the housework herself in the two-story, nine-room brick house. She also, despite her husband's objections, often worked as a cashier at the emporium because she always suspected that the "help" was cheating them.

As Demetrius prospered, he never forgot his little village on the island of Somos and, indeed, did a great deal of good through his financial support. As was usually true in small isolated villages, most of the inhabitants were related in one way or another. Demetrius was personally responsible for providing the necessary funds for the careers of several local boys as doctors and lawyers. His contributions helped enlarge the school and build a small but modern hospital. He was the godfather to countless namesakes and was regarded as a local hero by the people of Somos.

Having somehow kept these contributions a secret from his wife, whom he knew would resent them, it was quite a surprise to Eleanor upon accompanying her husband on a visit to Somos to discover his celebrity status. Having always heard of the great beauty of the Greek islands, Eleanor was looking forward to the trip. Whatever Eleanor might have been expecting, she was not prepared for Somos!

The sea voyage to Athens was a trial for Eleanor who did not prove to be a good sailor and was seasick the whole time. The beauty of Athens did somewhat alleviate her consternation. The Parthenon and other historic sights restored her enthusiasm while the sun and clean salt air restored her color and health. Her impatient husband was soon enough to dispel Eleanor's newfound contentment by reminding her that they must embark for Somos which was, of course, the whole purpose of the trip.

Trying to keep a stiff upper lip, Eleanor allowed herself to be put aboard a small foul-smelling fishing boat, which would transport them to the island. This voyage made up in roughness what it lacked in duration, and a very sick Eleanor disembarked on the island.

Having, of course, heard about how quickly military control of the island could change hands between Greeks and Turks, Eleanor was terrified to see a large rough-looking mob shouting on the shore. She was certain that the threatened hanging party from the 1884 war awaited them. As her husband set foot on shore, he was immediately seized and carried out of sight among the howling masses. When someone tried to grab hold of Eleanor, she fended him off with her omnipresent British umbrella. In her terror, she began to scream. Surely, somewhere on the island was someone who could stop these barbarians from executing them!

The confused townspeople, never having had any personal contact with an Englishwoman before but having heard of them having strange customs, wanted her to feel at home, and so they also began to scream in the belief that this must be a British sign of happiness. Thus, a very strange procession entered the heart of the town. While Demetrius was being carried victoriously on the shoulders of his compatriots to be welcomed by the town elders, the rearguard consisted mostly of women and children, all smiling happily and screaming along with Eleanor, who occasionally poked with her umbrella at the hands of those who tried to touch her golden hair and stylish clothing.

It wasn't until they reached what was supposed to be a dais that Eleanor realized her husband was actually being honored and not about to be hanged from the platform. While Demetrius had warned her that the village was primitive, the dirt, flies, and poverty appalled the normally fastidious Eleanor, and the eternal black clothing of the women depressed her.

Eventually, they were led to the house of one of her husband's many cousins. House, indeed! It was a little better than a hovel! Slowly, a terrible suspicion entered Eleanor's mind. Could this shack, by any chance, be the accommodations that her husband had provided for their stay? Was it possible that there wasn't a hotel or even a small inn somewhere on this godforsaken island? What could Demetrius be thinking?

Trying to get him aside to ask these troubling questions wasn't a simple task. In true Greek macho fashion, Demetrius was systematically ignoring Eleanor. Her husband had often commented that women knew their "places" in Greek households, but prior to this, he had never been foolish enough to try and impose these antiquated customs on her. Greek women were not only not heard; they were also seen as little as possible. Their only "proper places" were in kitchens and bedrooms, and if some of the rumors which she had heard about Greek men were true, even their places in the bedrooms were not sacrosanct!

To say that Eleanor's visit to Somos was not memorable would be a terrible lie. It was, in fact, so memorable that she swore never to return, and not only did she never forget it, but she made certain that Demetrius never did either!

Chapter 3

A Very Strange Greek Wake

> There's a new foot on the floor, my friend,
> And a new face at the door, my friend,
> A new face at the door.
> —Tennyson

As was the custom in those days, Father's body was to be laid out in the parlor. This was a relatively large very formal room used only for special occasions, and since my parents seldom entertained, those occasions were few and far between.

Sadly enough, although the whole family visited Father every day, the only ones present at the time of his death were Mother and my brother John. Richard was looking after the store, and I was on my way home from school. I had just begun to wash up preparatory to leave for the hospital when a very grave-faced Richard walked in and announced the news. Since someone had to telephone Arthur, I, being the younger of the two and therefore having no say in the matter, was naturally chosen. It was Alissa who answered the phone, expressed her condolences, and promised to break the bad news to Arthur.

With Mother prostrate with grief, someone had to tend to the funeral arrangements. Never having dealt with death before or, for that matter, with much of anything else either, our attempts to assist her proved unsatisfactory. The clothing that we picked out for Father's final rest was declared by Mother to be ill-chosen and mismatched. When she hysterically discovered that she owned nothing in black that was suitable for a widow, we were totally stymied. We had no female relations whom we could call on for help, and none of the neighborhood women had ever been more than nodding acquaintances with Mother. Recognizing her very real need for the comforting presence of another woman, Mother called us all together and said with a look of desperate defeat, "Get Alissa!"

Due to our shocked disbelief, it took us a few minutes before we could rouse ourselves to carry out Mother's order. Rushing to the phone, I again called Arthur's house and explained the situation to him. We all waited in considerable anxiety for Arthur's arrival. He hadn't committed himself over the phone to his wife's coming, and since she wasn't at home to ask, we didn't know what to expect.

"I don't think I'd come if I were Alissa," I said.

"Why not?" asked the as usually naive John.

"It's not the best conditions under which to pay a visit to someone's home after thirteen years. It wouldn't have been so bad if Mother had invited her after the hospital visit, but to summon her here now…well, it just doesn't seem right."

"I wouldn't worry. She won't come anyway. Just you wait and see," added Richard.

"You said that about the hospital too and were wrong."

"This is different. She only had to make an appearance then. Now she would have to do some work, act as a hostess, and make funeral arrangements. Besides, the hospital visit was to ingratiate herself with Father, whom I don't think she ever really disliked, but this time, she'd be doing Mother a favor, and you know how she feels about Mother."

My interest heightening, I hastily added, "But I don't know how she feels about Mother."

"Well, this is no time to go into all of that," Richard said, quickly squelching any hopes I might have had of learning about the feud.

Less than two hours later, Arthur and Alissa walked in carrying numerous parcels, which Alissa explained were food and the reason for their delay. She realized that while Mother probably wasn't thinking of eating, she was sure that the rest of us were hungry. Apologizing for the hasty fare, she proceeded to set before us breaded chicken, homemade potato salad rich with hard-boiled eggs, and a cranberry sauce mold. For dessert, she carefully unwrapped a very large three-layer fudge cake that literally melted in our mouths. She told us that she had first started cooking when she heard of Father's death. (This quickly put down Richard's insinuations of leftovers.) She even had the foresight to purchase a black dress, shoes, and veil for Mother, which was what she was doing when we phoned the second time, and she only hoped that she had guessed the sizes correctly.

She then made up a tray for two and went up to Mother's room where she remained until a strange disturbance brought everyone rushing to the parlor.

About an hour after Alissa had joined Mother, the doorbell rang. It was a very irate Uncle Theo who was surreptitiously pushing something into the front hedges.

"Edward, my boy, why was I not informed of your father's death? Is not a brother to know of such things?" he complained in heavily accented English.

"Gee, Uncle Theo, in all the excitement, it slipped our minds, but it only happened a few hours ago. We would have told you, of course. How did you find out?"

"I found out from here," he said, pointing to his heart. "Does not a brother know such things? Did not my own heart also stop for a second in sympathy with my brother's heart? Did I not feel the angel of death hovering over the house of Andros? Did a shadow not pass over the sun? Did not Joseph the florist who heard it from your father's doctor just finish a late lunch in my restaurant?" sheepishly asked Uncle Theo, putting his beefy arm around my shoulders and ushering me from the front door before I could lock it.

Moving into the dining room and eyeing the fare, he quickly sat down and began piling food on an empty plate. Eating with his usual gusto, he told us the often-heard stories of his early years with Father. The fact that he was talking while eating betrayed how upset he was by Father's death. Uncle Theo usually subscribed to the philosophy that talk confused the taste buds, which must, like all great artists, have silence for their work.

Appreciatively licking the last crumb of chocolate cake from his fork, Uncle Theo looked solemnly at us and announced, "All your troubles are over for I, Uncle Theo, have brought you a present—and no cracks from you, young Edward, about Greeks bearing gifts."

"Is that what you were shoving in the bushes?"

"Ah, you saw that! Such an observant boy! Wait here while I fetch it."

This took longer than we expected. Since Alissa had sent Arthur on some sort of errand, he had not eaten yet, so I decided to occupy myself with straightening out the table while we all tried not to look too apprehensively at each other, awaiting Uncle Theo's return. As I was clearing away Uncle Theo's used plates, the most unearthly shriek rented the air. It was a sound so inhuman as to actually make the hairs on the backs of our necks stand up and our blood run cold. Worst of all, it seemed to be coming from the parlor where Father's body was laid out. As we all ran in, the most horrible sight met our eyes. A black figure stood eerily in the flickering candlelight, rocking over Father's corpse and continuing the high keening sound.

Spotting Uncle Theo, Richard grabbed him and yelled, "My god! What is it?" while John and I, paralyzed with fear, watched the macabre tableau.

Before Uncle Theo could answer, Mother and Alissa raced downstairs.

"Oh no! It's the devil himself coming to take your poor father. I warned him about treating me so shabbily," Mother hysterically moaned.

"Don't be ridiculous, Mother," consoled Richard. "There must be a more logical explanation."

"Yeah, maybe it's the angel of death Uncle Theo was talking about," John added, being, as usual, no help at all and making Mother scream even louder.

"Why it's a professional mourner! How unique!" exclaimed Alissa, looking with interest at the wailing figure.

"Exactly, my dear," said a very gratified Uncle Theo. "And whom might this vision of loveliness be?"

"Let me introduce you to Arthur's wife, Alissa, Uncle Theo," I helpfully added.

"Ah, Alissa with an A, no doubt. What else would a woman with not only the beauty of Aphrodite but also the wisdom of Athena be called? Somehow you don't look like what I thought you would," he added, shooting a direct look at Mother, who had the grace to blush.

"She's lost some weight," Mother answered defensively.

"Of course! That would account for it," he quipped, winking at Alissa.

"This is my gift to you, Eleanor, and to my brother," he said, pointing to the mourner. "No true Greek can die without one."

"Your brother managed very nicely."

"This is no time for levity, Eleanor," Uncle Theo said, looking wounded. "What I mean, of course, is that the professional mourner makes certain that the dearly departed leaves this vale of tears for the glories of the afterlife."

"That I can believe. Even a dead person couldn't stay in a room with all that racket. In self-defense, they would be forced to leave."

Leading us back into the dining room, Uncle Theo turned his attention back to Alissa. "I have heard, fair lady, that you visited Demetrius in the hospital. It was good of you—all things considered."

"Well, by the time I arrived, Demetrius was already in a semi-coma, so I don't really know if he was aware of my presence."

"Have no fear! He knew you were there. If such a vision of female loveliness could not rouse a Greek man from his deathbed, then what could?"

"A pretty boy, perhaps?" suggested Mother.

With a look of exaggerated pain, Uncle Theo remonstrated. "Eleanor, what causes you to say such unkind things about your husband's countrymen? Ever since I gave her a book to read entitled *The Rites and Customs of Ancient Greece*, Alissa, she makes these horrible insinuations about me. Considering how many children she's had, although five of the poor little souls did not survive infancy, I don't think she has a legitimate reason to complain about my brother."

"Who's talking about Demetrius? But I notice you never got married, Theo."

"Ah, alas, that is true. When I was in England, I did not want to form any close attachments. All I wanted was to save enough money to come to America and maybe open a restaurant not too far from my only surviving brother. 'Maybe,' I said, 'I will marry an American flipper.'"

"Flapper," Mother corrected with disgust.

"Yes, but when I arrived here only five years ago, the sight which I beheld upon visiting my dear Demetrius was hardly conducive to emulation."

"Why you—"

"Tut! Tut! Eleanor, do remember your splendid English upbringing."

Just then, to everyone's relief, Arthur walked in.

"Arthur, my boy!" Uncle Theo rushed up to Arthur, enveloped him in a great bear hug, and kissed him smack on the lips.

"See what I mean?" Mother, smiling with satisfaction, asked Alissa.

In consternation, Arthur glanced quickly at Alissa, who had put a hand over her mouth trying to hold in the laughter which already had her body shaking convulsively.

As Uncle Theo seated Arthur at the table, he began to fill two plates with food. Seeing my surprised expression, he explained, "Ah, you forget that Arthur has not eaten yet, and no one likes to eat alone, so I do him the honor of joining him."

Just as Arthur was about to take his first bite, the wailing started again. "Relax, my boy, that is a professional mourner—my gift to your father. She must have stopped when you arrived to umm…ah, you know, relieve herself," Uncle Theo said, face reddening with embarrassment.

"What! Relieve herself, where?"

"What an excitable family! Relax, Eleanor. I showed her where the downstairs bathroom was when we first arrived and the entrance through the kitchen. Naturally, she would not have had to pass us in here. What in the world were you thinking of?"

"You're forgetting that I once visited Somos!"

"So it's a little primitive there."

"Is that where you got her from, Uncle Theo?"

He then went on to explain how upon first hearing of Father's mortal illness, Uncle Theo had arranged with his hometown on Somos to have their best mourner and a Greek priest, who spoke some English, shipped to the States. There had been a few problems, however, with the other passengers on the ship, who became frightened whenever Mrs. Popoulandropos, the professional mourner, would practice. After some negotiation between the priest and the captain, it was decided that Mrs. Popoulandropos would ride in steerage where she couldn't annoy anyone and would also entitle Uncle Theo to a substantial refund.

"Well, at least she would have felt at home in steerage," quipped Mother.

Refusing to acknowledge this last bit of sarcasm, Uncle Theo merely agreed. "Right you are, Eleanor. There was even a special breed of goats being shipped over. Being a shepherd's wife, Mrs. Popoulandropos did, indeed, feel at home camping among them."

"She smells like it!"

"Now, now, Eleanor, that is unkind. She has been off the ship for two weeks."

"Do you mean, Uncle Theo, that this woman has been living in your house alone with you for the past two weeks?"

"Only on and off, Arthur, my boy. As the name implies, my village of Athens Cove has a pretty large Greek population, and I have been able to rent her out for various funerals. To keep her in good form, of course," he added quickly, turning a guilty face away from Mother.

"And to earn you a nice profit to boot!"

"I only wanted her at her best for my brother Demetrius. Nothing is too good or too much trouble for an Andros!"

"Hmph!"

Turning with exasperation from Mother, Uncle Theo began complimenting Alissa on her good cooking. "But, dear child, do not trouble yourself further. Did you not know that I, Theophilus Andros, am the proud owner of Delphi's Oracle, that renowned establishment of exotic Olympian culinary delight?"

"Gee, Uncle Theo, you make it sound like a bawdy house," piped in John.

"What? I said exotic, not erotic, you nitwit! Besides, one does not speak of such things in the presence of ladies," he said, pointedly ignoring Mother and leering at Alissa.

"Tomorrow, sweet Aphrodite, we will feast on moussaka, spanakopita, pastitsio, and, as the pièce de résistance, my own baklava so thick with walnuts and honey that your mouth will water," he stated as Mother's fork shot out like lightning to intercept Uncle Theo, who was about to snatch the remaining potato salad.

Clutching his hand and muttering about British hospitality, Uncle Theo continued to compare notes with Alissa, who had a great interest in ethnic cooking.

"Had I known of your fine culinary skill, Alissa, I would not have worried about providing food for Mrs. Popoulandropos for tonight, but I did promise to return her in good health, and you know what stringy roast beef and Yorkshire pudding can do to one's constitution. Pudding, indeed! Only the English could call dumplings floating around in tasteless gravy pudding. Bah!"

"If you don't mind, Theo, it's getting late, and we have a long day ahead of us tomorrow. Demetrius, having been so popular, I'm sure that many people will be calling all day," Mother coldly broke in on Uncle Theo.

Knowing that he had gone too far this time, Uncle Theo abashedly rose from the table, tried to shake hands with Mother, kissed me and my brothers, enveloped Alissa in one of his 250-pound bear hugs, and departed.

After clearing off the table and escorting Mother to bed, Alissa and Arthur prepared to go home. Although we could have found room for them to spend the night, I was to learn that Alissa never left her cat without having previously arranged for someone to feed him and then only in the direst emergency. The last time she had made such arrangements, she lost her best friend when the hungry feline dug its teeth into the calf of the tardy substitute feeder. Since that time, nobody except her parents would agree to catsit for the nasty-tempered Tippy.

*****

The next two days passed without any real problems. Every morning, Mother emerged elegantly coiffed and attired, thanks to Alissa's assistance. A myriad of mourners came to view the body, drawn in part to honor Father and also by the novelty of Mrs. Popoulandropos. Except for the occasional sarcasm between Uncle Theo and Mother, everything proceeded in a dignified and orderly fashion. Well, perhaps I should amend that in as dignified a fashion as was possible with our own resident Greek screaming banshee in the background.

The day of the funeral dawned bright and sunny as was usually the case on an early September morning. There were none of the clouds or rain that one somehow foolishly expects, as if the elements acted in conjunction with our feelings.

In addition to the elegant floral arrangement that had arrived on the day of Father's death, Alissa had brought with her several roses of Sharon, which she explained were the only flowers still in bloom in her garden.

When the family was assembled to say its final farewell to Father, as an in-law, Alissa went first. Kneeling next to Father, holding the roses, Alissa was a vision of breathtaking beauty. Expecting her to place the flowers in the coffin with Father, Uncle Theo and I looked confusedly at each other as she reached out to do so but quickly withdrew her hand and stood up, still clutching the roses.

Next came John and myself followed by Richard and Arthur. Uncle Theo came last as he escorted Mother who was, I believe, too shaken to even realize whose arm was supporting her.

I noticed a strange thing happening. At most funerals, the people, after saying goodbye, would leave the room where the coffin was and would begin the journey to the cemetery. As anyone tried to leave our parlor, one of Uncle Theo's friends would signal him to remain. Thus, the room was filled with a great many people standing perplexedly along the sides and back of the room.

The reason for the delay soon became apparent. The minute Mother rose from her knees after kissing Father goodbye, the waiting priest slammed the coffin lid down in front of everyone. This evoked a gasp of shocked surprise from the white-faced Alissa and a scream of despair from Mother, who threw herself on Father's coffin while poor Uncle Theo tried unsuccessfully to pry her loose, explaining all the while that the public closing of the coffin was also a Greek tradition.

*****

The time spent at the cemetery was mercifully brief. No sooner had we been ushered from the cars than we were rushed back in. It was only at the cemetery that Alissa finally relinquished the roses, kissing them and placing them reverently on the coffin lid. Since a friend of Uncle Theo was acting as a sort of funeral director had given everyone who went to the cemetery a rose to leave, Alissa's action confused me until she turned to me with tears in her eyes and said a little defiantly, "Mine were given with love, not just because someone handed me a flower and told me to drop it on the coffin."

After the funeral, everyone returned to Mother's house for the traditional collation in gratitude to those who had paid their final respects to Father.

When all the guests had finally departed, I asked Alissa why she hadn't left the roses in Father's coffin before we left the house. Looking up at me in embarrassment, she said, "I didn't know if it would be resented. After all, I'm not really a member of the family."

"In that case," Mother replied, kissing Alissa's cheek, "may I be the first to welcome you officially into the Andros family."

"Hear! Hear!" we all shouted, and even Richard offered no protest.

They said that life was a continuous process. Nature would never take a life away without in some way replacing it. This was a very comforting thought that I believed to be true.

For many years after Father's death, new life was to be transfused into the Andros family through the love and laughter of Alissa.

Chapter 4

Big Al's Little Girl

> But he, the favorite and the flower,
> Most cherished since his natal hour…
> My latest care, for whom I sought
> To hoard my life, that his might be
> Less wretched now, and one day free.
> —Byron

Alissa was born on September 1, 1898, in Queenstown. Being the adored only child of Gabrial, alias Big Al, and Josephine Saronna, they would see to it that everything humanly possible was done to ensure a secure future for their beloved daughter.

The oldest of seven children of Italian immigrants, Gabrial learned at an early age while growing up on the lower east side of Manhattan to use both his fists and wits to get ahead. Being an ambitious lad, he took advantage of every opportunity that presented itself to him and learned to create opportunities where formerly none existed.

The post-Civil War period was a time of great job opportunities. While working conditions were poor and wages were ridiculously low, with seven out of ten industrial workers earning no more than ten cents an hour, everyone was working together for the process of Reconstruction. As the chronicler, Franklin Welsh wrote in 1874, "Work has sometimes been called worship and the dusty, smoky workshop a temple because there, man glorifies the great architect by imitating him in providing for the wants of his creatures." Even

Grover Cleveland in 1881, when accepting the Democratic presidential nomination, praised the philosophy of hard labor for the good of mankind when he said, "Honor lies in honest toil."

It was also, however, an era which would find that a certain honor even existed in dishonest toil. Despite the reputation for propriety, which the Victorian era would always call to mind, this was also one of the most corrupt periods in history. Men like Gould, Vanderbilt, Rockefeller, and Carnegie were to amass fortunes and social prestige despite the fact that little honor could be found in their methods.

It was a time of corruption not only among the lawless but also among those who should have been upholding the law. While New York City's police chief George Walling was dubbing them "the city's finest," the police department was to come under attack by such men as Dr. Charles Parkhurst, who would go undercover to expose political and police graft. Most of the city's gambling parlors, liquor dealers, after-hour saloons, and bawdy housekeepers were to be discovered, turning over a good percentage of their profits for police protection.

The absence of child labor laws also fostered a different kind of corruption. Infamous sweatshops which employed children to do grueling labor from sunrise to sunset would be commonplace. Inhuman working conditions, inadequate lighting and ventilation, and dangerous equipment which killed and crippled thousands of people would all be overlooked by the owners, who were looking for the biggest profit for the smallest outlay. The slogan of the day was "The factories need the children, and the children need the factories."

It wasn't only in the factories that children were abused in the name of "honest toil." Almost two million children under the age of fifteen were working along with their fathers in the mines under conditions little better than those Americans were denouncing in such places as Wales.

Other children were employed on cotton and tobacco plantations, taking the places of the emancipated slaves; the only difference being that the children earned about twenty-five cents a day for the backbreaking work. In many ways, the slaves had probably been better off since most plantation owners were diligent in providing them with decent homes, food, and clothing. It wasn't unusual at this time for whole hardworking families to die of malnutrition-related illnesses or to freeze to death from not being able to purchase enough coal if an unusually cold spell occurred.

It was into this paradoxical world of hard work, Victorian prudishness, and political and economic corruption that the young Gabrial Saronna would go to make his mark. Starting as a shoeshine boy at the tender age of seven, he began his lifelong career of self-employment. His independent nature and impatience would make it difficult for him to discover his proper niche in life. From selling hot sweet potatoes and chestnuts from a cart and various other sidelines, both legal and illegal, he soon had enough money to purchase his own hackney coach and horse.

With the busy lives of New Yorkers, getting fares was no problem, and by working long hours and concentrating on the banking and commercial districts, Gabrial found himself in a very lucrative occupation. With his two younger brothers also doing well, he found his own apartment closer uptown. It was in a soda fountain near his new home that he met his future wife, Josephine Di Marto.

Josephine was the nineteen-year-old daughter of a music teacher and his ailing wife. A gentle, petite, and pretty girl, Josephine was, at first, offended by the brash and rather arrogant Gabrial. After all, it was extremely improper for him to walk right up, introduce himself, and try to pay for her soda. He even had the effrontery, when she ignored him, to wait for her to leave and try to drive her home.

Gabrial was not a man to be easily discouraged. For the first time since he had started working at the age of seven, he found himself taking time off to hang around the soda fountain where he had first seen Josephine. Because of his persistence and also because music teachers didn't make much money, he soon convinced Josephine to allow him the privilege of paying for her sodas. Being impressed by his muscular good looks and his obvious adoration of her, Josephine allowed their relationship to develop. Despite her parents' objections to his lower working-class background and lack of formal education (even his first name was spelled strangely, her mother pointed out), true love reared its head—Josephine had found her Napoleon!

Josephine's initial fears about Gabrial soon proved to be justified. Once the honeymoon was over, he showed himself to be something of a tartar. Although he ignored the strict etiquette of the times when it suited him, he was insistent that his wife be a proper Victorian matriarch. In the presence of others, she was to address him as Mr. Saronna, and heaven help her if her household was not managed to his exacting standards.

As the two English observers, Rivington and Harris, in their Reminiscences of America wrote, "The husbands are content to slave in business in order that their wives and families may live in ease and affluence."

In exchange for the opportunities that this new affluence presented to her, the wife was to improve herself by reading *Godey's Lady's Book* and other publications which told her how to run every aspect of her life in case her husband had overlooked anything. It wasn't unusual for a lady to have a whole library of nothing but etiquette books, and indeed, with such strict rules of decorum governing every aspect of Victorian life, they were often necessary.

Despite Josephine's efforts to please him, Big Al was not an easy man to live with, and he constantly found fault with his timid wife's every effort.

When after four years of marriage and Josephine discovered herself to be pregnant, she viewed her new condition with mixed emotions. While the expectation of finally having someone from whom she could receive and give the love denied her by Gabrial pleased her, she dreaded breaking the news to her husband. He had, so far, shown no interest in children and, if anything, seemed relieved every month when she was again proven to have failed to conceive.

Gabrial was, in fact, furious when the news was first broken to him. He even illogically and unfairly blamed Josephine for "getting yourself in that condition just to spite me," as if she were some sort of sadistic hermaphrodite.

When he finally reconciled himself to the novel idea of fatherhood, he began making grandiose plans for his "son." Not wanting his child to be raised among the corruption of the city, he purchased a new house ornamented with the latest fretwork and peaked gables in outlying Queenstown. Being a lady of simple tastes, Josephine abhorred the elaborately crammed way in which fashion and Gabrial dictated that the house must be decorated. Every nook and cranny was stuffed with gimcracks of every description from plaster busts to Japanese paper kites and parasols. Every table and even the grand piano was skirted since "legs" were not supposed to be seen. All in all, each house was a housekeeper's nightmare. It was no small wonder that most middle-class homes required some sort of domestic help.

With the house completed, Gabrial began working seven days a week and even longer hours. He purchased two more coaches—one for Manhattan and one, ostensibly, for a transport service in Queenstown although neighbors suspected that it was really purchased to ensure someone's constantly being in Queenstown to fetch the doctor whenever Josephine went into labor. (After the baby's birth, the Queenstown hack was, indeed, reassigned to Manhattan.)

A lovely nursery was prepared for the special event. Josephine listened in gratified surprise as Gabrial regaled her with descriptions of the marvelous toys and baby's clothing which he had ordered. Being a superstitious man, he had insisted that the merchants hold his purchases until after the baby's safe delivery. For the first and, unfortunately, last time in her married life, Josephine was to be pampered by her stern husband who insisted that nothing was too good for his heir or his heir's mother.

After a stifling summer and an extremely difficult and long labor, Josephine gave birth to Gabrial's heir. While the doctor and nurse assured Josephine that the baby was perfect, her joy in having finally done something to please her husband was only too short-lived as the fatal words "It's a girl" were announced.

To the shocked horror of both the doctor and nurse, Josephine began to cry hysterically and refused to even look at the baby. So great were her fear and agitation that the doctor was forced to heavily sedate her to prevent her from injuring either herself or the child in her distraught state.

Having heard the baby's cry and then Josephine's hysteria, Gabrial, fearing that he had sired some sort of monster, rushed in to see the doctor struggling to sedate his wife while a wide-eyed young nurse clung fearfully to a little bundle which had again started crying due to the ruckus.

The nurse, who had never liked the stern-faced Gabrial, stared in horror as he approached her. Extending his arms, he announced in a no-nonsense manner, "Give me my son."

Speech failing her, the nurse unceremoniously dropped the baby in her father's arms and ran out of the room. The doctor, having heard what was going on but too busy with Josephine to interfere, now turned his attention to Big Al.

"Mr. Saronna, you are the proud father of a beautiful little girl." Seeing the father's stunned reaction, he hastily tried to reassure him. "I know, like most men, you were probably hoping for a son, but there's no reason why your wife can't give you many healthy sons. Enjoy your daughter while you can. They're a lot less trouble than boys. I have two sons and one daughter, so I know. Only a daughter can wrap her father around her little finger. Just you wait and see!"

Noticing the fixed expression as Gabrial continued to stare at him and fearing an explosion, the doctor quickly retreated from the room, promising to send the nurse back in and to return himself the next day. Walking out of the room with a sigh of relief, the doctor quickly went to locate the young nurse. Finding the frightened girl in the kitchen talking with the Queenstown hack driver and the cook, he tried to reassure her.

"Time to get back upstairs, young lady. No reason to look like that. Everything will be fine. By the way, I have a birth certificate to fill out. Did the mother ever mention what the child's name was to be?"

When the nurse shook her head negatively, the doctor considered going back upstairs to ask Gabrial, but thinking better of it, he decided to wait until the next day. He'd just leave that space blank for the time being. From the look on the father's face and the nervous collapse of the mother, they probably had only thought of boys' names anyway.

Accepting his hat from the maid, he walked out shaking his head sadly and muttering what sounded to the maid like, "That poor little thing"—a statement which when reported to the nurse, cook, and driver would provide hours of gossip and disagreement among the four of them as to whether the doctor had referred to the baby or the mother.

Returning reluctantly to the bedroom, the nurse was surprised to walk in and see Mr. Saronna still standing in exactly the same spot where she had left him, holding the baby and staring stony-eyed at his wife's recumbent form. Straightening her shoulders, the nurse approached him and tried to take hold of the baby.

Turning to face the intruder, Big Al merely pointed his hand at the door and shouted, "Get out!" thereby dissolving all the nurse's newfound courage as she scurried away.

Running back into the kitchen, she reported to the wide-eyed staff what had happened.

"What if he kills her?" she asked.

"Who, the mother or the baby?" the cook inquired.

"Does it matter?"

"W-well," she said philosophically, "there was a case not too long ago where a father killed his newborn infant, and since the child was considered his property, they didn't do much about it. On the other hand, if he kills his wife, he might go to jail for a few years."

"What nonsense!" Jim, the driver, said. "Sure, Big Al's got a hot temper, but he'd never hurt the little mite. You should see how he treats the horses. He's even warned us about overtiring them. He has a real soft spot for animals and little things."

Noticing that he hadn't mentioned anything about Josephine, the three women looked at each other and nodded their heads knowingly.

Being an honest man, Jim had deliberately made that omission. He truly didn't know what Big Al might do to his wife. He had often heard his boss speak disparagingly about his pretty little spouse, and he also knew that Big Al had no compunctions about violence. Remembering too how much Big Al had been looking forward to a son, he decided to follow the doctor's example and beat a safe retreat.

Grabbing his hat and hastily thanking the cook for lunch, he pretended to have just remembered a fare.

*****

As Gabrial's shock began to dissipate, he lowered his steely eyes to the face of the unwanted child in his arms, whom he had not even looked at yet. Pushing aside the folds of the blanket, his surprise was so great that he nearly dropped the baby. Instead of the smoky blue eyes of most newborns, he gazed into a pair of large green eyes, the exact mirror image of his own. Indeed, wasn't that also his chin and those lips were shaped remarkably like his? The tiny perfectly formed small pink hand that wrapped itself around his finger had the strength of a pair of manacles around his heart. Face and eyes as soft as marshmallows, Big Al began to rock the baby in his arms.

When the baby started to whimper, he worriedly rocked harder, and when she started howling lustily, he panicked. Placing her gently in the hand-carved cradle, skirted and decorated with white eyelet and organdy flounces, he ran out of the room.

Rushing down the stairs, he charged into the kitchen, grabbed the terrified nurse, and propelled her upstairs to the wailing baby.

"Do something quickly! She's either sick or dying!" he pleaded with the frightened girl.

Noting the genuine fear and love on Mr. Saronna's face as he looked at his daughter, the astonished nurse quickly reassured him that the baby was fine.

"She's probably only wet or hungry. That's all it is." After checking, she said, "Well, she's not wet, so she must be hungry."

No sooner had the word *hungry* been spoken that Big Al rushed over to the bed and tried shaking awake his sedated wife.

"No, no, Mr. Saronna! Please, leave her! The doctor says she's to rest. He left me some formula for the baby which I only have to heat. I'll fetch it. Besides, the doctor says your wife hasn't enough milk to feed the baby anyway," she blushingly reported.

"That figures! She's always messing things up. Well, hurry up and get the formula. What are you waiting for? No one makes Big Al's daughter cry," he roared.

As she heated the formula, the nurse reported the amazing change of heart to the others, who had been waiting expectantly. When they all broke into relieved smiles, only the cook remained dubious.

"If you ask me, that poor lady is going to have her hands full anyway in more ways than one. No one makes Big Al's daughter cry, indeed! Mark my words. Big troubles are a-coming!" she gloomily predicted.

Leaving the baby to the nurse's ministrations (after all, she mustn't be too bad; the baby had stopped crying and was greedily sucking on the proffered bottle), Gabrial realized that he had a lot to do. His daughter didn't even have one toy to play with when she finished eating! Until he could round up his three coaches and collect the things he had waiting in the city, he would have to do some shopping now. Getting into his new locomotor, the only thing available, he headed into the heart of Queenstown to make some purchases.

He returned with dozens of parcels. In his newfound good humor, he had purchased presents for everyone. He had even grudgingly bought some flowers for Josephine although as he told the embarrassed florist, "She messed things up again. She never does anything right. It was supposed to be a boy, you know. Not that I'm complaining. Oh no! Nothing like that! It's just the principle of the thing. You sure these flowers won't bother the baby?"

As the florist tried to convince him that fresh flowers were actually beneficial to breathing, Big Al tripled the order and red-facedly handed the man a tiny bouquet of pink rosebuds and baby's breath to add to the order, saying, "That's for my girl, you know!"

*****

Hearing a strange sound in her room, Josephine woke up. As she remembered about the baby, she timidly opened her eyes to be greeted by the startling sight of her husband sitting in a rocking chair, singing a lullaby (the strange sound) to their daughter.

Noticing that his wife was awake, he walked over to the bed, looked at his frightened wife in the eye, said, "You messed up again, but that's okay," and went back to rocking the baby.

Realizing that her husband wasn't really angry with her and seemed to love the baby, Josephine relaxed and took a good look around her room, which was almost unrecognizable with its masses of fresh-cut flowers. She also noticed with a bemused expression that a tiny but beautiful bouquet of pink rosebuds was placed on a low stool by the cradle.

Not having as yet even seen her daughter, she asked Gabrial to bring the baby to her. Reluctantly, he moved over to the bed and lowered the baby into her mother's arms with the warning, "Don't you wake her up now. I just got her to sleep again."

As Josephine gazed into her daughter's face, the reason for Gabrial's change of heart was immediately apparent. Giving a little gasp, she said, "My goodness, she looks just like you, Gabrial!"

"Do you really think so?" he asked proudly.

"You know she does."

"Well, yeah, she has my eyes all right, and now that you mention it, she does seem to have my chin and mouth. Hope she won't have my nose though. And she doesn't have much hair to speak of."

"Neither do you," Josephine mused, looking at her husband's hairline which had been rapidly receding for the past few years.

"Yeah, I guess even her head's like mine." He laughed. "What are we going to name her?"

Trying to further appease her husband, Josephine suggested the obvious name of Gabrielle.

"No, I don't want no daughter of mine to go around with a nickname like Gabby," he sensibly decided. "And I don't like Josephine," he quickly added.

"No, no, I wasn't even going to suggest that. How about a name using your nickname 'Al' in it? There are some very pretty names beginning with those letters."

"That sounds good to me. What names do you have in mind?"

"Well, let's see. There's Alberta and Althea." Seeing her husband's grimace, she suggested, "There are also all the variations on Alexander: Alexandra, Alexandria, or Alexandrina."

"Can't you think of anything better than that?" he asked impatiently.

"There's Almira, which means lofty or a princess in Armenian."

"I like the princess part, but the name stinks."

"There are always Alice or Alicia."

"Alicia's nice," he conceded. "But I had an aunt by that name whom I couldn't stand. It would always remind me of her."

"Well, that won't do then." Searching desperately for a name to please her difficult husband, her eyes fastened on one of the romantic novels by her bedside which she loved to read.

Looking up hopefully at her husband, she asked, "What about Alissa?"

As his face lit up, she gave him a happy smile, and he said, "Alissa, I like that! Gee, you didn't mess up!"

CHAPTER 5

A Match Made in Queenstown, Still Not Heaven

> The unicorn is noble,
> He knows his gentle birth,
> He knows that God has chosen him
> Above all beasts of earth.
>
> —Volkslied

The glory of Alissa's growing up years perfectly matched the glory of the new century. It was a time that would be known by such shining epithets as "The Age of Optimism," "The Age of Innocence," and "The Age of Confidence." The opening years of the twentieth century were years of booming progress and prosperity.

Senator Depew of New York said, "There is not a man here who does not feel 400 percent bigger in 1900 than he did in 1896, bigger intellectually, bigger hopefully, bigger patriotically."

Every twentieth century man was optimistic that he could bring the "good life" to his family and most were remarkably successful. Food and goods of all kinds were abundantly available, and prices were low. New inventions such as telephones, typewriters, and sewing machines were creating new employment opportunities for thousands. America was truly the new Garden of Eden, as Senator Beveridge of Indiana said, "God has marked the American people as his chosen nation to finally lead in the regeneration of the world.

This is the divine mission of America, and it holds for us all the profit, all the glory, all the happiness possible to man. We are trustees of the world's progress, guardians of its righteous peace." With such grandiose sentiments being promulgated all around them, it was not surprising that men such as Gabrial Saronna went out to claim their little piece of heaven.

Of all the wonders of the twentieth century, the one that would have the most impact on Gabrial was the automobile which, by 1900, was coming into its own with as many as eight thousand registered vehicles in the country. No inconvenience could dampen the enthusiasm of the novice motorist. Almost everyone loved the new "horseless carriage," and almost everyone wanted to be the proud owner of one.

Of course, like all new inventions, the automobile created as many, if not more, problems than it did pleasures. New traffic laws had to be enforced around the country. In 1902, Vermont required that a mature person waving a red flag must precede every automobile to prevent motorists from running down unwary pedestrians and colliding with horse-drawn carts. In Tennessee, a motorist had to post a warning of a week's notice before embarking on a trip.

Because of poor road conditions and the resulting dust which choked and blinded motorists, a whole new era in fashion was born. By 1904, Saks and Co. had a 270-page catalog filled with the latest in chic motoring garb. It also contained lists of all motoring necessities, including a beginner's kit of thirty-five tools which could be purchased for $25. Also recommended were the proper emergency food rations for four without which no true automobile connoisseur would be caught. Packard, Peerless, Great Arrow, Pierce-Arrow, and others became household words.

In 1908, the Locomobile won the Vanderbilt cup when it reached speeds of up to sixty-four miles per hour. People were so obsessed with motoring that there was even a melodrama entitled *The Great Automobile Mystery*, and everyone was singing such tunes as "Toot Your Horn, Kid, You're in a Fog" and "In My Merry Oldsmobile."

With the country in the grip of "motormania" and with the *British Herald* predicting, "If one could not have made money the past few years, his case is hopeless," Gabrial Saronna looked to the "main chance." Seeing the unlimited possibilities which the automobile presented to his business, Gabrial was determined to be one of the first, if not the very first, owners of a fleet of motorized cabs in New York.

If Gabrial had been an ambitious man before, the birth of his darling daughter, Alissa, drove him to new herculean efforts on her behalf. The driving force in his life was Alissa, and he was heard repeatedly stating, "Nothing's too good for Big Al's kid."

As an infant and toddler, Alissa was a true eldritch child. With her long blond curls and captivating smile, she won the hearts of everyone with whom she came in contact. The invention of the Kodak Brownie camera at this time allowed her proud parents to record for posterity every stage of her happy and carefree infancy. Despite the tactlessness of such comments as "What a beautiful child! She doesn't look like you," Gabrial and Josephine never got tired of displaying Alissa's charms or hearing her praises sung.

Alissa's first steps were filled with anxiety for her nervous and overprotective father. Josephine watched with bemused fascination every time Alissa slightly injured herself on one of the unsightly Victorian ornaments which crowded the house. She was not above steering the child toward a particularly hated grotesquerie since with every bump and bruise the tottering infant received, her irate father quickly discarded the offending object which was responsible for causing Big Al's daughter to whimper or cry.

The child's bedroom was a virtual fairyland. What else was worthy of housing such a precious princess? Her father had employed a well-known local artist to decorate the walls with beautiful murals. Alissa's favorite scene depicted a marvelous unicorn frolicking with beautiful maidens in a flower-strewn field. In the background stood a crenellated multi-turreted golden castle. When she went to bed at night, she could gaze in delight at the hand-painted golden stars which decorated the blue ceiling. Her furniture was hand-carved with fantastic mythical woodland creatures, and again, the unicorn played a prominent role. Was it any wonder that this fabulous creature should so dominate the young child's mind?

Despite these elaborate fixtures, no one could live in a perfect world. Even in Alissa's golden fairyland, an ugly dragon reared its head and shattered her spun-sugar world.

As the years went by, Josephine and Gabrial's arguments became more and more violent. It was not unusual for the child to be awakened in the middle of the night to the sounds of her father's yelling and her mother's weeping. This fact coupled with her father's migraine headaches, which demanded absolute silence, made the sensitive Alissa retreat more and more often to the safe haven of her room and the comforting presence of her painted friends. The once lighthearted and high-spirited princess soon became an introverted and frightened child whom any sudden loud noise, in the usually cloister-quiet house, could send into a panic.

She soon discovered that she could often divert her argumentative parents by the magic words "I don't feel well" and thereby avoid one of the all too common battles which usually followed their heated discussions. Thus, a pattern was set whereby the child would retreat into invalidism to rechannel her parents' energies into worrying about her rather than killing each other. Indeed, the child really was made physically ill listening to and watching her parents. Along with the love shown toward her, Alissa also received an early education in hate.

Josephine was able to escape the ugliness of her life by reading the currently popular books and magazines in which dashing suitors saved heroines from various mishaps. The romantic fiction of the day encouraged women to believe that love conquered all no matter what her everyday life might tell her to the contrary. At the same time, Alissa escaped through the fictional works of chivalry which her mother regularly read to her and which she later spent long hours reading to herself. Mallory's *Morte d'Arthur* and poetry such as Spenser's *The Faerie Queen* were among Alissa's favorites. At a very early age, she was able to explain all about troubadours and chansons de geste to her amused relatives. While providing hours of quiet diversion for the little girl, more importantly, they solaced her troubled spirit.

Although she was sent to expensive private schools, socializing with her classmates was not encouraged by Gabrial. His overprotectiveness prevented Alissa from visiting her friends, and not many children were willing to visit Alissa and play in her very restricted environment.

Alissa read with envy the newspaper accounts of the Roosevelt children and their menagerie of pets which included dogs, rabbits, flying squirrels, a badger, and even a small black bear. Not wanting his daughter to experience the heartbreak, which was the natural result of losing a pet, Gabrial's only concession to Alissa in this regard was a goldfish, which the lonely child joyously ran to feed every morning. He always kept a spare one secreted away so that she would never awaken to find her little friend floating on the top of the bowl. One day when Alissa remarked that her goldfish looked different, her father reassured her. "Balderdash! Just as you change as you get older, so does your goldfish."

As Alissa reached the age of ten, the beautiful elfin child slowly began to disappear. As if a bad fairy had attended her christening, Alissa's looks began to change. Her enforced inactivity resulted in a lazy overweight child who spent most of her time studying and reading while consuming large quantities of ice cream and candy. Her golden curls, which were bound to change since both her parents were dark-haired, turned a mousy brown; and her complexion, due to a lack of fresh air and exercise and an overabundance of sweets, became spotty. Alissa was to enter what she would later refer to as "the longest awkward stage ever known to man or womankind."

Being a naturally bright child, she did extremely well in school and continued to make her parents proud through her scholastic success; being overweight and isolated, her social life was a disaster. Although Josephine saw what was happening to her ill-fated daughter, she was unable to convince Gabrial of the error of his ways with regard to raising Alissa. He felt he knew best and would tolerate no criticism. Gabrial was blind to the changes taking place in Alissa and never realized that his sprightly fairy princess had turned into a fat dullard.

As Alissa reached her teens, she became more and more self-conscious about her social handicaps and would look wistfully at the photographs which proved what a lovely child she once had been.

Consequently, she would spend her time alternating between all-out beautification efforts, which would fail, and all-out periods of depression and overeating.

The second decade of the twentieth century was a difficult and puzzling time for Americans. Unlike the optimistic first decade, these later years were marked by labor unrest and increasing discontent even though economic growth continued. Americans were no longer self-assured or referred to themselves as God's chosen. In contrast to Senator Beveridge's words of only ten years before, William Howells wrote, "When our country is wrong, she is worse than other countries, and we ought somehow to make her feel that we are sorry and ashamed of her."

A new woman also emerged at this time, who was no longer content to stay at home. Besides entering the labor force in increasing numbers, she was also smoking cigarettes, driving automobiles, and bobbing her hair. Along with the right to vote, she was demanding of all things—the right to use birth control! To the Victorian male of Gabrial's generation, she was seen as the devil incarnate, and every effort was made to keep his wife and daughter from her demoralizing influence.

Despite Gabrial's fears of this new immorality, one memorable Sunday, five months before her sixteenth birthday, Alissa was allowed to accompany some school friends on a picnic. Since she attended an all-girls parochial high school, Gabrial saw no danger in this, providing he was permitted to drop the girls off at the park and again pick them up. He hadn't foreseen the possibility of one of the girls' brothers meeting them there with some of his friends. It was an oversight that Gabrial would always regret because it marked the beginning of his princess's rescue from her ivory tower.

Among the young men present was one Arthur Andros. Despite his knightly name, Arthur more closely resembled Don Quixote. At nineteen, Arthur was a lanky, self-conscious lad to whom the rescue of distressed damsels was the furthest thing from his mind.

Taking pity on the pointedly ignored Alissa, he introduced himself. "Hi! I'm Arthur Andros, a friend of Jack's."

"Hello. My name is Alissa Saronna. If my father finds out there are boys at this picnic, I'll be killed."

"Yes, I know."

"What do you mean 'you know'?"

"Everyone talks about how strict your father is with you. Is it true that you have a painted unicorn and castle in your room like Linda says?"

"Yes. Even though I was allowed to redecorate the room when I grew up, I didn't have the heart to paper over the unicorn scene. I even left the gold stars on the ceiling."

"No kidding! What did you do that for?"

"Well, it beats staring at plain white paint," Alissa defensively answered.

"Yes, I guess that's true," Arthur conceded, lapsing once more into silence.

Despite the stiltedness of their first conversation, Arthur and Alissa soon discovered that they had a lot in common, and a strong affection began to blossom as the two rather gauche, not too attractive youngsters found in each other a kindred spirit. Before the day was over, they had agreed to meet the next day after school at the library—the only place Alissa was unquestionably allowed.

Even when the other boys teased Arthur about his interest in the "Saronna Sow," as they unkindly referred to Alissa, he was not discouraged. Focusing on her only good features, her huge green eyes, Arthur was able to overlook her other physical shortcomings.

Although it was more or less a predestined fact for a romantic, lonely young girl, who was obsessed with visions of Camelot, to fall in love with an attentive young man with the unlikely name of Arthur, that famous question was being asked for the first if not the last time. What did Arthur see in Alissa? Besides her pretty eyes, what drew Arthur to the strictly reared, overweight Alissa? I really doubt if Arthur, who was never given to introspection, ever really bothered to analyze it. No doubt Alissa was both sympathetic and pathetic, but other motives besides romance might have played a part, even if only subconsciously, in Arthur's mind.

The role of knight in shining armor was not really a new one for Arthur. Eleanor and Demetrius's homelife closely paralleled that of the Saronnas' when it came to violence. The only difference being that Eleanor would unfairly run to her eldest son Arthur to take her part. Being raised in an age that emphasized the superiority of men and the helplessness of women, Arthur really resented his father's harshness toward his mother while, likewise, resenting his mother's emotional dependence on him. Despite the fact that Demetrius had always favored his eldest son, whom he expected to carry on the family business, Arthur's championing his mother's causes was driving a wedge between the two men. In truth, Eleanor herself was even more of a factor than Alissa's attraction for Arthur in alienating her son from his family. Eleanor's refusal to release Arthur from her emotional bondage to him would be the major cause of resentment between Eleanor and Alissa when Arthur switched Guineveres.

Despite her cautiousness, Gabrial soon discovered Alissa's duplicity, and despite the severity of her punishments, she still contrived ways of meeting Arthur. Realizing that he would either have to compromise or lose his daughter's love completely, Gabrial allowed the two to meet as long as they did so under his or Josephine's chaperonage, which was only proper anyway. Only too happy to agree, Arthur became an almost daily guest of the Saronnas. While Eleanor and Alissa remained hostile, Arthur was warmly welcomed into the Saronnas' home by Josephine, who was thrilled to see the change in her daughter.

Arthur's interest in Alissa soon gave her the self-confidence to begin dieting and improving her looks. Concentrating on her best features, she found ways of dressing and fixing her hair that again called to mind her former beauty. Discovering what she called "figure dressing," she stuck to styles which emphasized her full bosom and tiny waist while playing down her too round hips and derriere. As her looks improved, so did her self-esteem, and she developed her own unique flair. A proud carriage and good grooming combined with superior education and polished manners soon had people attributing to her that elusive quality known as "class."

While Arthur was proud of Alissa's transformation, he really missed the rather pathetic mess that he had first been attracted to. He couldn't help but resent the male attention that she was now receiving even though he couldn't truthfully complain that it was "turning her head." In her heart, no matter how attractive she might outwardly appear, Alissa would always see herself as the "Saronna Sow." (This was the only fact that Eleanor and Alissa, in the early years of their acquaintance, would ever agree upon.)

Eventually, even Gabrial's attitude toward Arthur softened. Arthur's love of engines was the main factor in accomplishing this seemingly miraculous feat.

In the early days of the automobile, motorists were expected to fend for themselves when breakdowns and accidents occurred. Gabrial's fleet of cabs had more than their share of mishaps, which Gabrial was at a loss to deal with. One day, to the gratification of both of them, Gabrial discovered Arthur's mechanical ability.

With over five million passenger cars sold between the years 1910 and 1915, the need for competent repairmen was obvious. By 1914, Ford's factories alone turned out over 240,000 cars due to his new standardized Model "T," which went a long way in making cars affordable to more people. While other auto manufacturers were raising prices, he was lowering them. As Henry Ford himself stated, "Every time I lower the price a dollar, we gain a thousand new buyers."

When these new statistics led Gabrial to suggest to Arthur the possibility of opening a repair garage with Arthur as chief mechanic and manager, he jumped at the chance. Never having had any real interest in merchandizing, he was only too anxious to leave Andros's Emporium for the possibility of working for Gabrial.

World War I had little direct effect on the Saronna family. Alissa and Josephine did what they could for the war effort by knitting socks, collecting books, and even packing peach pits that were used for gas mask filters. (It took seven pounds of pits for one gas mask.) Arthur, deferred because of a hearing disability, was busy with the new business while Alissa agreed to attend college in hopes of becoming a school teacher.

When Gabrial decided to move and expand his garage and cab business by branching out to Pine River Falls, a more affluent neighborhood, Arthur was more than happy to go with them. Although Alissa regretted leaving behind her unicorn room, she now had other interests in life and would soon have to leave her room behind anyway when she and Arthur got married.

Arthur's decision to leave Queenstown was a final bitter blow to his family who accused the Saronnas of bribing their son in order to "buy" a husband for their daughter. When Arthur pointed out that Alissa could now have her pick of husbands, his family refused to acknowledge this fact, and Arthur was ordered out of the house before he could even pack his belongings.

While the entire Saronna family was distressed to learn of the outcome of their offer to Arthur, Alissa was particularly incensed at the Androses' unfair treatment of him. When the Androses failed to acknowledge a formal announcement of the engagement between their offspring and Alissa, she swore to ban them from the wedding, which was to take place in April of the next year. Thus, the infamous Andros-Saronna feud which had begun in 1913 with a romance was to continue for a period of thirteen years until a funeral ended it in 1926.

On Sunday, April 20, 1919, Alissa and Arthur were married in a small but elegant ceremony in the Saronnas' new home in Pine River Falls. Big Al's little girl was now a married woman.

CHAPTER 6

Christmas in Camelot

> In Xanadu did Kubla Khan
> A stately pleasure dome decree.
> —Coleridge, 1926

It wasn't until Christmas Day, four months after Father's death, that the Andros family received its first glimpse of Arthur and Alissa's home. While Queenstown's rumors all agreed that the house was unusual, no one had actually seen it. In that unique way that rumors usually work, we were expecting anything from a Somos hovel to the Taj Mahal.

The drive out to Pine River Falls was a long one. It probably wouldn't have been too bad, but Father's 1918 Model "T" was not up to such a journey. It had snowed the night before—one of those picturesque storms that quickly blows over, leaving pristine postcard settings and ice slicks and mudholes. We spent as much time pushing the car back on the road as in progressive travel.

Upon reaching Pine River Falls, we had more problems. After making numerous inquiries (something not easy to do with all smart people snuggled in their own homes), we learned that Arthur and Alissa's house was located outside of the town itself—something Arthur's directions had failed to clarify. After having traveled about seven more miles east, we came to a dirt road with a large holly-decorated sign with an arrow showing that the Andros residence was one mile to the right.

While it was one of the bumpiest and most rutted roads I had ever traveled, Mother Nature had certainly cooperated with Alissa in providing a breathtakingly beautiful setting for her home. There in the midst of a snow-covered pine forest stood an impressive miniature Tudor manor. Pulling into the circular driveway, we all watched in fascination as a pair of dappled deer darted from the side of the house back into the surrounding woods.

As I assisted Mother from the car with her bags of Christmas presents, John impulsively ran ahead and began banging on the front door with an ornate brass knocker in the appropriate form of a deer's head.

It was Alissa who answered the door. In a time of short skirts, rolled-down stockings, and bobbed hair, Alissa was a lovely, if unconventional, sight. With her long dark hair hanging loosely down her back, she was dressed in a floor-length red velvet dress which was fastened around her waist with a braided gold cord. Except for the provocatively low scooped neck, she resembled some sort of medieval saint.

Amid the choruses of "Merry Christmas" and many hugs and kisses, Alissa led us into a very large foyer, which served as a sort of central courtyard for the house. The floor was of mottled pink-and-white Languedoc marble, and the walls were oak paneled. All these luxurious accoutrements were merely a setting, however, for at the top of the hand-carved staircase was the real focal point. We all stared up in awe at the landing which had for a backdrop a large Gothic-arched stained glass window that depicted in jeweled tones a unicorn rampant. Hearing Mother's gasp of appreciation, Alissa turned to her.

"Oh, you've spotted my unicorn. I was hoping to save the grand tour till later, but it's almost impossible to miss him. It was too much to hope that I could hustle all of you into the parlor before he was noticed. He was directly copied from an illuminated fifteenth-century manuscript—but what am I thinking of standing here lecturing while you're shivering? Come inside and get warm."

Noticing Alissa's puzzled expression, Mother quickly explained, "Richard sends his regrets, Alissa dear. I'm afraid that he had made some other plans for the holidays, which I knew nothing about. There will be other Christmases he can join us, I'm sure…"

"And Marcie had to spend Christmas with her family, but she said to wish you the merriest of Christmases," I added.

"I hope that the two dropouts won't upset your menu too much, dear."

"No, of course not, Eleanor." Alissa smiled, trying unsuccessfully to mask her disappointment.

Turning to the left, she led us through a massive oak door which was banded with heavy ironwork. The room which Alissa referred to as a "parlor" was unlike any parlor any of us had ever seen before. It was a large room about forty feet long. Walking in, we all made a beeline for the massive fieldstone fireplace on the far side of the room in which a Yule log was burning. A huge pine wreath was suspended above it, and pine roping was draped to each side. Both were decorated with tartan plaid ribbons, pine cones, and red velvet balls. I was especially impressed by the Gothic andirons and the fireback which bore a unicorn crest.

As I turned back to the room, I noticed Alissa trying to rouse my recumbent brother who was sleeping on a thickly cushioned red velvet sofa.

"Welcome, everyone," he sleepily greeted us. "Please do sit down as soon as you're warm enough."

As Alissa passed around hot mulled wine and cider in heavy pewter tankards, I seated myself in a comfortable red chair and took stock of my surroundings.

The white stuccoed walls provided an excellent background for several beautifully woven wall tapestries. The furniture was heavy and Spanish-looking. A Persian carpet with dominant shades of red, green, and gold covered the parquet floor. In front of one of the heavily leaded Gothic-arched windows stood a beautifully proportioned eight-foot pine tree decorated with the same bows, balls, and cones as the wreath and roping with additional gold angels and ornaments to fill it out. Fresh bunches of holly and ivy were festooned everywhere. But for me, the pièce de résistance stood at the other end of the room directly opposite the fireplace.

Behind an intricately worked pair of Spanish wrought iron gates stood a large anteroom which we had bypassed. Waiting for no invitation, I rushed in and stood dumbfounded. At the back of the room facing into the parlor was another large stained glass window; this one was depicting a scene from Camelot. Here, repeating the dominant red, gold, and green shades of the carpet were King Arthur and his knights seated at the Round Table. The other two sidewalls were covered with recessed shelves containing hundreds of books. In the center of the room stood a large refectory table surrounded by six comfortable dark leather upholstered chairs. The ceiling was beamed and painted with medieval hunting scenes.

"My god, Alissa, your house is really unique!"

"Thank you, Edward. It's unusual to find someone as young as yourself able to appreciate it. I'm afraid it doesn't follow the current vogue. After dinner, if you'd like, I'll show you around."

"Is dinner ready yet?" Mother asked.

"No, not for at least half an hour," Arthur responded.

"Then I'd really love to see it all now, if you wouldn't mind, Alissa."

"All right. First, I'll fill you in on the background. When Arthur and I decided to marry, my father offered us a home as a wedding gift—"

"Some gift!" interrupted John.

"I had visited Europe with my parents shortly after meeting Arthur and had fallen in love with the castles of Moorish Spain. Since Father, obviously, couldn't afford to build me a castle, he told me to use my imagination and compromise with something reasonable. After looking at contemporary homes, I was totally disappointed. While nice enough, they just didn't suit me. By asking around, I discovered that if we built outside the actual town and in what is known as the 'Pine Barrens,' I could save a small fortune which could then go into the design of the house. Medieval being my passion, I decided that I could have what I wanted if I scaled it down and didn't build on a 'prime property' site. Thus, what you see before you came about."

"These tapestries are lovely, Alissa. Did you make them yourself?"

"Yes, as you can see, there are seven of them. They are reproductions of the famed Unicorn Tapestries which tell of the hunt of the unicorn. The originals were woven around 1500 in Brussels. You probably read about them when John D. Rockefeller Jr. purchased them from the La Rochefoucauld family a couple of years ago."

"Yes, I think I do remember something in the *Times* about it. Weren't they supposed to have been used to keep potatoes from freezing during the French Revolution?"

"That's right. One of them was so badly damaged that only fragments of it remain. I was lucky enough to obtain a book on early tapestries which depicted the whole collection."

Leading us back across the foyer, Alissa led us into the dining room which was equal to the parlor minus the library in size. It was papered in a moss green velvet flocked pattern, and one whole side of the room was covered with Gothic-arched gold-veined mirrors. A huge octagon-shaped table surrounded by high-backed moss green velvet chairs stood in the center of the room. A heavily carved Spanish credenza, china cabinet, and sideboard were also included, and moss green velvet curtains hung at the three-arched, mullioned windows. At the far end of the dining room stood French doors, which Alissa explained led out to the flagstone patio.

Turning to the left, we were led into a very modern kitchen which contained all the latest electrical appliances—one of Alissa's few concessions to the twentieth century. The kitchen led directly into a small herbary which contained various apothecary jars and mortars and pestles. At one side of the room was a door which led outside to an herb garden.

"The garden contains not only herbs for seasoning food. I've also included medicinal herbs such as hyssop, horehound, belladonna, and foxglove from which digitalis is derived. There are also dye plants such as wood, weld, and madder which were used to make the Unicorn Tapestries."

"Gee, I feel like I'm in a museum," piped in John.

Exiting the herbary from another door opposite to the one in the garden, we came out underneath the foyer steps. As we climbed upstairs, we were again overcome by the beauty of the unicorn stained glass window.

On the left side of the landing was the master bedroom. Here again were heavy Spanish pieces of furniture and a large fieldstone fireplace. The walls were also flocked, but this time, the color scheme was royal blue velvet for the bedspread, canopy, and drapes. French doors led outside to a terrace. A modern blue marble-tiled bathroom was connected to the bedroom.

To the right of the landing were two more bedrooms each with its own connecting bath. The larger of the two bedrooms was done up in a very masculine style with browns and golds dominating. The other was equally feminine with pink, gray, and light green accessories.

What the house lacked in the number of rooms, it more than compensated for in luxury and style. While it certainly would not have appealed to everyone, I could immediately understand its appeal to Alissa. Where Arthur fit in was another question.

Leading us back to the parlor, Alissa excused herself to take care of some last-minute dinner details.

"Arthur, you must be very proud of your home," Mother said.

Arthur, not a man of many words, simply smiled and said, "Yes. It's a sort of dream come true for Alissa. She designed the whole thing herself. I really didn't have any ideas for a house."

"You sure were lucky. Imagine getting a keen wife like Alissa and then having a business and spiffy house like this thrown in on the side," John tactlessly said.

Before the silence could become too awkward, Alissa came in and announced that dinner was served. It was a fairly traditional if abundant spread. There was turkey soup to start followed by the choice of either chestnut-stuffed turkey or apple-stuffed goose. There were mashed potatoes, candied yams, squash, succotash, brussels sprouts, cranberry sauce, fresh baked rolls, and two kinds of gravy.

We all agreed to wait for dessert and retired to the parlor while Alissa cleared away the used Haviland china, Sheffield silver, and delicate Waterford crystal.

When she again joined us, we all gathered around the Christmas tree to exchange gifts. There were the usual "ohs" and "ahs" as carefully wrapped and decorated packages were ripped open in undisguised excitement. While all the gifts were beautiful and everyone seemed pleased, I think that the two hits of the day were the antique carousel music box which Mother had given to Alissa that played "Greensleeves" and the set of premed books which I had received from Arthur and Alissa. While we quietly reexamined our gifts, Alissa went to prepare dessert.

As we walked back to the dining room, it was obvious that Alissa had never lost her childhood sweet tooth. Covering the sideboard and credenza was a fantasyland of sweets. There were chocolate mousse; crème brûlée; an ice cream bombe; apple, pumpkin, and mince pies; cherry trifle; and chestnut Mont Blanc. Large bowls of fresh fruit and nuts were scattered across the table.

"I'm sorry that there's no plum pudding, but when I looked up the ingredients, the pig's blood decided me against it."

"Hmph! Leave it to the English to call something with pig's blood in it pudding," quipped John in his best imitation of Uncle Theo's Greek accent.

This had everyone laughing, and even Mother had a hard time concealing a smile.

"Did you know that Alissa had invited Uncle Theo too?" Arthur asked Mother. "But he was keeping the restaurant open today and doesn't trust anyone else to do the cooking."

"Yeah, it's really crazy. Who would want Greek food for Christmas?" John asked, slicing into the apple pie.

"Obviously, only another Greek," Mother announced, helping herself to a large dish of whipped cream-laden trifle.

After we were stuffed to bursting point, we returned to the parlor. While Mother and Arthur nodded in front of the fire, the rest of us tried to decide what to do next.

Suddenly, Mother looked up and asked, "Alissa, have they ever really proven if there was a King Arthur?"

"No, not really. He's supposed to be based on some sixth-century figure. He wasn't actually given prominence until the twelfth century by Geoffrey of Monmouth in his *Histories of the Kings of Britain*."

"Mother, I hope you're prepared for a history lesson. You don't know what you're letting yourself in for," Arthur interrupted a red-faced Alissa.

"Oh, hush, Arthur. It wouldn't hurt for all of us to learn something. I think it's wonderful that Alissa has these facts at the tips of her fingers."

"Yeah, I guess if you live in a medieval museum, you have to know something about it," John agreed. "Go on, Alissa."

"W-well, if you're really interested. It was Robert Wace, a Norman poet at the court of Eleanor of Aquitaine, who after reading Geoffrey's book, made Arthur a romantic hero and first mentioned his Round Table. Chrétien de Troyes, a poet at Eleanor's daughter, Marie of Champagne's court, moved Arthur's court from Caerleon to Camelot. He also shifted the emphasis from Arthur to his knights, especially Lancelot and Percival. Because of this shift, he eventually created the romance of Lancelot and Guinevere."

"Where did this Geoffrey of Monmouth hear about Arthur?" I asked.

"I really don't know. The legend of Arthur was supposed to be a dominant theme in folklore, and generally, where there's smoke, there's fire, so I think it's safe to assume there probably was an Arthur although I doubt if we'd recognize him from the elaborate legend that now surrounds him."

"Speaking of legendary figures, where's this Tippy we've heard so much about?" I asked.

"He's probably hiding under the bed. We have so little company that with the exception of my parents, the poor cat's frightened by anyone else who comes in."

"Do you mean that he'll actually remain under the bed until we leave?" Mother queried.

"Probably. He's really a misanthrope like his father," Alissa answered, gesturing toward Arthur.

"A misan—what?"

"Alissa had to explain that one to me too, John," Arthur explained. "She felt that being half Greek, I would know that it comes from the Greek word *misanthropos*, which means a hater of mankind."

"That's not nice, Alissa," Mother chided Alissa with the severest rebuke she would ever give her new favorite. "Maybe he is a little antisocial, but I don't like to think that any son of mine could actually 'hate.'"

"That's dumb, Mom. Edward and I hate lots of things, and as for Richard, I sometimes wonder if there's anything he doesn't hate. So why not Arthur? Everyone hates. Even you once hated Alissa," John continued in his usual tactless fashion.

Trying to change the subject and alleviate the embarrassing silence that now hung over the room, I suggested we sing Christmas carols.

Starting out with a rousing chorus of "Jingle Bells" and "Deck the Halls," we then proceeded to the mellower "Silent Night" and "O Little Town of Bethlehem." Mother soloed "The Holly and the Ivy" and Alissa with "Oh Holy Night." I chose "O Christmas Tree" and John with "God Rest Ye Merry Gentlemen" with Arthur opting for "The First Noel." After these, Mother and Alissa sang "Barbara Allen" apropos of nothing.

When we had exhausted our rather large repertoire, we decided on charades. Mother and Alissa wrote book titles on slips of paper which we drew from a large Sevres vase. Since we were an uneven number, we couldn't work in teams, which made it more difficult. After books, we tried current songs and plays.

Alissa told us that she and Arthur had continued a childhood custom of hers after they married. Every year on Christmas Day, they read aloud to each other Dickens's classic *A Christmas Carol,* with each of them taking different parts. Liking this idea, we agreed to participate. Drawing for parts, Arthur got Scrooge and I got Tiny Tim, which John sarcastically said was good typecasting. The remaining minor parts were divided among the three of them with John taking Bob Cratchit. Since besides reading the parts, we also decided to also act them out. We were all soon reduced to helpless laughter as John tried to put me, Tiny Tim, on his shoulders.

While Alissa, fearing an injury to either of us, said that we could skip that part. Mother, who had partaken of too much of Alissa's favorite Amaretto liqueur, insisted that we "do it right," and so a grumbling John had to carry my rather bovine body around the room.

"It's a good thing I lift weights every day, or I'd never be able to lift this tub of lard," John insultingly said.

"Stick to your script" and "No comments from the sidelines" greeted his complaint.

After Scrooge's reformation, even the usually inventive Alissa was at a loss for suggestions, and so we all agreed to just sit back and relax before the long return trip to Queenstown.

"I really wish you didn't have to go. We could easily put you up for the night, you know," offered Alissa.

"Maybe some other time, dear. I hate leaving Richard all alone for the entire holiday."

"But, Eleanor, you said that Richard had plans. Surely he's still out with his friends."

"Well, yes, Alissa," began Mother, trying to cover up her faux pas. "That's probably true. What I meant was he'll undoubtedly be home early, and he's most likely going to be hungry," Mother finished, lamely looking to John and me for help, which we both were too embarrassed to give her.

"All right," Alissa said resignedly. "I'll just pack up some food for him. It's really too much for just me and Arthur."

"Yeah, that should really make Richard feel guilty," agreed John not as sotto voce as he thought.

As I helped Mother gather the gifts together, I took one last look around the room. It really was a uniquely beautiful home, and I couldn't wait to describe it to Marcie who had been adamant about me remembering every little detail. On second thought, although I would tell her how beautiful it was, I would save the description till she could see it for herself. After all, every fair maiden deserves to spend some time in Camelot.

CHAPTER 7

Family Relationships Strengthened

I am the lion, and his lair!
I am the fear that frightens me!
I am the desert of despair!
And the night of agony!
—James Stephens, 1927

The New Year was heralded in with the same optimistic bang that had been welcoming every year since the end of World War I. It was an adolescent time in an adolescent country, and everyone lived according to the adage "Eat, drink, and be merry," forgetting its follow-up "for tomorrow we die."

The famous Volstead Act or Eighteenth Amendment did a great deal in adding to the excitement of the times. Like anything which was suddenly taken away, it quickly reached such paramount importance that it became an obsession. Even formerly staunch teetotalers were not now above setting up their own portable stills. Libraries were well stocked with newly published books and pamphlets explaining the best methods of accomplishing this. Every newspaper ran countless ads on new products such as solid blocks of grape by-products which, when mixed with water, became a fairly drinkable wine.

Accounts of the daring exploits of the "rumrunners" were avidly read, and new heroes of rather shady if not downright criminal character came into prominence. The South Shore of Long Island where the Saronnas and Arthur and Alissa lived was gaining notoriety for liquor smuggling.

After our Christmas visit to Arthur and Alissa's home, Arthur began visiting us on a fairly regular basis. At least once a week while passing through Queenstown on business, he would stop by to say hello and have dinner.

We didn't get to see Alissa as much as we would have liked to though since Arthur's visits were mostly during the day when Alissa was teaching her fifth-grade class at the Pine River Falls Elementary School.

"I do wish we could get to see Alissa more often, Arthur."

"Sorry, but she's pretty busy with her teaching and research."

"What research?" I asked with interest.

"Her unicorn research," Arthur reluctantly admitted.

"She doesn't really take it seriously, does she? I mean how can anyone spend hours researching a fantasy figure?"

"I don't know, Edward. Why not ask Alissa? She'd love any excuse to talk about it, but don't forget what I told you when Mother brought up King Arthur. Be prepared for a long-winded scholarly discourse."

"Yeah, or be prepared to cut her off and change the subject real fast," cut in John who had just walked in.

"Hi, brudder!" John said, slapping Arthur on the back. "Why don't you bring your better-looking half more often? At least she's a treat to look at. Yep, she's really the cat's meow. Too bad you saw her first, big brudder."

"John, you should show a little more respect when speaking of your sister-in-law. After all, she should be to you like one of your own poor dead little sisters," Mother remonstrated.

"Nerts! She ain't no sister of mine, and she sure is alive. Just looking at Alissa gives me the heebie-jeebies," John continued in his usual eloquent way while Mother winced.

"Thank God none of my other sons speak like him. It would just be too, too much!"

"That's because I'm the only 'hep' one in the family. The rest of you are 'all wet.'"

"Speaking of 'all wet,' John, go upstairs and get washed for dinner. You look like you've been rolling in mud all day," Mother admonished.

"His usual habitat," I added sotto voce so only Arthur could hear.

"Righto!" answered John, running up the stairs, doing an improvised Charleston and singing "Ain't She Sweet" all at the same time.

*****

It wasn't until Easter vacation that we finally had a visit from Alissa. Everyone was glad to see her, and even Marcie, who hadn't seen Alissa since the funeral, was there.

It was a beautiful, if pale and thin Alissa, to whom I answered the door. "Hi, Alissa! Long time no see," I tritely greeted her.

Kissing me on the cheek, she quickly called together the whole family to show us her new Niagara blue roadster.

"It's the latest thing," she proudly announced to the admiring crowd, and since it had only two seats plus a rumble seat, it took a while before we had all gone for a spin. Even Mother wanted a ride in the new car and shocked us all by insisting on riding in the rumble seat. The one thing that always particularly pleased me about this new and close relationship between Mother and Alissa was how quickly Mother's icy sense of propriety could melt under Alissa's sunny exuberance.

Even Richard surprised us by sitting in front with Alissa, a concession he agreed to when she pleaded a headache and asked him to drive.

When we finally all got back to the house for dinner, Mother remonstrated with Alissa.

"You really aren't looking quite the thing, Alissa. You've lost weight and are looking very tired and pale."

"She sure looks good to me."

"I'm not talking about her good looks, John. Even lovely people get sick. Why are you getting such severe headaches so often? Shouldn't you see a doctor?"

Smiling gratefully at John, Alissa went on to explain, "I usually get these headaches after a long drive, and as for seeing a doctor, I have, and it's a waste of time."

"Why do you say that?"

"It seems that I am a victim of what my mother refers to as 'The Great Saronna Genetic Conspiracy.'"

"The what?" I asked.

"Mother has always felt that I totally take after my father. Along with his other traits that I inherited, it looks like I've also inherited his migraine headaches."

"How awful for you, Alissa dear. Are they inheritable?"

"The doctors don't really know although the headaches do seem to run in the same families. I just wonder if it's a sex-linked characteristic."

"Sex-linked! What a vulgar expression!" Mother predictably protested.

"All it means, Eleanor, is that the sex who has the trait can only pass it on to an offspring of the opposite sex. You know…like hemophilia. You remember when the poor Czarina Alexandra passed on hemophilia to the czarevitch? They say color blindness is another sex-linked characteristic."

"Oh, that poor, poor martyred family. To kill not only the czar and czarina but also the young grand duchesses and that poor frail little boy! The horror and shame of it!" Mother wailed, still thinking of the Russians.

"Yes, it was horrible. It was just one of the things that made me very happy to see the end of the second decade," announced Alissa.

"Can't the doctors do anything for your headaches?"

"No, nothing helps. They are becoming so frequent and so severe that I'm thinking of giving up teaching. It's impossible to remain calm and patient with your head splitting and your stomach upset."

"Will you last out the term?"

"Hopefully, Eleanor. If I've lasted this long, I guess I can hold out till late June."

Alissa and Mother had made an agreement not to help in each other's houses with dinner preparations. So while Mother cooked, Alissa worked on a crossword puzzle.

"Do you do them often?" I asked.

"Yes, I really love them. Along with mah-jongg, some kind of new tile game, they are the latest fads. I was just reading about a minister in Utah who wrote his sermon in the form of a crossword puzzle which his congregation then solved during the service."

"You're joking!"

"Not at all. Even the Baltimore and Ohio Railroad has placed dictionaries in all its trains for the use of commuters to help solve their puzzles."

"Do you work with a dictionary?"

"Sure! See my latest. It's small enough so I can wear it on a band around my wrist. I see more of them being worn than conventional bracelets."

"Gee, that's nifty!"

"Thanks, John. Would you care to take a closer look?"

"No thanks, Alissa," said an embarrassed John, who realized that he had been caught peering over her shoulder and trying to peek down her V-neck sweater.

After Mother's predictable dinner of roast beef and Yorkshire pudding, Richard further surprised us by leaving his room and joining us for dessert. The spin in Alissa's new roadster seemed to have improved even his mood.

By this time, unfortunately, both Mother and Alissa had partaken of too much Courvoisier, which Alissa had brought with her in two flasks. When Richard came down, she offered him some, and I thought the poor guy would faint when Alissa seductively lifted the side of her skirt and extracted a flask from a frilly thigh-high garter.

Trying to make Richard relax, Alissa began discussing music with him. Although their likes and dislikes differed, it soon became apparent that Richard respected her musical knowledge if not her taste.

"I'm afraid my tastes aren't very sophisticated, Richard. In fact, with the exception of Debussy's 'Clair de Lune,' my favorites are the Russian composers. While I enjoy the beauty of Mozart and the serenity of Bach, I love the barbaric emotions of Rimsky-Korsakov's 'Scheherazade' and the powerful fantasy of Tchaikovsky's 'The Nutcracker.' When I was in college, I could spend hours just listening to the music majors practicing. I always felt that they were, by far, the happiest and most content students on campus."

"Surely with your grandfather having been a music teacher, you must have some talent," Richard guessed.

"I'm afraid not. When I was about a year old, the piano, unfortunately, was one of the first things that I bumped into, so I never learned to play."

Seeing the confused looks on his family's faces, Arthur elaborated, "Whenever Alissa would hurt herself on some object while learning to walk, her father would simply throw it out in retaliation for hurting her even if the object was as large and expensive as a piano."

"My goodness! That must have been very hard on your poor mother, my dear."

"Well, Eleanor, it seems that Mother never really had much talent, and like most children who are forced to take lessons, she ended up hating the piano and was just as happy to see it thrown out."

"My Richard is a very talented musician," Mother said proudly.

"Are you really?" Alissa asked, her eyes shining with enthusiasm.

"I'm all right. I'd be happy to play a few pieces for you. If you wait a few minutes, I'll just straighten out my room upstairs where the piano's located and call you when I'm ready."

"Oh, Richard, I'd just love it!" Alissa gushed.

While Richard got ready, Alissa tried to rouse my omni-sleeping brother Arthur.

"Maybe we should leave him, Alissa. My son Richard hates to be kept waiting. Since he really is being unusually gracious, I'd hate to ruin things. I can't even remember when he last played for anyone."

"That's why I'd hate for Arthur to miss it. Besides, he sleeps too much."

"Even Calvin Coolidge spends two to four hours a day napping, so it can't be all bad," Mother defended while looking fondly at her horizontal son.

Just then, all disagreement ceased as Richard called for us all to come upstairs. Richard's music room was fully equipped, and Alissa stared around in fascination. As she admired the piano, it seemed that this was certainly a night for miracles as Richard asked her if she'd like to try it even though his reluctance was obvious.

"Thank you, Richard, but no. My whole musical repertoire consists of 'What Can You Do with a Drunken Sailor,' which I had to learn to play in college in order to get my teaching license."

"What an absurd song for children."

"Yes, isn't it?" Alissa giggled. "Well, I didn't choose it, you know," she told an accusatory Richard.

Just when I thought that Alissa had blown her one chance for a private concert, Richard squared his shoulders and sat down. He then proceeded to play "Clair de Lune," the first two movements of "Scheherazade," and the overture and divertissement of the "Nutcracker" to a starry-eyed Alissa.

When he finished playing, Alissa was overcome with emotion. Profusely thanking him and sincerely admiring his talent, she made the faux pas of asking him why in the world he hadn't gone into music professionally.

As we all held our breaths for Richard's reaction, he turned a tight-lipped face toward Alissa and then, without a word, slammed down the piano lid and strode furiously out of the room.

Seeing the shock and hurt on Alissa's face, we all tried to alleviate her guilt and embarrassment.

"As soon as Richard calms down, he'll realize that you didn't mean anything by it," Mother said, trying to comfort Alissa.

"But that's just it. He is talented enough to be a professional. Why was he so angry? I was just so grateful that I wanted him to know how much I appreciated his playing. I never would have said it if it weren't true. I never lie… I hate liars." Alissa sobbed.

"Please don't cry. What you don't understand is that Richard did intend to go into the musical field."

"What happened?"

"Well, after Arthur went to work for your father, Richard, as next in line, felt obligated to take over the emporium."

"No wonder he resents me so much! But surely, he still could have done what he wanted."

"Sure, he could have," John consoled Alissa. "He just wanted to make points with Father. He was old enough to make his own decisions. All the rest of us did."

"That's not exactly fair," I said, uncharacteristically defending Richard. "It's all a matter of favorites. Arthur, despite everything, was always Father's favorite. John is Mother's favorite, and I, as the youngest, have always been John's and Richard's favorite, but poor Richard, no matter how hard he tries, has always been unappreciated. Thus, he keeps trying harder to be appreciated. It's why he's still hanging on to the emporium even though Father's dead. He wants to please Mother now."

"That's not true!" Mother protested.

"If you'd just be honest with yourself, you'd see it is true."

"I can see now why poor Richard always seems to have the weight of the world on his shoulders," Alissa commiserated.

Trying to divert Alissa, Mother served her usual custard and fruit dessert. In this way, she hoped to at least appease Alissa's notorious sweet tooth.

The little contretemps with Richard combined with the Courvoisier, unfortunately, brought out a darker side of Alissa that we had never seen before.

To me, Alissa epitomized the age we lived in. She was provocatively gay, sometimes almost with an underlying desperation.

In order to overcome Alissa's self-proclaimed guilt over having ruined the evening, Mother changed the subject by asking about Alissa's parents. Despite Arthur's (who was finally awake) signals to avoid the subject, Mother persisted.

As it turned out, Alissa was very depressed over her parents and was soon again in tears. It seemed that they were fighting more than ever, and somehow Alissa blamed herself for not being able to alleviate her mother's misery. When Alissa went into a whole tirade against herself, Arthur interrupted.

"Don't listen to her, Mother. When she gets depressed, she always feels like this. She's no worse than any other son or daughter. Just because she didn't turn out perfectly, she tortures herself with guilt."

Mother walked over to Alissa and hugged her.

As I watched the genuine love and warmth between these two former enemies, I was reminded of the words of Ecclesiastes about there being a time for every season under heaven.

When Mother and Alissa first met, the time wasn't ripe for friendship to blossom between them. I'd always thought that the overweight, insecure Alissa must have been intimidated by Mother's forbidding and obviously critical manner. In retaliation, Alissa might very well have tried to influence Arthur leaving the family although I certainly didn't know this for a fact.

Years later, when meeting as equals, the time was ripe for deep love and respect to blossom through Mother's new vulnerability and need and Alissa's natural kindness and genuine caring.

CHAPTER 8

Rum-Running in Suffolk County

King John was not a very good man,
He had his little ways,
And sometimes no one spoke to him
For days and days and days.
                      —A. A. Milne, 1928

While it was generally acknowledged that the early Plantagenets had their black sheep of the family in the person of Prince John, later King John of Magna Carta fame, it was an equally acknowledged fact that the Androses had their family scoundrel in the person of my brother John. The maternal heartache experienced by Eleanor of Aquitaine was nothing compared to that experienced by Eleanor Andros, which was perhaps why Mother always referred to the former as "that dear saintly queen."

Historians, of course, differ greatly in their opinions of Eleanor of Aquitaine, and few, other than Mother, would have ever seen anything saintly in that rather infamous lady. But as Mother would always indignantly retort, "What do they know of a mother's sorrow?"

Prohibition offered new and varied outlets for anyone of criminal inclination, and, unfortunately, John was one of the many who "never looked a gift horse in the mouth."

The idea of prohibition was nothing new. As far back as 1735, Georgia experimented with it. While it only lasted until 1742, it had planted a new idea in the fertile soil of a virgin nation. The Pennsylvania temperance movements began about 1800, and by 1823, a temperance journal, *The Boston Recorder*, was being published. The idea of total national abstinence didn't appear, however, until 1819, and it wasn't until 1830 that total abstinence actually became the main object of temperance advocates.

The efforts of three New England preachers, among whom was the Reverend Lyman Beecher, father of Harriet Beecher Stowe, finally made the idea of temperance as a religious issue; and by the middle of the 1840s, every state legislature had its temperance lobbies. And who could forget the early days of the Anti-Saloon League when such termagants as Carry Nation made their hatchet-swinging attacks on the liquor dispensaries in Kansas?

It wasn't until World War I began in Europe in 1914 that it was discovered that the German-American Alliance had been a major clearing house for anti-prohibition propaganda because of the influence of German brewers. On April 6, 1917, when Congress declared war on Germany, the Anti-Saloon League made the most of this fact and helped speed up the ratification of the prohibition amendment in January of 1919. Even with all the pressure being put on Congress, it still took a whole additional year before the Volstead Act finally went into effect on January 16, 1920.

As was to be expected with so much advance warning, hoarding, and frantic private purchasing took place. Even with all of this preparation on the public's part, no one really expected that the so-called "Noble Experiment" would actually last fourteen years—fourteen years during every minute of which it was broken on a widespread scale despite everything that the Federal government and its numerous agencies did to enforce it.

Since the youth had always enjoyed "putting something over" on those in authority, the major criminal elements involved in rum-running and bootlegging had no trouble enlisting young jerks like my brother John to assist them in their nefarious activities.

It was on a warm, clear night in July of 1928 that Alissa, of all people, informed us that John had been arrested in Suffolk County for taking part in a rum-running operation.

Unable to get ahold of Arthur, she was at a loss as to how to deal with the police who came to inform her that someone claiming to be a relative of hers had just been arrested less than one mile from her home.

Hoping to contact Richard and learn the name of the family lawyer, she naturally called our house.

"Richard, a terrible thing has happened. John has been arrested for rum-running. We have to get him a lawyer, and Arthur isn't home, so you have to do something," Alissa said frantically.

"Calm down, Alissa! It's two o'clock in the morning. As soon as it's reasonable, I'll give Mr. Lewis, the attorney who handled Father's estate, a call and see what's to be done."

"You can't make him spend the night in jail. Your mother will be frantic when she realizes he hasn't been home all night. What will she say when she finds out he's in jail?"

"She'll probably say, 'Poor unfortunate John. Look what trouble his friends have gotten him into now,'" Richard calmly answered. "Don't worry, Alissa. Mother's sleeping, and I promise to catch her first thing in the morning before she becomes worried. It really is too late to do anything tonight anyway, so why wake her up? Go to sleep, and I'll phone you as soon as I learn anything."

Unfortunately, Mother did awaken before Richard, and upon discovering John's unslept in bed, she became hysterical. When Richard explained to Mother what had happened, I also learned for the first time about John's nocturnal activities. Upon hearing that her favorite son had spent the night in jail, Mother promptly fainted. When she finally came to after the application of spirits of ammonia, her reaction was "Why does everyone pick on my poor, unfortunate John? I told him that his friends were not good enough for him. Look what they've led the poor boy into doing." (It's a wise son who knows his own mother.)

With a half-awake Mr. Lewis in tow, we all rushed out to the Pine River Falls jail in Suffolk County where Arthur and Alissa were to meet us at 10:00 a.m. When we were led to the cell where my brother was eating a substantial breakfast, Mother ran past the guard who had just unlocked the cell door.

Hugging John to her bosom as he tried to get up from his breakfast tray, Mother shot venomous looks at the guard and said, "My poor son! Have they abused you? Show Mother where they beat you to force you into making that false confession!"

While the confused guard watched us all piling into the small but neat cell, he tried to assure Mother that no one had abused John. He had been very well looked after.

The sheriff, whose curiosity had been aroused by all the commotion, kindly transferred the lot of us into his private and more spacious office. As Mother advanced on the poor man in her best Boudicca manner, the sheriff quickly took refuge behind his desk and asked Mother and Alissa to be seated.

"This is all a mistake," Mother informed the sheriff. "And if you don't immediately release my son, I'll see that Big Al hears about it. Then you'll be sorry!"

Looking impressed, the guard asked Mother, "Do you mean you really know Al Capone?"

"Of course not! I mean Big Al Saronna."

"Oh, you mean the old guy who owns the taxi and repair shop businesses," said the disappointed young guard. "Now take it easy, Mrs. Andros," warned the sheriff. "As to Big Al, he runs a clean operation, and he'd be the last person to help your son. Matter of fact, Mr. Saronna is the one who put us wise to last night's caper."

"What?" asked an astonished Alissa. "Are you saying that my father is the one who called the police to arrest John?"

"No, no, not exactly. It seems that the last few times your father was out visiting you in the Pine Barrens, he noticed some suspicious lights in the vicinity of your house."

"He never said anything to me. Did he mention it to you, Arthur?"

"Come to think of it, he did mention something sometime after New Year's Eve," admitted Arthur. "I didn't pay too much attention to it though. You know what a fanatic your father is where you're concerned."

As Alissa was about to protest, the sheriff cut her off, probably hoping to avoid a family quarrel which would only complicate things even more.

"I guess he didn't want to worry you. Your father thought it was probably poachers using their headlights to blind the deer for an easy catch. He told us that you're an animal lover, and if you thought that someone was out hunting on your property, you'd never have a moment's rest. You'd be likely to stay up all night looking for lights. Said you also have a nasty temper, and he was afraid that if you caught them at it, he wouldn't put it past you to either run them down or put a bullet through their heads... Though I think he was just joking about the last part...or at least, I hope so," the sheriff said worriedly, scratching his head.

"So what do poachers have to do with my poor boy?" Mother impatiently urged.

"I was just getting to that, Mrs. Andros. It didn't make much sense to me and my men for poachers to be hunting so near a house when there are miles of uninhabited forest in Suffolk County. Why would they take the chance of their lights being spotted or their shots being heard? My deputy and I figured that either someone was casing Alissa's place or something else was going on. We decided to keep a tighter patrol on the Barrens. While we spotted lights several times, we never could find the source."

"Yeah," the deputy added, "that's a lot of woods out there with miles of firebreaks running through them."

"Right. It was actually just a fluke that made us think there might be some connection to liquor smuggling. As you probably know, the Coast Guard doesn't have an easy time of it, trying to patrol both shores of Long Island. That's a lot of shoreline and a lot of deserted beaches. Just for the heck of it, we started marking down the dates when we saw lights in the Barrens and asked Mr. Saronna to do the same. We would have liked to have gotten the cooperation of Arthur and Alissa, but there are some rough elements involved in this business, and the fewer people who know about it, the better.

"Anyway, we decided to check our dates with the Coast Guard and any suspected liquor landings. Sure enough, there did seem to be a connection! Just last month, one runner, the Island Belle, was caught about fifteen miles east of here as her crew was unloading contraband liquor. The Hampton Police were unable to catch the waiting drivers, however, and reported losing the cars just east of Pine River Falls somewhere in the vicinity of the Barrens."

"I remember that," Alissa piped in. "It was about three in the morning when a patrol car with two policemen woke me up and asked if I had seen anything suspicious around lately. They told me not to open my door to anyone else that night and not to mention them having stopped by to anyone. Since Arthur slept through the whole thing anyway, I didn't even tell him."

Arthur seemed entirely nonplussed by Alissa's revelation and merely shrugged his shoulders.

"Last night," the sheriff continued, "the Coast Guard had gotten a tip that another ship was expected to make a landing somewhere along the South Shore. They wanted to get the middlemen too this time and asked us to keep watch around the Barrens.

"They let the ship come in, and after it was unloaded, the Feds tailed the five cars loaded with liquor. Again, they lost them in the vicinity of the Barrens. But this time, my men and I were ready! We had the entrances to the firebreaks heavily patrolled, especially the area around Alissa's house. Sure enough! This turkey"—the sheriff pointed to John—"drove right into our open arms."

"I was only going to visit my brother and sister-in-law," swore an innocent-looking John. "It was so dark that I made a wrong turn."

"Sure you were! At 2:00 a.m. and bringing them a present of ten cases of illegal liquor," snorted the sheriff.

"A little hostess gift," John explained.

"How could you, John?" moaned Alissa.

"It was real good stuff! Same quality as Captain Bill McCoy brings in. You know, 'the real McCoy,'" bragged John.

"Sheriff Macklebee, isn't there something you can do? He's only a dumb kid," Alissa argued. "He's never been in trouble before."

"Sorry, Alissa. I know now that he really is your brother-in-law, but it's a Federal case, and there really isn't anything I can do except try to get an early hearing. If he's never been in trouble before, like you said, he probably won't get much more than a rap on the knuckles and maybe a light sentence to teach him a lesson in using better judgment when choosing his friends."

"My poor baby! In jail!" Mother cried hysterically.

The sheriff looked at us in embarrassment. "Look, folks, you've got your lawyer with you. Why don't I leave all of you alone for while so you can talk this thing over and decide what's best to do. I'll even leave the prisoner—heh, heh!—unguarded. I don't think he'll try to escape," he said, looking uncomfortably at the window behind his desk and walking out.

After an awkward silence, Mr. Lewis spoke his first words since we had arrived. "Well, now, John, why don't you explain to us exactly what happened?"

"Nothing to explain," John remonstrated.

Just then, I noticed the deputy outside the window, supposedly pruning some shrubs.

"Do you mean this really isn't a mistake?" Mother asked, the dawn finally breaking through. "Are you telling me that my own son has been involved in criminal activities?"

"What are you so shocked about, Mother?" Richard asked. "It's not the first time, as you well know."

"It's not?" asked a confused Alissa.

"No," Richard added. "John's been getting into trouble since he was about five years old."

"He was only a baby." Mother sobbed.

"Yes, a baby gangster," I retorted while Mother and John gave me dirty looks.

"You can't have forgotten when the emporium was broken into so many times that Father was forced to hire a night watchman?" Richard relentlessly continued.

"Don't you remember how embarrassed father was when the guard caught a ten-year-old John breaking into the delivery entrance?"

"It was only a boyish prank," Mother insisted.

"That's what you used to say when at five years old, he was robbing money from your purse and breaking open Edward's piggy bank," Richard protested. "And why do you think the cash register was short so often?"

"I always said the employees couldn't be trusted. That's why I used to insist on being cashier myself even though your father felt it wasn't proper."

"Oh, Mother, why don't you admit it? You wanted to be cashier because as John got older, you knew that he was helping himself to the till, and this way, you could replace the money before Father got wise. Why don't you stop protecting him? He only goes on to bigger and worse things the older he gets."

"Didn't you ever feel guilty, Mother, firing those innocent cashiers?" I asked in shocked disapproval.

"I paid them off and gave them excellent references. No one was hurt. I even personally arranged better jobs for some of them," Mother tried to justify herself.

"Poor, poor Eleanor," Alissa crooned sympathetically, hugging Mother. "How very difficult it must have been for you! How long has this rum-running thing been going on, John? It was your first time, wasn't it?" pleaded Alissa.

"Heck, no! Ever since I saw that great setup when we visited your house at Christmas, we've been using the Pine Barrens as part of our operation. If it wasn't for your nosy father, we probably would still be doing it."

"You leave my father out of this, John. He's not used to dealing with criminals. Sorry, Eleanor," Alissa quickly added for Mother's benefit.

The result of John's attempts at liquor smuggling was a six-month sentence in a nearby Federal prison. Upon hearing the sentence, Mother surprised no one by fainting. She did, however, surprise us when she came to and cried out, "Now he'll miss Uncle Teddy. I just received a letter before we left home that Uncle Teddy and his family are coming to spend the rest of the summer with us. Now they'll miss seeing John." She sobbed. "How will I ever explain it?"

Speaking of missing, I'd been wondering where the missing Arthur had been at 2:00 a.m. when John was arrested but wisely refrained from bringing it up at this time.

It once again was proving true that while the Lord takes with one hand, he gives with the other. While John was being taken away from us to serve his well-deserved six-month hitch, Uncle Teddy and his family were on their way to us and to America. As I considered this, I felt confident that as trades go, the Andros family couldn't help but come out as winners this time.

Chapter 9

An Alien Invasion

> With rue my heart is laden
> For golden friends I had,
> For many a rose-lipt maiden
> And many a lightfoot lad.
> —A. E. Houseman

Uncle Teddy's arrival was enthusiastically anticipated by the entire Andros family. Mother was especially thrilled. If anyone could comfort Mother over John's absence, it was her gay younger brother Teddy. The prospect of seeing Teddy's family was also pleasant, but for Mother, everyone else palled in comparison with Teddy's golden aura.

Family life had been a lonely affair for the seven-year-old Teddy after Mother's marriage and defection to America. Teddy's father, although proud of his only son, took little enough interest in the boy except as his heir apparent. His mother, who was much younger than his father, was busy with her own hectic social life, and thus, Teddy was left almost entirely in the care of various nannies and tutors.

The only one who had shown any real interest and affection to the neglected young boy had been his older half sister Eleanor. She had served both as a mother and father figure to him, and he would spend most of his early years subconsciously searching for a substitute to fill the void in his life.

Being at heart a very affable and jolly fellow, Teddy had little trouble making friends when at an early age, he was sent to the finest public schools that his father could afford. While no intellectual giant, he at least did well enough in school to prevent him being "sent down." His generous and amiable personality, combined with his athletic prowess, won the respect and approval of both his teachers and peers.

It was in his first term at Eton that Teddy met Henry Eversleigh. Teddy and Henry were roommates, and immediately, the two young men hit it off. Their mutual interests, which included sports, good times, and women, did a great deal to cement their new friendship.

Henry was the son of a country squire. His father owned vast acres of farmland in Hampstead Heath and had several tenant farmers attached to his estate. Being the only son, Henry was, like Teddy, the heir apparent to his family's fortune. Unlike Teddy, however, who had no interest in banking, Henry liked farming and considered his time at Eton a chance to sow his wild oats before settling down to sow the real thing.

Both Henry and Teddy, although they differed very much in appearance, were definitely ladies' men. While both were fashionable and dapper, Teddy was dark, debonair, and slender; Henry was tall, powerfully built, and auburn-haired.

It was one day soon after their first meeting, while discussing their families, that they learned they even had older sisters in common.

"I really do miss Eleanor, Henry. You should see her—tall, blonde, regal...just as stately as her name implies."

"Yes, I miss Henrietta too although, mind you, she's probably about as opposite of Eleanor as a gel can get."

"Did you say Henrietta?"

"Yes, my mother was a frail little thing who had a devil of a time with my sister's birth. When the midwife told my father that there probably wouldn't be any more children, he insisted on naming her after himself—Henry, you know. When I came along some years later, my father again couldn't resist naming another child after himself especially since this time, there definitely wouldn't be any more children... You see, my mother died at my birth."

"Oh, I am sorry, old man."

"Yes…well, Henrietta, even though only two years my senior, always mothered me and my father. To do him justice, never held any unfair grudges where I was concerned. Actually, the farm is quite an interesting place to visit… Maybe you'll be able to see it sometime."

It wasn't until Christmas vacation two years later that Teddy finally did get to see Eversleigh Manor.

"Do you think your parents would object to you spending the holidays with my family this year?"

"Object! They'll probably be ecstatic. Father really hates the evenings which he feels obligated to spend away from his club when I come home for the holidays, and Mother somehow, unintentionally I'm sure, always makes me feel like I'm cramping her style. If it weren't for me, there would be so many other things which she'd prefer doing."

"Good show! That's settled then. You spend the holidays with us."

It was with a light heart and happy anticipation that Teddy accompanied his friend a few days before Christmas to Hampstead Heath. Instead of being let in by a servant, it was Henrietta herself who threw open the front door and gayly welcomed both young men.

Henrietta was indeed, as Henry had warned, the exact opposite of Eleanor in both manner and appearance. She was a great strapping redheaded lass whose joviality and lack of formality were well-matched by her father, the squire.

Squire Eversleigh was a hard-drinking, hard-riding old fellow, who was only too happy to have another man in the house, and as for Teddy…why the more, the merrier!

After the greetings and introductions were concluded, they all settled down with cider and ale around a huge fire in a large comfortably shabby room. Teddy admired the hunting prints which decorated the walls, and he certainly couldn't help but notice the four large dogs of various breeds, one of which he had tripped over as he entered. While at first surprised, due to Henrietta's presence at the lack of any feminine touches, he soon discovered that she fit in with the decor as comfortably as the rest of them.

While Henrietta's looks were not the kind that attracted Teddy, who preferred the feminine ideal of the day, he couldn't help but warm to Henrietta's easy manner and the sense of comradery which pervaded the house.

All in all, that Christmas holiday was one of the most memorable of Teddy's whole life, and it was with feelings of loss and disappointment that he returned to Eton. He was consoled by the fact that Henry was returning with him and that the Eversleigh family, being charmed by Teddy, had extended sincere invitations for him to visit them again soon and often.

Back at school, things went on as usual with the two friends "mucking through" their studies and having more than their share of peccadilloes. Now, however, when Henry read his letters from home to Teddy, there was always some warm greeting for Teddy from either the squire or Henrietta, but most often, both asked to be remembered by him and reminded him of his promise to return.

It was just before spring vacation, when both Henry and Teddy were looking forward to another long holiday at Eversleigh Manor, that tragedy struck.

The Thursday before Easter, a large group of friends decided to have a last preholiday fling by forming two teams and having a boat race. Since the members of the opposing teams were drawn by lot, it was simply kismet that placed the two good friends on opposite sides. With much good-natured joking between them, they boarded separate crafts.

As the race progressed, it looked very much as if Henry's team was going to be victorious. Just as Teddy was musing over the ribbing he was going to receive from both Henry and Henrietta, the leading boat capsized.

Although Henry was normally a strong swimmer, a cramp, the cold temperature of the water, or perhaps an injury made him go under. Despite the rescue attempts of both parties of young men, it was a black day for Eton when two drowned and two more came down with pneumonia.

A guilty and shamefaced Teddy met Henrietta when she came to claim her brother's body. Her father had suffered a stroke upon hearing the news, and the prognosis wasn't very favorable for his recovery.

"I can't tell you how very sorry I am, Henrietta… If only we hadn't decided on that fool race. I really did do all I could to save him," swore the distraught Teddy.

"I'm sure you did. Please don't feel guilty. It wasn't your fault… Who could have known that such a tragedy would occur," commiserated the brokenhearted Henrietta. "I understand that two of the chaps came down with pneumonia. Are they going to be all right?"

"I'm afraid one died this morning, but the other fellow is expected to pull through."

"I certainly hope so. I'll pray for him."

"If only it had been me instead of Henry. He had so much to live for…so much to look forward to."

"You mustn't talk like that, Teddy, or I shan't be able to stand it. You also have a promising future ahead of you, and I couldn't bear for anything to happen to you too."

"Forgive me, Henrietta. How is your father doing? I know about his stroke, of course…"

"It doesn't look too good, I'm afraid… I'm sorry, Teddy, but I really must leave now if I want to reach Hampstead Heath before dark. Do remember us, Teddy, and if you're ever in our part of the world, please do stop by. Father and I would love to see you."

"I will. Goodbye, Henrietta," Teddy said brokenly.

Nearly two years would pass before Teddy was to see Henrietta again. During those years, they had exchanged cards and letters, and both were kept abreast of the news—the most tragic of which was the death of the squire six months after his son's death. Teddy, who would have liked to attend the funeral, was unable. He was bedridden with a congested chest and so was only able to send his condolences to the very disappointed Henrietta, who, even in her grief, had been hoping to see her late brother's friend once again.

Henry's death had a marked effect on Teddy. While outwardly, he seemed his usual devil-may-care self, those who knew him best sensed a new maturity about him. Even his family noted a gentleness formerly lacking in him combined with a seeming need to settle down.

It was toward this "settling down" that Teddy announced his engagement to a popular society "deb" the following Christmas. Priscilla Marlow was a petite flaxen-haired blue-eyed beauty who, many people felt, resembled a Dresden shepherdess. It was only too bad that it was not only her looks that bore this resemblance.

Almost two years to the day of Henry's death, Teddy found himself not too far from Eversleigh Manor at a house party with his fiancée. When he mentioned the Eversleigh to his hosts, they quickly recalled the tragedies of both the squire's and his heir's deaths. When Henrietta's name was brought up, it was discovered that while she was "a good enough gel" and they respected the way she was managing the estate on her own, she was just "not quite the thing."

"After all, my boy," his host said, "any gel who rides around in breeches and insists on managing her lands personally without proper chaperonage, mind you, can never be expected to mix in fashionable society."

"And those dogs," sniffed his hostess, "I can understand a little lapdog, like my Caroline's Puff Puff, but to be trailed constantly by four large hunting dogs… I mean…really! What can that gel be thinking of?"

When Teddy came to Henrietta's defense and even expressed a desire to pay a visit to her the following day, not a few eyebrows were raised in disapproval.

"It just isn't done, dear boy! After all, Ms. Eversleigh is living without adequate chaperonage. It would be considered highly improper."

"I'm sorry to disagree, Lady Holmsby, but the servants along with my fiancée, Priscilla," Teddy said, shooting a direct look at the cowed girl, "whom I am sure will accompany me, will provide all the necessary decorum. I do promise that all the proprieties will be observed."

"Is this true, Priscilla?" Lady Holmsby asked with disapproval.

"Of course, Lady Holmsby. I would be only too happy to accompany Teddy on a visit to Ms. Eversleigh. He has often mentioned his deep abiding friendship and gratitude to the Eversleigh family because of their kindness to him."

"W-well, I suppose that will be all right then," Lady Holmsby reluctantly conceded. "Although I would prefer if Caroline didn't accompany you," she quickly added.

It was with mixed feelings that Teddy approached Eversleigh Manor the next day. While he had informed Henrietta of his engagement and she had responded with the appropriate good wishes, the presence of Priscilla only served to underline how dramatically the past years had changed their lives.

In contrast to his last visit, it was a somber butler who opened the door this time. He led them into the drawing room while he went to fetch the "mistress" who was expecting them.

It was an ecstatic Henrietta who unceremoniously rushed into the drawing room and hugged Teddy.

"Teddy, welcome! I couldn't believe it when I received your note that you'd be calling. I can't tell you how happy I am to see you… Why you haven't changed at all except for getting more handsome, I do believe." And then turning her head in some surprise, she noticed Priscilla.

"Forgive me! Why you must be Teddy's fiancée. Priscilla, isn't it? You should have mentioned that you were bringing her, Teddy," Henrietta scolded. "I'd have prepared a proper tea. As it is, I only have some of the rum cake that you and Henry favored."

"Didn't I mention Priscilla in my note?" asked the abashed Teddy.

"I'm afraid not, but I'm certainly pleased to make your acquaintance, Priscilla," Henrietta said graciously. "Whatever am I thinking of? Why I'm so excited that I forgot to even invite you to sit down! Please excuse me for a few minutes while I inform the cook to set out a proper tea."

"Please don't bother on my account," Priscilla protested. "Rum cake will be just fine."

"Nonsense! I so seldom have guests that I want to do this correctly," Henrietta explained, rushing back out of the room.

As Teddy and Priscilla sat together in awkward silence, he nostalgically looked around at his surroundings. Until this moment, he hadn't realized just how much he had missed Eversleigh Manor. After all, how could a place that he had only visited for one holiday come to mean so much to him...but maybe it wasn't just the place. After all, a house was only as fine and warm as the people who inhabited it, and Teddy had never known three finer or warmer people than Squire Eversleigh, Henry, and...yes, Henrietta.

It was a teary-eyed Henrietta who bade them a fond farewell, promising to come to London for the planned October wedding.

When Teddy finally returned home, his mind kept recalling the visit to Eversleigh Manor, and he couldn't help but compare Henrietta and Priscilla. While he remonstrated with himself to be fair to Priscilla, somehow, no matter how many excuses he made for his fiancée, she always came out the loser. Her docile insipidness was just no match for Henrietta's genuine warmth.

When Teddy tried to discuss his second thoughts with his family, they were horrified. While it was true that they had never met Henrietta, Teddy's descriptions of her left a great deal to be desired.

After all, Priscilla was a real beauty—gracious, popular, and accepted in all the best circles, they pointed out. From what they understood of Henrietta, while seemingly nice enough, she certainly hadn't much to commend her.

"A girl who lives alone with just servants and dogs and carries on like a common field hand certainly isn't the proper partner for you, my son," Teddy's father persisted, making the projected union sound like an unfavorable banking transaction. "And worse of all, think of how offending the powerful Marlow family will affect business," his father moaned.

Despite his family's and friends' objections and despite his reluctance to hurt Priscilla, who really was a sweet, if dull, girl, Teddy was made of stronger stuff.

It was on a sunny, warm Sunday in August in the little chapel at Hampstead Heath that a beaming Henrietta Eversleigh became Mrs. Edward Busby.

Chapter 10

Teddy Busby, Bon Vivant

> A knight was with us, and an excellent man,
> Who from the earliest moment he began
> To follow his career loved chivalry,
> Truth, openhandedness, and courtesy.
> —Chaucer

It was a noisy and expectant group who had assembled in Mother's parlor. Even Mother considered her brother's first trip to America of enough importance to warrant parlor usage, and although we were, at first, uncomfortable in such grand surroundings, the good food and drink combined with a general air of joviality soon relaxed everyone.

Every time we heard a vehicle approaching, we would all race to the windows in the hope that they had arrived. Even Mother, who had scolded us for such undignified behavior, could be seen comically wiggling in her seat with anticipation every time the rest of us ran to look outside. Nothing could ruffle Eleanor Etiquette's demeanor!

Finally, a vehicle pulled up in front of the house, and a knock was heard on the front door. As Mother couldn't contain herself any longer, she flew out of her chair, rushed past Marcie, who had gotten up to open the door, and threw herself into the arms of a very startled Uncle Theo.

"Control yourself, Eleanor. I know you are glad to see me. After all, I haven't been around for many months, and it's only natural that you should miss me," Uncle Theo sympathetically patted Mother's shoulder.

With a shriek of outrage, Mother quickly pulled away and shouted, "What are you doing here?"

"What am I doing here? Why I come, of course, to see your brother Teddy and to see again my favorite niece Alissa," he said, winking at Alissa, who with the rest of us, had rushed to the door.

"I suppose I'll have to ask you in," Mother reluctantly grumbled.

"Of course, Eleanor. It is only good manners."

Pushing his way into the parlor, Uncle Theo looked around perplexedly. "Well, where is the boy wonder whom I always hear so much about?"

"He hasn't arrived yet, and you'd do well to remember that he's no longer a boy. He's a man."

"What! Do you mean to say that England's Childe Teddy ages like the rest of us? Can it be that the boy wonder is no more?"

Trying to divert the usual argument as Mother's face became suffused with red and her eyes had murder in them, Alissa tried to distract my uncle. "Uncle Theo, just the person I was hoping to see! Could you possibly help me with the hors d'oeuvres? Yours are always so much more attractive than mine."

"Of course, lovely Alissa! I would be happy to help you. I will show you how to make them pretty and dainty," my 250-pound uncle said as he lumbered off after Alissa into the kitchen.

"Yes, leave it to Theo to make them dainty," Mother couldn't refrain from shouting after them.

"Now, Eleanor, please do not start that nonsense tonight," Uncle Theo said, turning and starting back into the parlor. Fortunately, Alissa grabbed his arm and, with a strength surprising in such a small person, dragged him back into the kitchen.

It was while Mother was fuming, Marcie and I were playing backgammon, Arthur was sleeping (as usual), and Alissa and Uncle Theo were in the kitchen when the long-awaited aliens finally landed at our front door.

Richard, who had met Uncle Teddy several years before in England, led the entourage with Jack, one of Mr. Saronna's drivers, trailing the parade, balancing two heavy trunks on his broad shoulders.

The years had been kind to Uncle Teddy. At least, I believed that they had. Of course, never having met him, I could only judge by Mother's old photos and even older daguerreotypes of him. At the age of forty-two, Uncle Teddy was still the dashing gay blade of whom Mother had always regaled us with tales. Maturity and a few gray hairs at the temples had only added to his attractiveness. Even Marcie and I, who usually considered forty as "over the hill," had to admit that Uncle Teddy was a very handsome and charming man.

As to Aunt Henrietta... Well, that was another story. Although it's only fair to say from the start that upon getting to know her, she would become one of my favorite people, her appearance was a shocking contrast to her youthful-looking husband. Age, hard farm labor, and an excess of drink had coarsened Aunt Henrietta to such an extent that the thought of her being married to Uncle Teddy absolutely boggled the mind.

My cousins were the biggest surprises of all. Roderick was about my age and the spitting image of his father but without Uncle Teddy's natural amiability. In fact, Roderick's charm, when he bothered to use it, was so phony as to be actually repellent.

His twelve-year-old sister Melinda was a skinny, freckled, owlish carrottop. She was a child of many moods. During the course of her visit, she would develop a close affection for Marcie and Mother and an especially deep attachment to Alissa. Uncle Theo would be able to reduce her to giggling shyness and Richard to a trembling ball of fear, and she would regard Arthur and myself with a very adult aloof disdain.

Uncle Teddy was immediately overwhelmed by a sobbing mother, who rushed into his arms with such force that she almost knocked the poor man off his feet.

Aunt Henrietta kissed me and introduced herself and my cousins while Roderick looked down with his nose in disdain at us and our home. Melinda stood behind her mother with her eyes tightly closed. Whether wishing that she'd disappear or because she couldn't stand the sight of us, I wasn't sure. And all the while, poor Jack struggled to squeeze around everyone, bringing in the rest of the luggage.

While all of this was going on, in walked Uncle Theo with two trays of his dainty hors d'oeuvres, which he immediately set down and rushed over to Uncle Teddy, snatching him from Mother's embrace, and kissed him smack on the lips.

"Teddy, I'd have known you anywhere! You haven't changed much from the sassy seven-year-old who introduced my dear departed Demetrius to this...," he said, pointing rather rudely to Mother.

"And you, Theo, are still that same great, wonderful big gladiator of a man whom I remember!"

"And the same unnatural clod whom I remember," Mother added sotto voce.

"Sit down! Sit down, everyone! Where are your manners, Eleanor? Your family comes all the way from England, and you leave them standing in the hallway."

Before Mother could protest, Uncle Theo led everyone into the parlor where hors d'oeuvres, little sandwiches, and cakes were scattered on trays all over the room. Presently, Alissa walked in carrying a tray with a silver tea service and a carafe of port (Aunt Henrietta's favorite wine).

As Uncle Teddy spotted Alissa, his eyes lit up, and he ran to take the tray from her. "You, my dear, can only be Alissa," he said, smiling charmingly at her.

"How do you know that?" Uncle Theo asked perplexedly. "She cannot possibly look like you expected her to," he said, shooting a glance at Mother.

With a knowing look on Uncle Teddy's face as he realized what Uncle Theo was up to, he said, "But of course, she does." Then Uncle Teddy, always the diplomat, added to assuage Uncle Theo's disappointment at being thwarted, "She is just as lovely as I would expect the wife of an Andros man to be." At this, Uncle Theo brightened considerably.

After being introduced by Aunt Henrietta to Marcie and me, Uncle Teddy looked around and said, "Let's see. I believe there are still two members of the family missing. Where are Arthur and John?"

At these magic words, Mother sobbed. "Oh, my poor, poor baby." Then she ran out of the room.

"What did I say?" asked a contrite Uncle Teddy. "Was it the mention of Arthur or John who caused that reaction?"

"John," I answered.

"Well, what happened to him? Is he in trouble? Has he run away? Someone please?"

"He's in jail," I volunteered.

Upon hearing this, Roderick, who had been looking bored, suddenly perked up. "For what?" he asked.

"He got himself into trouble for rum-running."

"Rum-running? Oh, that's right. You have that dumb prohibition thing over here," Roderick said with disdain.

"Prohibition amendment," I corrected.

"Or Volstead Act," Marcie piped in.

After explaining the whole story with Alissa's help, she excused herself to try and comfort Mother.

"No, no, don't bother, my dear," Uncle Teddy offered. "I've always had a way with Eleanor. Let me give it a try."

From downstairs, we could hear Uncle Teddy's argument with Mother.

"No sense getting yourself sick over this, old gel."

"But, Teddy, he's only a baby. His friends did this to him. They set him up because he's so good-natured."

"I don't know anything about that, but John is twenty-one years old and certainly no baby. As to the rest of it, it's too late to do anything about it now. So I insist that our visit not be ruined by any more idle lamentations… Foolish bit of business, if you ask me," Uncle Teddy said sternly to Mother. "Now wash your face and come downstairs. This is no way to treat me and my family after such a long journey. So hop to it, old gel. We'll be awaiting your gracious presence downstairs."

Sure enough, in about fifteen minutes, Mother came back downstairs. She smiled brilliantly at all of us, and except for an occasional escaped sob, she showed us her determination to keep a stiff upper lip.

As was usually the case with people who hadn't seen each other in some time, Uncle Teddy and Mother reminisced, and their conversations were liberally sprinkled with "Do you remember when's." While this could be very boring for those who didn't—I, for one—find it very interesting, we discovered some new sides to Mother's character, which I never would have guessed at.

"How long will you be staying with us, Uncle Teddy?" I asked.

"Either three or four weeks. I'm not sure which."

"I guess your banking firm really depends on you," Richard speculated.

"Not really, Richard, my boy. It's the farm that can't do without Henrietta." He laughed. "This is the first time since our honeymoon that Henrietta agreed to leave the farm for longer than overnight... Isn't that so, my dear?"

"Well, Teddy, animals and crops are not like pieces of paper, you know. They don't react favorably to everyone," Aunt Henrietta defended herself.

"Admit it, my dear. It's not the crops' or animals' reactions you're worried about. It's you missing those darned horses and dogs," he affectionately corrected her.

"All right. I do admit it. I worry when we're away too long."

"Don't you have a good manager now?" Mother inquired.

"When Teddy first decided to take this trip, I had to look for one. Normally, I prefer to manage the manor and farm myself."

"I can understand that," agreed Mother. "I've always preferred managing the emporium myself too. Good help is so difficult to come by," she insensitively continued, not seeing Richard's wounded expression.

"I was just fortunate that a neighboring farm was letting their manager go now that their older son was taking over. Otherwise, I wouldn't have known what to do. One simply cannot allow an unknown into one's home."

"I should say not," Mother vehemently agreed.

"Enough of this business talk!" Uncle Teddy remonstrated. "I believe you have only one more year of school left, Edward. Any plans for afterward?"

"Oh yes!" I answered enthusiastically. "I want to become a doctor."

"That's a fine ambition, my boy," Uncle Teddy said with interest. "Any specialty in mind?"

"No. I just want to be a good general practitioner. You know, a family doctor."

"And I want to be the queen of England," Mother piped in acerbically.

"You already are a queen, Eleanor, but why so sour on young Edward's future plans?" Uncle Teddy asked in surprise.

"It costs too much to go to medical school."

"There are always scholarships. Aren't there, Edward?"

"Yes, but they're really hard to win, and I doubt if I'd score that highly on the exams."

"I guess it's what Alissa would call 'A Unicorn Dream.'"

"What's that?" Uncle Teddy asked.

"A Unicorn Dream refers to the elusive goals that we establish for ourselves but seldom achieve."

"That's what I mean," explained Mother. "Even though I don't like to discourage you, Edward, you must be realistic. You've never really distinguished yourself academically. I think you should try for something easier."

At this point, Alissa, who had been unusually quiet all evening, joined in. "Eleanor, I'm sorry but I must strongly disagree. I think he should become a doctor because he has the most important quality of all."

"I agree with Alissa," added Uncle Theo. "What quality is that?" he asked sotto voce.

"Compassion, of course."

"Of course!" echoed Uncle Theo, shaking his head emphatically as if he had known all along what Alissa was talking about.

"Edward truly cares about people. He's sensitive enough not to treat them just like impersonal slabs of meat. I'd rather have a doctor who really cares about me as a person any day than some top-notch specialist who hasn't the time to get to know me but only studies me through a set of x-rays," Alissa continued passionately.

"Bravo, Alissa!" Uncle Teddy said. "Needless to say, Eleanor, if Edward does have the qualities that Alissa speaks of, then he must, by all means, be encouraged in his professional ambitions."

With that speech, Uncle Teddy quickly joined Alissa on Marcie's and my list of favorite people.

It was at this point that Roderick, who seemed vexed at me being the center of attention, decided to turn the conversation away from me.

"Didn't you say that you have another brother named Arthur? Where is he?"

As we all looked at each other with embarrassment, Alissa piped in, "Oh, Arthur! He's asleep around here somewhere."

As if on cue, a loud snore erupted from a couch on the far side of the room.

"There he is!" Mother said proudly. "Such a tired boy! I'll wake him so you can meet him," Mother said, rushing over to the couch and shaking him violently.

"He's hard to awaken," explained a red-faced Alissa. "I'm afraid that in all the excitement, I forgot all about him."

"Do not worry, sweet Alissa," consoled Uncle Theo. "In Arthur's case, that is very easy to do."

Looking back over the years, I would say that the fact that he was either overlooked or asleep during the most important of life's events was probably my brother Arthur's biggest problem.

Chapter 11

Pygmalion

> Out upon it, I have loved
>   Three whole days together!
> And am like to love three more,
>   If it prove fair weather.
>
> —Sir John Suckling

A few days after the arrival of the aliens (which I jokingly took to calling them, much to Roderick's chagrin), Alissa arrived driving her father's biggest cab and announced that we were going sightseeing.

"But first, I have an announcement to make. On the last Saturday evening of this month, I'm giving a costume party, or fancy dress ball, as I believe you refer to it," Alissa said, smiling at the aliens.

"What jolly good fun!" approved Aunt Henrietta. "Do you have a theme?"

"Yes. That's the best part," Alissa enthused. "In honor of my newly met relatives, the theme is to be 'Famous People from English History.'"

"How far back can we go?" Roderick asked.

"Do they have to be very famous?" queried a worried Melinda.

"You can go back as far as you like. It doesn't matter if they're very famous, Melinda...just so everyone has heard of them. They can even be fictitious figures or figures associated with English folklore. Try to pick your favorite person or perhaps someone you would have liked to be or feel some special kinship with... The most important thing is for everyone to have a good time. I've brought some books on English folklore and myths and a copy on *Kings and Queens of Great Britain* to help you."

"That was very considerate of you, Alissa," Mother smilingly approved. "Who will be invited?"

"Just the family, I think, and of course, Marcie. I'd also like to try to get Uncle Theo to come."

"Oh no!" groaned Mother at Uncle Theo's name.

"Now, Mother, I think it's a good idea to invite Uncle Theo. Since Father died, he seems so lonely… You can always ignore him, you know. Just don't bait him, and everything will be peaceful enough," I naively asserted.

"What do you mean 'bait him'?" Mother indignantly demanded.

"What is your costume to be?" Melinda tactfully broke in on what could have been a sound verbal whipping from Mother to me.

"Oh yes! That's something I forgot to tell you. Each of us must keep his costume a secret. Only if you're coming as a famous couple, such as William and Mary or Robin Hood and Maid Marian, can you work on your costumes together. In this way, everyone will be surprised."

"What if we end up with duplicates?" Roderick inquired.

"We'll just have to take that chance, but with so many people to choose from, surely that won't happen, especially if we each have a good reason for our choice."

"I think that's an excellent idea," Uncle Teddy said approvingly. "And a very original form of entertainment. It gives us over two weeks to work on our costumes too."

"Well, if that's settled, let's begin today's itinerary," Alissa said with relief.

"What is today's itinerary? I wasn't aware that we had one," Mother perplexedly confessed.

"I thought we'd all pile into my father's cab and visit Manhattan… if everyone agrees."

A volley of yesses met her suggestion, and we all hurried outside to begin our tour.

All in all, it was a very pleasant day. We visited the Statue of Liberty, Central Park, St. Patrick's Cathedral, and various other landmarks. It was a good opportunity, as Alissa pointed out, for us native New Yorkers to really see New York.

Uncle Teddy was especially interested in Wall Street, and so Alissa dropped him off there. Roderick and I opted for the American Museum of Natural History, and the ladies decided to explore the famous Fifth Avenue shops with Tiffany's at the top of their list. We all agreed to make our own ways back to Central Park where we'd meet for the return journey.

The following Sunday, we decided to take a boat trip up the Hudson so that Arthur and Richard could join us. Although Richard declined, Arthur accepted.

Majestic and stately scenery met our eyes, and Alissa entertained us with stories of Dutch folklore. Her relating Rip Van Winkle soon had everyone roaring with laughter since Arthur, as usual, had slept through the whole trip.

The women were especially pleased by our stop at Bear Mountain, and Melinda's enchantment with the bears made her large bespectacled eyes appear even larger.

Roderick, Uncle Teddy, and I favored West Point, and even my snooty cousin made fewer derogatory comments about "the colonies" after a film and lecture on US military power.

The sea air stimulated everyone's appetite, and the three large picnic baskets, which we had brought along, had to be supplemented by numerous snacks at the concession stands.

"I think that more than one type of appetite has been stimulated by the sea air," Roderick opined on the return trip.

"What do you mean?" I asked, relaxing on a deck chair next to Marcie. Aunt Henrietta, Melinda, and Mother had gone inside, claiming the sea breezes were too cold. Arthur, needless to say, was sleeping in a deck chair across from us, and Uncle Teddy and Alissa were standing in the prow while she gaily pointed out various landmarks.

"I think that what I mean is obvious," Roderick sneered. "Have you been watching my father and Alissa?"

"Of course, I have," I snapped with annoyance. "After all, they're standing less than ten feet in front of us. What about them?"

"I'd say that Father's having a hard time keeping his eyes off Alissa. She certainly is a beautiful woman," Roderick leered.

"What rubbish!" Marcie protested. "I think you're vile to even make such a suggestion. The only reason your father is interested in Alissa is because she's a very intelligent and informative person."

"Besides my sister-in-law, you're talking about your own father," I reminded Roderick as I began to uneasily observe the two under discussion. Alissa was a fetching picture with her skirt and long hair blowing in the wind, and now that Roderick had pointed it out, Uncle Teddy did seem to be finding Alissa the most interesting scenery on the tour.

Catching myself, I decided it was just the power of Roderick's nasty insinuations that was making me imagine things that weren't really there... But I couldn't help suddenly wishing that Arthur would wake up and stay awake for a change.

*****

During the following weeks, as the weather became hotter, we went on various excursions to such places as Coney Island and Sunken Meadows. It was the evening following one of these beach excursions that Aunt Henrietta reminded us that Melinda's thirteenth birthday was only two days away.

"We'll certainly have to do something special for that," Mother said happily. "What about dinner at Delmonico's?"

While everyone else seemed delighted with the suggestion, Melinda suddenly looked up from the copy of *Vanity Fair* that she had been reading and stubbornly announced, "I'm not going!"

"But, Melinda," Alissa tried to reason with her, "it's a very fashionable restaurant. The food is absolutely delicious...and wait until you see their dessert carts. Why my mouth's watering already!"

"Sure, it's fine for you to go to places like that. No one laughs at you. I tell you, I'm not going!" Melinda reasserted and ran out of the room crying as if her heart would break.

"Whatever did I say wrong?" Alissa asked bewildered.

"Oh, it wasn't you, Alissa dear," Uncle Teddy consoled, placing an arm around her shoulders.

"But, Teddy, what did she mean about people laughing at her?"

"That's probably my fault," confessed Aunt Henrietta. "Before we came here, Teddy gave me money to take Melinda into town to buy her a proper wardrobe. Somehow...with one thing or another, I never got around to it. I'm afraid that our visit to Manhattan's fashionable shops made her even more aware than ever that she just doesn't look quite the thing."

"Poor Melinda," Uncle Teddy sympathized. "Between her spectacles, freckles, red hair, and outdated clothes, the poor child does, I'm afraid, resemble a funny little red spotted owl."

"If that's all that's bothering her, would you give me carte blanche to completely do her over for the big day? It will be my birthday present to her."

"That might not be so easy, Alissa," Roderick pointed out. "She really does need the spectacles to see with, and if you can't eliminate them, I doubt if you can really do much good."

"The problem isn't so much the fact that she wears spectacles as the style of them. They do make some nicer ones over here. As to her hair, I'm afraid that her long sausage curls went out of style with the Victorians as did her lovely frilly dresses. While I really would like to help, you must understand that...you might not be too pleased with the results."

"It's Melinda's happiness that matters. If you can please her, that will be good enough for us. Right, Teddy?"

"Yes, Henrietta, of course. We give you free rein with Melinda and salute your efforts with Pygmalion."

"I'd like to start tomorrow if it's all right with you, and if you wouldn't mind... I'd like to tell her myself right now."

"Go at it, old girl," Uncle Teddy laughingly said.

*****

By now, Alissa's party was only a few days away. Marcie and I had decided to work on our costumes at her house since they were related and her mother was a dab hand with a needle. We needed all the help we could get since we soon learned that our costumes were too ambitious for two amateurs like ourselves to make alone.

On the day before Melinda's birthday, Marcie and I were just returning to my house after a day of costume fittings and shopping for a gift for Melinda. Alissa and Melinda were out working on the "Great Transformation." Mother had gone to the hairdressers, and she was to meet Uncle Teddy and Roderick downtown for sodas and then on to their own birthday gift shopping. We had been invited to join them but were just as happy to avoid Roderick as much as possible. Richard was probably working in the emporium. The only one expected to be home was Aunt Henrietta who was alternately nursing a bad case of sunburn and a hangover.

As we opened the front door, the raised voices of Richard and Aunt Henrietta froze us in our tracks.

"Don't be so blind, Aunt Henrietta!" Richard shouted. "Surely, even you can see the way he looks at her. Of course, I'm not saying it's all Uncle Teddy's fault. I've always felt that Alissa was little better than a slut."

At this remark, a resounding "slap" filled the air.

"Unless you have proof to back up your ugly insinuations, I would watch my words if I were you. I happen to be very fond of Alissa and won't just sit back and have her slandered."

"Instead, you'd rather your husband have a little adulterous adventure on the side," Richard sneered.

"It won't be his first."

"What!"

"You heard me. What do you expect? Your uncle spends five days a week in London. He only comes out to the farm on weekends and holidays. You, yourself, have pointed out his virility and love of feminine beauty… Do you honestly believe that after being married to him for almost twenty years that I fool myself into thinking that he lives celibately while we're apart?"

"Do you mean to say that you know of these things and you just put up with them?"

"What would you have me do, Richard? Leave him? Oh, I tried that when I first discovered his romantic liaisons shortly after Roderick's birth. He's an honorable man, your uncle...in his way. When I confronted him about the gossip I had heard, he didn't deny it. He admitted it was all true. It was just his nature, and since I knew what he was like before I married him, I should have expected it.

"He agreed to move back to London and stay there until I should summon him. If he didn't hear from me in one month's time, he would presume that I had decided to start divorce proceedings. He insisted that he loved only me and that his little affairs were just harmless adventures, but he acknowledged my right to break our marriage contract since he had broken our vows.

"I kept him waiting the whole month, and I... I took stock of myself. I'm certainly no prize to look at now and wasn't one when I was younger either. Oh, I had land and means and could always get one of the neighborhood bachelors or widowed farmers, who would be only too happy to increase their holdings, to wed me. I even had a few little affairs of my own... Yes, does that also shock you, Richard? Well, you can look just as embarrassed as you please, but since you started this, you can hear me out! Unlike your suave, sophisticated uncle who knows all the pleasures and nuances of lovemaking, these other clods mounted me like...like rutting stallions on a brood mare.

"After these experiences, I had no doubt at all that I'd opt for your uncle any time. He made me—yes, me...an overweight, coarse, uneducated bumpkin—feel like I'm the sexiest, most attractive woman in the world. When your uncle walks in the door, even if it is only two days a week, my whole world lights up because no matter what problems I've encountered during the other five days, I know that your uncle will dispel all the gloom. He has the special gifts of laughter and joie de vivre."

"Well, that's all very commendable, I'm sure, but what about Alissa? And Arthur... Are you willing to have him cuckolded by his own uncle?" Richard persisted.

"Alissa, my heart goes out to that poor child."

"What are you talking about? That poor child, as you refer to her, is seducing your husband."

"We have no proof of that! And I do feel sorry for Alissa married to a man like your brother Arthur. You claim Richard to be such a judge of human nature. If that's so, then why don't you see the emptiness in your own sister-in-law's eyes? She's hungry for love and affection. Something is very wrong with that marriage. Mark my words! No man should have a beautiful wife like Arthur does and treat her with such indifference."

"Why? Because he's always sleeping?"

"That's part of it, but have you ever seen him make any sort of affectionate gesture toward her—either touch her hand, tussle her hair, or slip an arm around her shoulder or waist? Well, neither have I, and if he doesn't start waking up to what he's doing to that marriage, then he deserves to lose her to someone…yes, like Teddy, who makes her laugh and feel good about herself. She's very beautiful as any man should be able to notice. Good Lord, Richard, I don't understand your hostility to her, or maybe I do, but Arthur's indifference, I don't understand at all, and it…it sickens me."

"Are you saying, Aunt Henrietta, that you would actually approve of an affair between those two?"

"Of course not, you fool! No woman approves of such a thing, but God knows Alissa does deserve some romance in her life, and I hope she finds it with someone…hopefully other than Teddy. I love her and want her to at least have one romantic interlude in her life that she can look back on. Alissa also is fond of me, and for that reason, I don't feel like she'd try to take Teddy away from me even if she could, which I doubt.

"Teddy needs me. He needs someone who will nurse his ills be they physical, emotional, or financial. He needs both a mother figure to cosset him and a father figure to tell him what to do. I can do all those things and more. Alissa is too young. She'd want more of Teddy than he's able to give anyone. He's a will-o'-the-wisp and must be enjoyed for what he is."

I didn't know how long we'd been standing in the hallway, but suddenly, I felt a hand touch mine; and as I looked up into Marcie's tear-filled eyes, she said, "I want to go home, Edward."

"We can't just leave like this. What if Alissa and Melinda come in and overhear what they're saying? It would kill them!"

"You're right." Marcie sobbed. "What can we do?"

Grabbing her hand, I quietly led her outside again. This time, upon reaching the front door, I knocked sharply and walked in, yelling, "Hello! We're back. Is anybody home?" and thereby averted what could have been a complete disaster for several people whom I dearly loved.

Chapter 12

New York! New York!

Haste thee, nymph, and bring with thee
Jest and youthful Jollity...
Come, and trip it as you go,
On the light fantastic toe.

—John Milton

No sooner had we announced our arrival than Mother, Uncle Teddy, and everyone's favorite cousin, Roderick, walked in. They all seemed very pleased with themselves and informed the rest of us that they had been very successful on their shopping expedition. Roderick naturally bragged that he had found the perfect gift for his sister and swore that no one's gift could possibly outdo his.

"Have Alissa and Melinda arrived yet?" an anxious Uncle Teddy inquired.

"With the overhaul that Melinda will need, I wouldn't expect them till sometime around Melinda's fourteenth birthday. Despite what Father may think, I doubt it even if Alissa is a magician," Roderick snidely remarked.

"How have you and my son Richard spent the afternoon? I hope the two of you have taken the time to become well acquainted," Mother asked Aunt Henrietta while four very red faces looked back at her.

"Yes, indeed! Richard and I have spent the entire afternoon exchanging various viewpoints and getting to know each other very well."

"I'm so glad! Conversing with Richard can be such a broadening experience...if you can get him to talk," Mother said proudly.

It was Uncle Teddy who noticed that neither Aunt Henrietta nor Richard would meet each other's eyes during the entire conversation. When he looked questioningly at Marcie and me, I simply shrugged my shoulders and mouthed the words "We just walked in" to him.

It was by now close to dinnertime, and Mother was fretting that Alissa and Melinda would be late, having to eat leftovers. Since Alissa would be in Queenstown most of the day, Arthur was also expected, and Mother always liked to make Arthur's dinner a little special... I supposed that was due to some lingering remnant of the Prodigal Son syndrome.

As we were all seated in the dining room, about to start on the traditional company fare, the front door was heard to open. All of us, except Arthur, immediately put down our forks and awaited the entrance of Melinda and Alissa.

"Do you think it's them?" Marcie, who was invited to stay to dinner in honor of the great occasion, asked and then answered, "Of course, who else can it be?"

No moment in history had ever been met with greater anticipation than Melinda's entrance by the Andros-Busby clan. With imaginary fanfare and drum rolls, in walked Alissa with a "cat that ate the canary" grin.

"I would like to introduce to all of you that English femme fatale... Melinda Busby!"

While we all waited expectantly, even Arthur from whom mother had taken his fork away, an empty doorway met our eyes. With a little sigh of exasperation, Alissa left the dining room, and suddenly, Melinda was literally propelled by what looked like a violent push in the back from Alissa into our midst.

When no one made any comment, indeed, we were all too stunned to do so, a red-faced Melinda said, "You don't like it!" and turned to leave.

"Don't like it?" Uncle Teddy jumped up. "We're overwhelmed! You look absolutely smashing, Melinda! Who said Alissa wasn't a magician?" Uncle Teddy shot at Roderick.

Melinda did look marvelous. She was dressed in a fashionably short blue pleated dress, white silk stockings, and even white shoes with straps and small heels. Her long sausage curls had been cropped, and a cap of short shiny red curls enhanced the before unnoticed piquancy of her features, but best of all, my cousin Melinda had one of the greatest pairs of legs that I had ever seen. She had the trimmest ankles, cutest knees, and shapeliest calves. Even Roderick seemed surprised by his sister's unveiling.

Seeing the direction of all our eyes, Alissa laughingly said, "With legs like that, the rest is probably superficial, but do try to notice her nice new clothes, hairdo, and spectacles too."

I had often heard of the metamorphosis of caterpillars into butterflies, but the actual experiencing of such a transformation was a wonderful thing.

As the rest of us finally got around to voicing our approval, the so-far anxious Melinda finally relaxed. Always the gentleman, Uncle Teddy escorted Melinda to her chair with a flourish.

"May I serve milady some roast beef? Or what about some Yorkshire pudding or the moon or the stars?" he joked, delighting our new little swan.

Laughing with pleasure at Melinda's genuine happiness, Alissa seated herself next to Marcie, and dinner finally commenced.

Since Arthur had to work the next day, it was agreed to make the evening a short one. As they were about to depart, Alissa told everyone to wait while she ran outside for a minute. We hardly had time to wonder at her strange departure before she came running back in carrying a very large package wrapped in a gold foil-type paper and decorated with a large pink bow. Handing it to Melinda, she explained that it was really a birthday present, but it would be better if Melinda received it today.

"Should I open it now?" an excited Melinda asked.

"Not until you're alone in your room. It's a new dress for tomorrow's dinner at Delmonico's."

"My goodness! In all the excitement about the 'new me,' I had forgotten that I never did shop for any clothes other than what I'm wearing. But when did you get it?" Melinda inquired.

"It was while you were getting your haircut. Don't you remember?"

"You said you had to shop for a new outfit."

"Well, I did…for you," Alissa laughingly explained.

"Can't we even have a peek?" Aunt Henrietta pleaded.

"That's up to Melinda."

Seeing my cousin's face light up, I had no doubt what her decision would be. As she carefully unwrapped the fancy package and dug through layers of cushiony tissue paper, a white sleeveless chemise-style dress emerged. It was of a silky material and had a pink low-slung sash around the hips, as was the fashion of that time. Below the sash were three tiers of pale pink flounces.

"Why it's just beautiful, Alissa!" Melinda stared transfixed at the dress.

"But do you really think the pink will work with Melinda's red hair?" Mother asked skeptically.

"Isn't it a little too long?" I asked as Melinda held it against her and pirouetted for our approval.

"The pink will look lovely on her, and the length is just right for a fancy evening. Of course, it's a little longer than the dress she has on now, but it's supposed to be. Just wait till tomorrow, and you'll see."

Turning to Melinda, Alissa smilingly said, "Just as long as you're pleased."

"It's the best present I've ever had," Melinda said brokenly as she rushed to hug Alissa.

*****

Melinda's birthday dawned sunny and hot. Our reservations for Delmonico's weren't until 8:00 p.m., and Alissa and Arthur were expected between 5:30 p.m. and 6:00 p.m. Melinda wanted Alissa to help her dress, and the adults of the party wanted to gather early enough to get what Aunt Henrietta referred to as "a rosy glow." It would also be a good time for the rest of us to give Melinda her presents. Although this was a difficult thing for a thirteen-year-old to do, she chose to wait for Alissa's arrival before opening them.

Alissa phoned at noon and said that she and Arthur would definitely be in Queenstown by 6:00 p.m. Since it was such a warm day, Mother had asked her to phone us as to the exact time since no one wanted to don evening clothes before they had to.

I'd never understood this reluctance on the part of women. Their evening clothes were always so much barer than their daytime wear that one would expect them to be anxious to put them on in hot weather.

Unlike Alissa's house in which there were three bathrooms for two people, trying to arrange equal time for seven people in one bathroom in our house was a major undertaking. We ended up drawing lots for bath times, and the poor unfortunates, among which I was numbered who drew the earliest times, were again uncomfortably sweaty when it was time to change.

Despite these difficulties, everyone, including Melinda, who had decided not to wait for Alissa after all, was waiting in the parlor when Alissa and Arthur arrived.

Alissa looked so ravishing that to this day, I couldn't recall exactly when Arthur entered although it was undoubtedly after his wife. While all the ladies looked charming in their evening dresses, there was no doubt that Alissa was clearly the "belle of the ball." The expression on Uncle Teddy's face when he saw her assured me that he shared my views.

Seemingly unaware of her effect on us, Alissa ran over to Melinda, wished her a happy birthday, and more or less reminded everyone why we were assembled there sweating in the first place. As Arthur began opening several bottles of imported champagne, which Mr. Saronna had donated to the occasion from his private stock, Mother passed the glasses around, and everyone sang "Happy Birthday" to Melinda who was allowed half a glass.

Melinda was very pleased with her gifts which included a mother of pearl vanity set from her parents, a copy of the poems of Emily Dickinson from Richard, a beaded evening bag from Mother, a new cardigan from Marcie and me, and a book on self-improvement from Roderick. Although Alissa had given Melinda her dress yesterday, she now presented her with a cameo locket from Arthur and herself for which Roderick offered to supply his picture. When Melinda adamantly refused his offer, Roderick became grossly insulted.

Since a spat was about to break out between his two offspring and spoil the evening, Uncle Teddy suggested that they roll back the carpet and do some dancing. Mother protested that it was much too hot, and besides, there was only a half hour left before we had to leave.

While Mother and Uncle Teddy argued it out, the doorbell rang, and before anyone could answer it, in walked Uncle Theo.

"Hello, everyone! How happy and surprised you must be to see me so unexpectedly." Before anyone could either agree or, as in Mother's case, disagree with him, Uncle Theo continued. "I have come to bring little Melinda a birthday present."

"How did you find out it was her birthday?" asked Mother, looking accusingly at us.

"The owner of Queenstown Imports from whom you bought that pretty beaded evening bag told—"

"I know," interrupted Mother. "He told a friend who just happened to have lunch in your restaurant."

"Almost correct, Eleanor. It was the owner himself who ate in my restaurant."

After Melinda excitedly unwrapped the present and took it out of its small box, she looked confusedly at all of us. Remembering her manners, she prettily thanked Uncle Theo, saying, "It's just what I've always wanted."

"Of course you have," sneered Roderick. "So tell us what it is."

As Melinda turned her usual unbecoming shade of fire engine red, Uncle Theo came to the rescue. "Roderick, you ignorant boy, of course, Melinda knows that they are worry beads, and with you for a brother, I am sure she will make good use of them."

"I sure will," Melinda agreed, hugging Uncle Theo for both the gift and the put-down to her brother.

"And how is my favorite beautiful niece?" Uncle Theo asked Alissa. "No, don't bother to answer. Anyone who looks as beautiful as you can only be perfect… And what about you, Eleanor? Looking at you leaves one with a totally different feeling," he teased.

Before Mother could retort, Uncle Teddy diplomatically broke in and explained to Uncle Theo, who was looking in some consternation at our partly rolled up rug, that he had wanted to dance but Mother was against it.

"Oh, I too love to dance," Uncle Theo said happily. "Eleanor is always the party pooker, I am afraid."

"Party pooper," Mother corrected.

"Yes, you are that too, Eleanor," Uncle Theo solemnly agreed.

"Alissa also loves to dance," Arthur added. "She and her father often go to the Roseland Ballroom on weekends and dance for hours."

"I didn't know that, Alissa. Does your mother also like to dance?"

"No, Eleanor. She and Arthur keep each other company watching and talking while Father and I trip the light fantastic."

"I too trip," Uncle Theo proudly beamed.

"And over more than just the light fantastic," Mother agreed.

"Uncle Theo," Alissa invited, "why don't you come with us to Delmonico's, and afterward, we can all come back here for some dancing. Melinda's too young, or we could all go to a nightclub."

"Alas, sweet lady, I must return to the restaurant. Some other time, I will show you some real Greek dancing."

"Maybe you could come with us some weekend to the Roseland?" Alissa suggested.

"I am afraid I do not know fancy ballroom dancing."

"Why not, Theo?" Mother asked. "I can just see the sensation you'd cause standing in the middle of the ballroom floor with a glass of water on your head."

"What do you mean, Eleanor?" a confused Alissa inquired.

"It's the way Greeks dance," Mother explained.

"Do you mean that the man and woman face each other with glasses of water on their heads?"

"No, no. Greek men only dance with other Greek men," Uncle Theo indignantly corrected.

"From the horse's mouth himself." Mother smiled smugly.

Seeing the direction this conversation was taking and noting the time, I reminded everyone of our eight o'clock reservations.

"Yes, I leave you good people to your dinner, but you must promise to visit my restaurant before you go back to England. I have a big surprise for all of you that I will tell you about next time I see you," Uncle Theo said cryptically as Mother ushered him out the door.

*****

Dinner at Delmonico's was an aesthetic as well as culinary feast. Its lavish decor met everyone's expectations and was only surpassed by the food and service. Melinda was especially enchanted as Uncle Teddy must have tipped off (both monetarily and orally) the waiters that Melinda was the birthday girl because a great fuss was made over her.

As exciting as our evening proved to be, the real fun—or should I say trouble—did not begin until we had returned home. No sooner had we walked in the door than Uncle Teddy suggested that we should burn up some calories by dancing. Even though it was 9:30 p.m., I agreed to give Marcie a call and see if she could come over.

Since Richard had the biggest record collection in the house, he agreed to bring them downstairs for us to use—a big concession for Richard who hated having his possessions handled by other people.

Marcie—who, like most women, was always anxious to dance—was over before I could bat an eye. It was great fun as everyone danced to such popular tunes as "Ain't She Sweet," "Baby Face," and "Yes, Sir That's My Baby." Marcie and I were soon joined in the Charleston and Black Bottom by Alissa and Roderick and then Uncle Teddy. Even Richard did a sedate waltz with both Mother and Aunt Henrietta. Only Arthur refused to dance at all.

It was quite late, and everyone was near exhaustion when Uncle Teddy asked a casual question which changed the whole tone of the evening.

"What's your favorite dance, Alissa?"

"Oh, that's easy." She smiled. "It's the tango."

It took Uncle Teddy a while before he found something appropriately called "Green Eyes" in the stack and invited Alissa to tango with him. Perhaps it was the fact that they were the only two on the floor since no one else tangoed, but there was something in the way their two bodies came together to start the dance, which made me take a second look at Alissa. She was wearing a pale green gown of the thinnest possible material. It was cut low in front and back and slit quite high on both sides to facilitate dancing, I supposed, although the slits were serving a better purpose than just that.

Except for Richard's two waltzes, this was the first contact dance of the night, and the effect of that contact was felt in reverberations which echoed all around us. Only Mother, Melinda, Aunt Henrietta, and Arthur (naturally) didn't feel them since the food, drink, and exercise had put them to sleep.

As I had already mentioned, Alissa wore her hair longer than the current fashion. It hung several inches down her back and curled slightly under at the ends. In front, it hung seductively over one very green eye and was pushed behind her ear on the other side with a jeweled comb.

As Uncle Teddy stepped forward and Alissa back in the first movements of the dance, Roderick whispered to me, "Ten to one, your sister-in-law isn't wearing any underwear."

While this suggestion shocked me, I couldn't help looking even more closely at Alissa, and although I'd never admit it to Roderick, it didn't seem as though she possibly could be wearing any as the lines of it certainly would have been seen through the onionskin-like material of her gown. And I must admit that the only lines showing on the gown were Alissa's own.

Marcie and I had always previously thought that our dances were daring, but there was something so sensual about Uncle Teddy and Alissa's tango that I felt like a voyeur watching them.

The record was a long one which Roderick made even longer by restarting it so quickly that no one except Marcie, Richard, and I realized what he was doing.

It soon became apparent that even Uncle Teddy and Alissa were no longer aware of the rest of us as his hold on her tightened and their bodies undulated provocatively in perfect time to the primitive rhythms of all mating dances from time immemorial.

Marcie, who was by this time too embarrassed to watch, began carrying empty glasses into the kitchen while I was too fascinated not to watch.

"Jesus," Roderick whispered huskily to me, "I'm getting so excited just watching them that I'll never get to sleep."

As Richard started to walk out the door to leave the room, Roderick wondered aloud what was bothering him. Richard's reason for leaving was soon revealed to us as he slammed the door and said, "They're disgusting!"

This caused several things to happen at once. Melinda, Mother, and Aunt Henrietta all awoke startled by the loud noise. Shouts of "bravo" and "good show" met Uncle Teddy and Alissa's performance since all three were too embarrassed at having fallen asleep not to pretend that they had been awake the whole time.

Uncle Teddy came to his senses, unfortunately, as he was into a deep dip with Alissa where he was bent provocatively prone over her body. He reacted so suddenly that he actually let go of Alissa, who was rudely awakened from her trance with a start as her lovely, shapely derriere hit the floor.

"Teddy, you dog," Aunt Henrietta chided him, "you've dropped her."

"No, no," Alissa quickly arose, protesting. "My hands got sweaty, and I'm afraid they slipped… It's the heat, you know," she finished lamely.

"It must be," Mother agreed. "Your face is so red. You and Teddy have had enough dancing in this heat. Go out in the garden and cool off."

Since I had reason to believe that going into the garden would do anything but cool the two of them off, I offered to go too.

"No, no," Mother protested. "Look at the time. You escort Marcie home this minute."

"Yes," Aunt Henrietta agreed. "Up to bed, Melinda, and you too, Roderick. I'll thank you now for a lovely demonstration of ballroom dancing, Alissa, and for helping to make Melinda's party so festive. I'm off to bed also."

After we all kissed each other good night, everyone was off to bed except me, who had to walk Marcie home; Arthur, who had never awoken; and Uncle Teddy, who quickly escorted Alissa into the garden.

By the time I got back from Marcie's, almost forty-five minutes had passed. Alissa and a sleepy Arthur were just leaving, and Uncle Teddy was seeing them to their car.

What happened in those missing forty-five minutes, I would always wonder about…but never really know.

CHAPTER 13

An Elizabethan Costume Party

> Gather ye rosebuds while ye may,
>   Old Time is still a-flying;
> And this same flower that smiles today,
>   Tomorrow will be dying.
> —Robert Herrick

We didn't see much of Alissa or Arthur the week before her costume party. She phoned us often to keep us up to date on the progress she was making. Although she had wanted more of a medieval decor, she explained that she had settled for Elizabethan since it was a lot more civilized.

While the rest of us were making last-minute alterations to our costumes, our curiosity was by now really peaked. Everyone had kept their promise to Alissa about keeping their costumes a secret. Except for those working in pairs, like Marcie and me, the rest of us had no idea whom the others had chosen. There was many a squeal of protest to be heard every time one of us walked into a room unannounced and caught someone working on his costume.

There were many things which Alissa needed ahead of time from Mother, and whenever she phoned in a list, Uncle Teddy was only too happy to volunteer his services as messenger. When I first learned of this, I immediately felt a twinge of apprehension until one day, looking out the window as Uncle Teddy set out for Alissa, I spotted a small curly redhead seated next to him.

Noticing my curiosity, Aunt Henrietta also looked outside and said, "Poor Melinda is so attached to Alissa that she takes every opportunity to see her. I'm afraid she sticks to Teddy like lichen every time she learns that he might be dropping something off at Alissa's for your mother. Our departure next week will really break Melinda's heart."

Nodding in agreement with my aunt's statement, I wondered if Melinda, who was a great deal more perceptive than most people realized, was actually sticking to her father for the reason stated, or was it possible that she hadn't really slept through the little birthday performance which Uncle Teddy and Alissa had put on.

With one thing I did agree completely with my aunt, hearts were going to be broken over their imminent departure…and I doubted if it would just be Melinda's.

*****

The afternoon before the party, Marcie and I were over her house eating lunch while her mother put the finishing touches on our costumes. Looking worriedly at her, I said, "Everything will be all right tomorrow night, don't you think?"

"What do you mean? Oh, you mean Alissa and Teddy. I wish you would stop that, Edward," she complained. "Do you realize that in trying so hard to prove their innocence, you have become as obsessed as Roderick, who's trying to prove their guilt. I can't believe that you really have so little faith in your uncle and Alissa."

"Do you mean to say that you saw nothing wrong in that tango they were doing?"

"All I saw were two adults, who had too much to drink, get a little carried away," she said, averting her eyes from mine.

"This is all your cousin Roderick's fault, you know. He could be Johnny Appleseed with the way he persistently plants seeds of suspicion in everyone's minds… And Richard is no better! Why if it hadn't been for the sick insinuations of those two, I wonder if we would have seen anything more than two people doing the tango. It is a very sexy dance, you know," she defended.

"Perhaps you're right… I just don't know. All I am sure of is that I have very serious qualms about the party."

*****

The day of the party was hot and humid, and the reason for Alissa's warnings to keep the costumes as cool as possible were belatedly understood. But when your theme was historical, this really wasn't very possible since dressing for the seasons was unheard of in days of yore.

The party was to start at 8:00 p.m., and we all agreed to meet fully costumed in Mother's parlor at 7:00 p.m. Marcie and I had dressed at her house, and by the time we arrived, the rest of the family was already assembled. Mother was dressed in light blue medieval robes with a fleur-de-lis and a lion rampant sewn across the bodice. Over her dark blue wimple, she wore a gold crown.

Because of the fleur-de-lis, the lion, and the hint of her name, Melinda, who was quite the history buff, soon guessed that Mother was Eleanor of Aquitaine. When I confessed that the logic behind her guess still eluded me, she explained with some disgust at my ignorance that everyone knows Eleanor of Aquitaine was married to both the kings of France and England, thus, the pictures on her bodice.

Melinda's costume was more obvious. She wore a long elaborately embroidered and bejeweled black-and-gold brocade gown. Her hair was severely pulled off her forehead and then tightly frizzed in a sort of aureole effect. She also was crowned and wore elaborate chains around her neck with a jeweled pendant. In her hand, she carried an ornate feather fan with an ivory handle. No one could fail to guess her identity for around her neck, she wore the famous Elizabethan stiffly starched ruff, which stuck out about a foot all around and made her resemble a red-haired pig's head on a platter. Her face was painted white, and the effect was certainly reminiscent of Elizabeth I, the Virgin Queen.

Uncle Teddy was dressed in a plain black suit with a striped black-and-white vest. Although the suit was clearly outdated, if it wasn't for Aunt Henrietta, I'd have never guessed who he was supposed to be. Aunt Henrietta's rather squat figure was also clad in black. She had on a plain black gown which belled out all around her with a little white lace cap and veil on her head. When they stood together, there was no mistaking them for anyone but Victoria and Albert.

We also had two knights in the room. One was dressed in the traditional silver coat of arms which we usually associate with knighthood. Over this, he wore a white tunic with a large red cross emblazoned on it like the Crusaders. Here also, the person's name helped, and we found ourselves in the awesome presence of Richard Coeur de Lion. It's a good thing my brother Richard was in good physical condition because his discomfort must have been as monumental as his costume.

Roderick wore chained mail over a medieval type of tunic. When everyone's guesses failed to uncover his identity, he gleefully explained that he was Mordred.

"Why Mordred?" I asked in confusion.

"I've always sympathized with the poor unwanted son of King Arthur, and my reasons might become more obvious as the night progresses," he mysteriously said.

Before anyone could really start wondering about this, the doorbell rang, and in clanked another knight. This one weighed about 250 pounds, undressed, and had a thick Greek accent.

"I didn't know that you were invited, Uncle Theo," I said in delighted surprise.

"Of course, Edward, my boy. Sweet Alissa never forgets her Uncle Theo."

"I wish I'd have known you were coming," Richard complained. "The only reason I'm going is that Mother said we needed two cars, and I would have to drive Father's car while Uncle Teddy drives John's."

"You mean, you do not want to visit your brother Arthur and his dear wife?" Uncle Theo asked in disbelief.

"I really would rather stay home and play the piano instead of walking around in this heat, feeling and smelling like a can of sardines," Richard grumbled.

"Nonsense!" Mother said angrily. "You look splendid, Richard. You chose the costume, you know, and I will not have you backing out of another invitation like you did at Christmas."

In order to prevent a family squabble before we even set out, I pointed out the ingeniousness of Marcie's costume. She wore a dark blue square-necked gown decorated with large white pearls. Around her neck, she wore a pearl choker from which the letter *B* dangled. The best part of the costume was the fact that the neck of the gown was elongated with flesh-colored material tipped in red to give her a beheaded appearance. In her arms, she carried a head on which perched a matching blue beaded hat. She also had six fingers on her left hand and was clearly recognized as the second wife of Henry VIII, Anne Boleyn.

In truth, although my six-foot rather rotund figure closely resembled Henry VIII's, I felt rather ridiculous in white tights, green velvet doublet, and a fur-trimmed cape to set it all off to perfection. I was also falsely bearded and wore an elaborate square-linked chain around my neck. On my head, I wore the large-plumed soft hat with upturned bejeweled brim usually associated with that infamous monarch.

As everyone complimented our costumes and Marcie's mother's needlework, I finally took a close look at Uncle Theo.

"Uncle Theo, I just realized that your armor is different from either Richard's or Roderick's. Isn't that a Roman pleated tunic and an Imperial Eagle on your helmet? I guess you forgot that the theme was English."

"No, no! Uncle Theo forgets nothing. I fear you, Edward, have forgotten the theme. It was 'Famous People in English History,' and who is more famous than Hadrian? After all, I saw his wall many times when I lived in England," he smugly stated.

With a final look of exasperation at Uncle Theo, Mother reminded us that we had a long drive ahead of us and should get started.

As we were about to walk out the door, Mother noticed a grisly object left on the coffee table. "Marcie dear, don't forget your head," Mother reminded.

Walking back to retrieve the forgotten object, I sighed with resignation and tried to accept the fact that a pattern had been set for the evening with Marcie misplacing her head all night.

The journey to Pine River Falls was long but very pleasant since we had no trouble finding it this time. Aunt Henrietta, Marcie, and Roderick were especially enthusiastic as they had never been there and only had our descriptions to go by.

The doorway to the house was elaborately festooned with spices, leaves, and flowers, and many candles festively shone through all the windows.

Alissa was clad in a gold-trimmed white medieval-styled gown, with a heavy gold chain around her neck and a small gold crown made a lovely Guinevere. Arthur, for once surprisingly awake, was dressed in tights and a red tunic with a dragon on it. He also wore a fur-trimmed cape and a gold crown. He made a rather dashing King Arthur.

Theirs were the only costumes that everyone had correctly guessed ahead of time, and suddenly, a sharp pang of fear went through me as Roderick again explained his costume with a sly grin on his face. I hoped that his connection with Arthur's and Alissa's costumes was only coincidental, but a sick feeling in the pit of my stomach confirmed the fact that this was too much to hope for. The look on Alissa's face also confirmed the fact that she was thinking along the same lines as I was. She was more familiar with Arthurian lore than most people and couldn't possibly fail to see the implication.

When everyone finished admiring everyone else and after those who were visiting for the first time were shown around the house, Alissa led us outdoors where her elaborately time-consuming preparations were even more evident.

A true "groaning board" was set up on a very large flower-decorated, wooden trestle table, especially constructed for the party. On it was an impressive and bountiful buffet. There were ham, turkey, salmon, a large leg of lamb, and stuffed breast of veal. Boiled pumpkins, carrots, turnips, beans, and sweet potatoes were also in abundance with mounds of artichokes and peas especially prominent. A roll of parchment written in Gothic script explained that artichokes and peas were new imports of the sixteenth century and that asparagus, kidney beans, and white potatoes were not familiar foods of that time and, therefore, not on the menu. Apricots, peaches, and almonds were also imports of Elizabethan times and played an important part in Alissa's desserts. The most impressive item among this gastronomic array was a large beautifully decorated marchpane unicorn which formed a table centerpiece.

A separate table was used for beverages which included brandy, beer, and all kinds of wine. There was sack served in the medieval fashion, heated and flavored with spices. It was then served in a cup nearly half full of sugar, forming a kind of syrup. Punch bowls of cider, perry, metheglin made of honey, and hippocras, a cordial loaded with spices all added to the authenticity of Elizabethan times.

Oil lamps in dozens of tall candelabras provided enough light to play shuffleboard and shuttlecock. Different parchments placed strategically around the garden explained various Elizabethan customs. One even told about the brutal sport of hanging a cat in a leather bottle in order to shoot crossbows at it.

"Is this really true about the cat?" I grimaced.

"Yes," Alissa admitted. "It was a barbaric time with barbaric customs. Don't worry. I intend to spare Tippy that ordeal." She laughed.

Everyone seemed to be having a really good time, and it seemed as if my worries had all been for nothing...at least so far.

I was glad to notice that Alissa hadn't been drinking, but it was with some apprehension that I noticed Uncle Teddy, Richard, and Roderick all heavily sampling the beverage table. While there was music and dancing, not one tango was played and Uncle Teddy and Alissa weren't paying undue attention to each other.

It was only as the evening progressed and Uncle Teddy was becoming more inebriated that I would catch him staring for long periods of time at Alissa. Whenever she looked up and their eyes met, she would quickly avert her gaze but not quickly enough for any astute observer not to notice the special softness that would glow in her large green eyes. It was that certain look that could only pass between two people who know each other in a special way. It was with acute distress that I realized I had never seen that look exchanged between Arthur and Alissa. I was reminded of Browning's famous lines from *My Last Duchess*: "Sir, 'twas not her husband's presence only called that spot of joy into the duchess's cheek."

With these uncomfortable thoughts running through my head, I noticed Roderick and Richard were also watching Uncle Teddy and Alissa.

I was glad when dinner was eaten around 9:30 p.m. and hoped this would counteract any inroads all the alcohol was making on the "Tiresome Trio."

"Aren't your parents coming, Alissa?" Mother inquired.

"No, I'm afraid Father wanted no part of a costume party and Mother, poor dear, couldn't come without him. I'm hoping that they'll show up for a while around 10:00 p.m. when I have some special entertainment planned."

After our tremendous meal, one of Mr. Saronna's cabs pulled up followed by Alissa's parents in their Bentley. While everyone was pleased to see the Saronnas, it was the woman and three men accompanying them who drew everyone's attention.

"Look! It's Robin Hood, Maid Marian, Friar Tuck, and Little John," said the ever-astute Melinda.

As the little troupe walked to the middle of the garden, we could tell that they were more than just four tardy guests, as I had originally supposed. Their arms and legs were decorated with tiny bells which jingled with their every move.

"They're morris dancers," explained Alissa. "This was a very popular sixteenth-century form of entertainment. It's a sort of ballet but similar to pantomime."

We all watched with interest the elaborate gestures and dance steps of the players. I was glad to see that even the "Tiresome Trio" had slowed down their drinking while watching the performance. Afterward, when the players mixed with the guests gathered around the buffet for dessert, I noticed Roderick taking a particular interest in Maid Marian and hoped this would keep his mind occupied. If only it were that easy with the other two…or should I say four? I certainly belonged to a complicated family.

Alissa's parents and the dancers left sometime after midnight. Since there was so much food remaining, they were invited to take some home, and Mother intended to take enough to make cooking a forgotten art for the coming week.

It was only as the women and Arthur were packing up the food preparatory to leaving that the trouble began.

"Since we all knew that Alissa would be dressed as Guinevere, Uncle Teddy, I'm surprised that you chose Albert as your costume," Richard said.

"What do you mean?" asked a wine-befuddled Uncle Teddy.

"I would have thought Sir Lancelot would have been more appropriate."

"Do you mean because of my gallantry?" Uncle Teddy asked, preening.

"No, I mean because of the legend. After all, everyone knows what Sir Lancelot was and why he couldn't find the Holy Grail."

"Damn you, Richard!" complained Roderick. "Mordred was supposed to destroy Camelot, not you."

"You're too drunk to destroy an ant," Richard sneered contemptuously.

"Didn't you hear me, Uncle Teddy? I said that everyone knows what Lancelot really was."

"And everyone knows what King Richard I really was. Is that your problem too, Richard? Is that why you feel compelled to make nasty insinuations about Alissa and me?"

"I don't know what you're talking about," Richard said uneasily.

"Well, here's a little historical fact for you. In the sixteenth century, Parliament passed an act for the punishment of buggery. It was considered a felony punishable by death and forfeiture of property."

"What's that have to do with me?" Richard furiously shouted.

"Did I say it had to do with you? I just said, 'Here's a historical fact.' Take it as you like... After all, Alissa has little Elizabethan facts of interest written all over the house and garden. Just thought I'd mention one that she seems to have missed up on."

"Ve-r-ry educational," agreed Uncle Theo, completely missing the point.

As the women approached, the conversation was dropped, and we all got up to leave. It was with a sigh of relief that I realized how closely we had come to disaster.

Although I had grown to love my uncle, aunt, and even Melinda, I was glad that they would be leaving within the week. My nerves couldn't take much more of this!

Chapter 14

Goodbye, Dear Friends, Goodbye

> When we two parted
> In silence and tears,
> Half brokenhearted
> To suffer for years.
>
> —Lord Byron

The final days of the Busbys' visit were strained for everyone. Mother and Melinda were already mourning the imminent departure, and every once in a while, a little sob would escape from one of them. Aunt Henrietta was wary and nervous. She hated sea travel and dreaded the return voyage. Uncle Teddy was in poor spirits and would lose his temper unexpectedly over the most trivial of incidents. And Roderick—well, the best way to describe him would be…vigilant.

The increasingly hot and humid weather accompanied by a rising barometer made the atmosphere like that of a pressure cooker—and Uncle Teddy was the most likely to explode from it. While the rest of us were content to sit in the backyard, trying to catch any suggestion of a breeze, Uncle Teddy had the unenviable task of running around and making departure arrangements. He would be gone in John's car for hours at a time and would return home to lock himself in the bedroom, more often than not, skipping dinner and pleading exhaustion.

On Wednesday evening, Arthur stopped by for his usual weekday dinner sans Alissa, who he claimed was suffering from daily migraine headaches due to the sultry weather.

"Poor Alissa," Melinda commiserated. "You're going to be a doctor, Edward. Why don't you do something for her?" she illogically asked as if I were already a doctor who had discovered a cure for migraines and was spitefully refusing to give it to my suffering sister-in-law.

Since it was too hot to bother refuting her statement, I simply turned over in my hammock and fanned myself harder.

Uncle Teddy, who had joined us for dinner in honor of Arthur's visit, became visibly agitated. "If your wife is in so much pain, Arthur, do you think it was wise to have left her alone?" Uncle Teddy asked.

Looking as if that aspect had never occurred to him, Arthur simply shrugged.

"She will be coming to the dinner Friday night at your Uncle Theo's, won't she?" asked Melinda with concern.

Again Arthur shrugged and said, "Guess it depends on the weather."

"What about the bon voyage party? She can't miss that," Uncle Teddy persisted, not bothering to hide his annoyance with Arthur's disinterest.

When Arthur again shrugged since he really couldn't know how Alissa's head would feel, Uncle Teddy slammed back into the house and went upstairs.

"Don't mind him, Arthur," Aunt Henrietta apologized. "It's the heat, and all the running around seeing the arrangements are getting to him, I'm afraid."

Changing the subject, Arthur asked about Uncle Theo. "Mother, did you ever discover what Uncle Theo's big secret is? You know, the one he mentioned several weeks ago but refused to go into detail about."

"Hmmph! I certainly have," Mother sniffed with disapproval. "He's making Delphi's Oracle into a speakeasy with live entertainment. Fortunately, it isn't ready yet, and we're about to have dinner at Theo's home on Friday."

"He must be very disappointed. I imagine he wanted to have the grand opening while Uncle Teddy's family was here."

"Yes, but if you ask me, it's just as well. You know my opinion of lawbreakers," she righteously continued, conveniently forgetting where dear brother John was spending his summer.

"What kind of entertainment?" Roderick asked.

"That's the most disgusting part of all—a belly dancer!" Mother indignantly informed us. Seeing Roderick's face light up, she soon dispelled his hopes. "You won't get to see her, of course. She won't be at his home...at least she'd better not be!"

At this, Roderick's face, which had begun to frown, lit up anew with resurging hope.

"What about you, Melinda? Are you looking forward to returning to England and seeing your friends?"

"I don't know, Arthur. I guess I have mixed feelings. I have no friends who live close to the farm, so I won't see anyone until school opens in September. While I can't wait to show them the 'new me,'" she said, preening, "I'm going to hate leaving everyone... I don't see why we can't stay longer." She shot a pleading glance in Aunt Henrietta's direction.

"We've already stayed a week longer than we really intended. You know very well that I can't leave the farm any longer, and your father has to get back to work. So no more of that if you please, young lady."

Noticing Melinda's rapidly reddening cheeks, I asked her if she'd like to walk over to Marcie's with me.

"Good show!" Roderick quickly exclaimed, rising from his lounge chair and uninvitedly accompanying us.

"Since we probably won't be back before you leave, Arthur, I'll say goodbye now," I said.

"Oh, me too," added Melinda. "And please give my love to Alissa. You really must try and get her to visit us soon. After all, we only have a few days left. Do tell her that I'll be ever so miserable if she's not, at least, at the bon voyage party. Father's really throwing it for her... Well, I mean in appreciation for all she's done to make our trip so lovely and for you and Aunt Eleanor and your whole family too…" she trailed off lamely.

Grabbing her by the hand, I quickly propelled her toward the gate, and with a final wave at Arthur, we started for Marcie's house. Glancing at Roderick, I couldn't miss his sneer of satisfaction and, not for the first time, came very close to wiping it off with my fists. Fortunately, for him (or perhaps for me), we had reached Marcie's front door, and Melinda was already ringing the doorbell.

Marcie was pleased to see us. "Melinda and Edward, what a nice surprise! Do come in and have some lemonade…and you too, Roderick," she added with less enthusiasm as she noticed my cousin.

Sitting outside on her patio, we all relaxed (at least as relaxed as we could get in Roderick's presence).

"Isn't this Arthur's visiting night?" Marcie asked me. "Of course, it is," she likewise answered. "How's Alissa?"

"She didn't come. Arthur says she's been suffering all week from migraine headaches due to the heat," I explained.

"Poor Alissa. You're going to be a doctor, Edward. Why don't you do something for her?" Marcie asked while a feeling of déjà vu overcame me. I would never cease to be amazed at how catching illogical thoughts were in women and had no doubt that Melinda had infected Marcie…or was it vice versa?

I was glad when some friends of ours arrived, thereby preventing the necessity of me having to answer Marcie's dumb question.

Seeing the admiring glances the "new" Melinda was receiving from the male members of the party, I wished Alissa were here to see the results of her efforts. If the Busby family had nothing else to remember Alissa by (and I strongly doubted if this was the case), Melinda's newfound happiness and confidence were something which no one could overlook. All in all, I felt that a debt of gratitude was owed to my sister-in-law.

*****

It was a soggy disgruntled group who assembled for dinner at Uncle Theo's on Friday evening. The weather had broken, and a violent thunderstorm was raging. While Mother had wanted to call it off, Uncle Teddy pointed out that this wouldn't be fair to Uncle Theo, who had probably spent all day cooking.

Uncle Teddy was the only one in high spirits as he drove to Uncle Theo's home in Athens Cove.

Uncle Theo greeted us all exuberantly and quickly began plying us with drinks. When Uncle Teddy realized that we were the only guests, his spirits plummeted again.

"Theo, haven't Arthur and Alissa arrived yet?"

"No, Teddy, and I have been trying to reach them all day, but I keep getting the buzzy signal."

"Busy signal!" Mother corrected disgustedly.

"Yes, busy signal. Maybe the lines are down. It is still early. We will give them some extra time in case the roads are bad. I will not start serving until 8:30 p.m., if that is all right with you, lovely ladies…and you too, Eleanor?"

It couldn't be more than fifteen minutes later when the doorbell rang, and Uncle Teddy rushed out of his chair, beating Uncle Theo to the door. He couldn't suppress a gasp as Alissa walked in followed by Arthur.

I didn't believe I had ever seen Alissa looking more beautiful and, certainly, Uncle Teddy hadn't either. She was wearing a pale silver Grecian chiffon evening dress which perfectly accented her tan. It had a low V-neck in front and back, which was trimmed with black-and-silver metallic braid that also served as a tie belt. Large individual rhinestones randomly adorned her auburn hair, which was dressed in cascading Grecian curls. A large diamond pendant hung suspended from a thin silver chain around her neck, diamonds sparkled in her ears, and rhinestones adorned her silver chiffon-covered pumps. For a lady who had been sick all week, she looked magnificent.

Rushing in from the kitchen, Uncle Theo broke the spell by giving Alissa one of his bear hugs and kissing Arthur.

"Welcome! Welcome! How glad I am to see you both. Alissa, my beauty, even Aphrodite is eclipsed by you tonight. You are looking truly breathtaking!"

"Thank you, Uncle Theo. I'm feeling wonderful too. This break in the weather finally got rid of my headaches." She smiled, her green eyes sparkling as brilliantly as her jewels. "And how happy I am to see the rest of you," she graciously added, kissing all of us hello.

Uncle Theo had surpassed himself, and we enjoyed (all except Mother who had a lamb chop), an appetizer of stuffed grape leaves in a creamy lemon sauce. There was pasticcio for the entrée accompanied by a large Greek salad and pita bread. This was followed by baklava for dessert and thick dark Greek coffee (Mother had tea).

While we relaxed in Uncle Theo's parlor after dinner, the phone rang. As we listened to the angry spate of Greek, Uncle Theo was looking increasingly worried. When he finally hung up, his anxiety could not be hidden from the rest of us.

"Whatever is wrong, Uncle Theo? Can we help in some way?" Alissa offered.

"Thank you, child…but no. No one can help Uncle Theo now. I am a ruined man!"

"Oh, stop being so dramatic, Theo, and tell us what happened. You know you're dying to," Mother snapped with annoyance.

"You are wrong, Eleanor. I do not like to upset my guests."

"But you will anyway," Mother finished smugly.

Ignoring Mother's sarcasm, Uncle Theo told us that the belly dancer he had hired for the nightclub had slipped on the rainy street and broken her leg.

"How can I open up without the promised entertainment? All of my deliveries are scheduled for next week. All the posters and engraved invitations are mailed out already, so what can I do?" he moaned. "As soon as the newspapers open in the morning, I will advertise for a new dancer…but how many unemployed belly dancers are there around here?"

"Don't worry, Uncle Theo," Arthur said. "In a pinch, Alissa could always help you out, I'm sure."

"What are you talking about, Arthur? Have you had too much ouzo? I need a belly dancer, not a goddess."

"I can belly dance," Alissa confirmed.

"You, Alissa!" Mother said scandalized.

"Yes, Eleanor. I took several classes in belly dancing. I really did it for the exercise, but I liked it so much that I went on to advanced belly dancing. I'm really quite good, if I do say so for myself."

"Would you really do this if I can't find someone else?" Uncle Theo asked, looking relieved.

"Why not? I love all types of dancing."

"Did you take dancing lessons as a child?"

"Yes, Henrietta, but I'm afraid they were wasted. When my parents had to buy two pairs of ballet laces to tie together in order that they'd fit around my ankles, they finally admitted I was too fat and dropped the classes," she said, smiling sadly. "It wasn't easy looking like a fat stuffed bologna in my pink tights and leotard while all the other little girls looked like dainty graceful butterflies."

"I can't believe you were ever that heavy," Uncle Teddy gallantly protested.

"Well, it's true."

"It certainly is," Mother vehemently, if tactlessly, agreed.

"You couldn't give a little demonstration of belly dancing, could you?" Roderick cajoled.

"No, I'm not dressed correctly, and it's getting late… Thank you so much for the lovely dinner, Uncle Theo, but we really must be going."

"You will be at the bon voyage party tomorrow?" Uncle Teddy asked anxiously.

"Of course, we wouldn't miss it. Will you be there too, Uncle Theo?"

"No, no, my dear. I must try to find a new dancer although I will take up your generous offer if I can't find one. I will call you in a few days, my dear girl, and thank you for allowing us to feast our eyes on you tonight… Drive carefully, Arthur, you have a rare jewel in your safekeeping," he finished with a flourish.

*****

Departure day was sunny and breezy. Yesterday's storm had gone far in clearing the air—at least the meteorological one. Over the Androses' house, a pall of gloom hung suspended that no mere storm could hope to dissipate.

Amid the hubbub of packing, spontaneous sobs could be heard intermittently escaping both Mother and Melinda. All too soon, Mr. Saronna's largest cab was outside being loaded for the trip to the pier where Arthur and Alissa were to meet us. Since Richard was driving Father's car, there was more than enough room for Marcie to join us.

All of Uncle Teddy's arrangements were worthwhile. They had been provided with deluxe first-class accommodations aboard the luxury liner *Queen Beatrice*. The large mahogany-paneled stateroom was on the upper deck and flanked by three large beautifully appointed bedrooms and a handsome tiled bathroom.

While I was admiring the flowers and baskets of fruit and assorted goodies sent by Arthur, Alissa, and Uncle Theo, my brother and his wife walked in. Alissa was dressed conservatively in a white, green-sprigged cotton dress and a large white straw picture hat with long green streamers adorning her long loose shiny hair. Although she greeted everyone happily, it was evident that she was feeling as miserable as the rest of us. Melinda ran into her arms and sobbed while Uncle Teddy quickly turned away and made an elaborate show of opening one of the bottles of vintage champagne, which Mr. Saronna had so generously supplied with the cab.

When several waiters arrived carrying trays of food which Uncle Teddy had especially ordered for the party, he laughingly reminded us that we were here to celebrate, and since the ship would be leaving in less than two hours, we'd better begin. After the elaborate party fare had been consumed, Uncle Teddy proposed a walk around the ship. While Mother, Aunt Henrietta, Arthur, and Richard declined, the rest of us enthusiastically set out to explore the good ship *Queen Beatrice*. Marcie, Melinda, and I enjoyed browsing around the duty-free shop, and Roderick busied himself by making unwanted advances to the shop's pretty salesgirl. Uncle Teddy and Alissa strolled the decks.

Catching sight of Alissa's hair and skirt blowing in the breeze while she and Uncle Teddy stood at the rail, gazing into each other's eyes, Marcie touched my arm and, with tears in her eyes and a catch in her voice, said, "My god, they look so beautiful together, if only—"

"Don't say it," I cut in.

"If only it weren't for Arthur and your Aunt Henrietta," she continued heedlessly.

Watching them turn around and begin walking back toward us, I was forced to agree with Marcie. They were beautiful together, if only…

As the ship's horn blared its warning for all visitors to disembark, we all hurried back to the stateroom for our last goodbyes. Quickly kissing everyone, Alissa shoved small boxes in each of the Busby's hands, and turning away from them, she said something that sounded like, "They're to remember us by. God loves all of you… for I do." She then raced back to the deck and down the gangplank.

Standing on the pier and holding on to the streamers which the Busby family had thrown to us, we walked along the pier as the ship pulled away. I noticed Alissa, who was holding the end of Uncle Teddy's streamer in one hand and Melinda's in the other, quickly kiss one of them. As we all released the streamers we were holding, I saw Uncle Teddy quickly pull his back up and pocket it before anyone else could notice. But he needn't have worried because everyone else, each for his own private reason, was too blinded by tears to have noticed.

CHAPTER 15

Uncle Theo's Den of Delights

> With dazed vision unawares
> From the long alley's latticed shade
> Emerged, I came upon the great
> Pavilion of the Caliphat.
>
> —Tennyson

Alissa didn't have much time to brood over the Busby's departure. She spent the following week preparing for her debut as a belly dancer in Uncle Theo's club. Despite Mother's protests, Alissa was determined to keep her promise to Uncle Theo, and finally, Mother had to resign herself to the fact that her own daughter-in-law was going to appear in public with her navel bared.

It was with an air of excited anticipation that we set out for the grand opening of Theo's Den of Delights as Delphi's Oracle had been renamed. Except for the white Doric columns which still decorated the outside of Uncle Theo's former restaurant, it would have been impossible to know that we were in the same place.

Mother was not with us. She had insisted on arriving early in order to help Alissa dress (or undress) in her costume and, I suspect, to put in a last-minute plea as well. We were greeted and ushered in by Uncle Theo. He was incongruously dressed in his traditional Greek folk costume of white pleated skirt, white bell-sleeved shirt, striped black vest, red velvet embroidered slippers, and white tights which he used to greet the patrons of Delphi's Oracle. As I surveyed the interior of his new enterprise, it struck me that an Arabian burnoose or a caliph's robe would have been more appropriate.

All signs of the classic Greek decor that Uncle Theo had been so proud of had disappeared, and in its place stood a sort of Arabian tent. In fact, the ceiling had been decorated with a striped material which was draped in such a way as to leave no doubt that you were, indeed, in some sort of tent. This impression was so strong that I kept expecting the late Rudolph Valentino to come slinking in through one of the beaded doorways in his sheik costume.

All of Uncle Theo's advance publicity certainly seemed to have paid off. The club was filled, overflowing with a majority of male customers who spoke a hodgepodge of Greek, English, and several indistinguishable languages.

As we sat at our small crowded table, waiting for the show to begin, I asked Uncle Theo where Mother was. At this, he merely rolled his eyes and raised both hands in supplication to heaven as he rushed to welcome more customers who were waiting to be seated although where he hoped to put them was beyond my limited comprehension. It was so noisy, smoky, and crowded that I had doubts as to whether anyone would notice the show when it finally began.

I needn't have worried about this. Suddenly, all the lights were extinguished and a large spotlight appeared in the middle of the dance floor. This was the cue for the music to begin.

The band consisted of seven pieces among which I recognized an oud, kanoon, bouzouki, doumbek, and three other instruments, which I didn't know the names of even though Uncle Theo had, at one time, taught me what Middle Eastern musical instruments looked like.

Not a sound was heard as the spotlight slowly crept over to a beaded doorway at the far side of the room as the zither-like kanoon played a prolonged wailing note. As the other instruments joined in the Beledi section of the piece, a gold-bangled arm seductively snaked its way through the beaded draperies. A blur of lime green and gold spun in front of our eyes, and before we could focus on the undulating vision, an unrecognizable Alissa was standing absolutely still in the middle of the floor, knees slightly bent and arms upraised as she went into the first movements of the dance.

If it weren't for her green eyes, I never would have recognized her, and even Arthur looked a little uncertain as he stared at his wife. While she had been nicely tanned at the bon voyage party, she was now such a deep bronze that she must have spent all week in the sun. Her costume consisted of a rather skimpy bra and low-slung girdle completely covered with gold coins which also looped around her body under the bra and across her otherwise bare rounded hips. A skirt of lime green gossamer trimmed with a gold band around the hem and slitted in front of each leg was attached to the girdle. As she went into the Beledi, a veil of the same gossamer as her skirt made a demure cover-up as it draped over her left shoulder across her torso and attached to her right hip in front and back. A short veil covered her face below the eyes, and gold bangles covered her upper and lower arms and ankles.

Just as I was beginning to think that belly dancing was a pretty modest affair as I watched Alissa perform some hip lifts and torso circles, the tempo of the music picked up as the band went into the Taksim. Alissa's movements had been so subtle during the first part that I hadn't realized that she had danced the veil off until a large bare stretch of taut brown torso stared at me in the face as she performed figure eights, shimmies, and the more intricate movements.

During the Tsifteteli, her prowess and agility were showcased as she performed what looked like spine-breaking backbends in which she knelt down and bent backward, grasped her heels with her hands, and then brought her head to the floor with her arms outstretched in front of her. During this part of the dance, she also used her zills or finger cymbals which were attached to the thumbs and second fingers of each hand as she continued her snakelike undulations.

By this time, Uncle Theo had joined us at the table, and he beamed proudly while cries of "opa" and "yasu" greeted Alissa's act.

"Delightful, is she not?" Uncle Theo asked no one in particular. "The only disappointment is that she doesn't have much of a belly. We, Mediterranean men, prefer more substantial women like your Aunt Henrietta. But such breasts, hips, and derriere! Just look at her!"

I seriously doubt if anyone needed Uncle Theo's directive as all eyes were already fastened to Alissa's shapely and supple body.

As the audience became more and more caught up in the performance, I noticed a great deal of money being tossed at Alissa. Uncle Theo explained that this was the custom, and most belly dancers were paid from a percentage of the money that they collected. As several of Uncle Theo's patrons became overexuberant, some of the men tried to get close enough to Alissa to tuck money into her flimsy costume. She very neatly sidestepped these advances by dancing away from their outstretched hands. Once in a while, a highly suspicious groan or curse was heard in the background. As the groans and curses became more frequent, everyone began murmuring and trying to discover what was wrong. Even the members of the band looked confused and played a few off-key notes as they too tried to locate the source of the disturbance.

Just then, Uncle Theo groaned, hit his head with closed fists, and yelled out, "That woman is trying to ruin me!"

Simultaneously with this announcement, the spotlight moved from Alissa to a shadowy black figure which had been trailing her around the dance floor out of sight on the periphery of the spotlight.

A tall angular figure in a black aba with a black head covering which came down low over its forehead and a black veil across its face could be seen smacking a wandering pair of hands, which had crept up in the back of Alissa with what strangely appeared to be an umbrella. Realizing that it had been spotted, the figure turned directly into the spotlight, and cries of "Mother!" escaped from Arthur, Richard, and me as a pair of icy blue eyes stared back at the crowd. The years hadn't changed her very much as Eleanor Andros again protected virtue (this time, Alissa's) against roaming Greek fingers.

Instead of the outrage, which Uncle Theo had feared, laughter resounded in the room, and Mother was forced to take a stiff little bow as rounds of applause greeted her performance.

Even Alissa, who had been wrapped up in her dancing and the music, looked taken aback as she realized what had been going on. As she twirled into the final Beledi of the dance, she knew that it would now be safe to get closer to her audience. With Mother faithfully trailing, Alissa began provocatively teasing the members of the audience with her veil and then haughtily stepping back when any of the men showed signs of becoming unruly although they always had second thoughts as Mother threateningly shook her umbrella at them.

As the dance came to a close, Mother gathered the tossed bills into a pouch she had strapped to one of her wrists while Alissa took several bows. As the spotlight again focused on Mother, she graciously acknowledged her own applause with a stiff nod of her head.

Although the audience yelled for an encore, Alissa had vanished behind the beaded curtain with Mother right on her heels. As Uncle Theo tried to appease the disappointed crowd with promises of more entertainment to come, the band began playing some contemporary music as an invitation to the audience to dance. When several brave couples got up, the tension was broken, and we could all relax as a mob scene was neatly averted.

"Is there really going to be more entertainment?" I asked a sweating Uncle Theo.

"Oh yes. We have several folk dance performers in addition to Alissa," he said, nervously wiping his brow.

"Does Alissa have to dance again?" Arthur inquired.

"No, no. I promised her she'd only have to dance that one time."

"I guess if you really need her, she'll perform again," Arthur suggested. "She really did seem to enjoy it."

"Especially when she realized she had a bodyguard." I laughed.

Uncertain applause was heard from some of the tables at the other side of the room as Alissa emerged sans veil and costume dressed in a gauzy caftan and sandals and headed for our table.

"Damn!" she complained. "I didn't think they'd recognize me."

"Most of them didn't," I assured her. "And even the ones who clapped looked unsure of themselves. I think it was your deep tan and hair which gave you away."

As everyone at the table congratulated Alissa on her fine performance, Arthur asked, "Where's Mother?"

"Oh, she'll be right here. She stayed behind to count the money and to change out of that ridiculous black robe."

Uncle Theo approached the table carrying a bottle of wine. "Mavrodaphne, sweet nectar of the gods for you, Alissa. Did you enjoy performing as much as we enjoyed watching you?"

"Yes, I really enjoyed dancing, Uncle Theo. Did I look nervous?"

"Not at all," I assured her. "I was kind of surprised at that. Do you remember that day in the emporium when that man kept staring at you?"

"I remember that," groaned Richard. "Alissa walked up to one of my best customers and told him to keep his eyes to himself because his staring was making her nervous," Richard explained to Arthur and Uncle Theo. "How come all this staring didn't bother you?" he asked with righteous indignation.

"That was different. When I'm dancing, I get so wrapped up in the music, I forget anyone is watching."

Thinking back to another performance of hers, I was about to testify to this fact when I thought better of it and held my tongue.

It was at this point that a conservatively dressed Mother joined us at our table. Ignoring the daggers which Uncle Theo's eyes were shooting at her, Mother happily told Alissa that she had collected $525.

"Not too bad for less than twenty minutes work," Mother crowed with satisfaction.

As the notes of the "Misirlou" were played, Alissa urged the women in the audience to form a long line while she showed them the steps to this slow stately dance. After watching her for a few minutes, Mother surprised us all by joining in. This was followed by a rather frenetic "Hava Nagila," which the women again danced to.

As we men sat back smugly, watching the women, the music changed. Alissa and Mother grabbed Uncle Theo and Arthur by the hands, and they, in turn, dragged me and Richard to the middle of the floor. As Mother and Alissa demonstrated the steps of the Dabke, a sort of Mideastern bunny hop, the audience was invited to take part in the simple walk-walk-walk-hop-step-hop which wound around the room.

While I had, at first, some doubts as to Uncle Theo's new scheme, I was now fully in accord with his idea. His new Mideastern hodgepodge speakeasy nightclub was a lot of fun, and except for the threatened assault and battery lawsuit which one irate member of the audience intended to bring against Mother, all in all, a good time was had by everyone.

CHAPTER 16
Touring Suffolk County

> Beauty and quiet
> (As I sail'd by it)
> Of sweet Long Island—
> Its low and high land.
>
> —John Orville Terry

As the summer drew to a close, I found myself dreading that annual inevitability—the reopening of school in September. It's not that I hated school (and considering that I wanted to be a doctor, that was a good thing) or that I was so occupied with interesting and fulfilling activities (in truth, I was getting bored), but what red-blooded American student who doesn't feel his stomach sinking at the first reminders of the return to the classroom?

I still remember one night in late August when I was ten years old and Andros's Emporium was displaying school supplies. I snuck in and covered up all their signs and took down their displays in the hope that this would make everyone forget the coming day of disaster. Needless to say, it didn't work, but, to do Father credit, he didn't get angry when he realized what had happened to his painstakingly arrayed pyramids of composition books and other school supplies. He was surprisingly sympathetic.

Perhaps that was why when I was a father, I could sympathize with my own children's disgust with the Robert Hall commercials heard during the late summer: "School bells ring and children sing it's back to Robert Hall again." Were falser words ever spoken?

Somehow, this vision of happy singing children rushing off to outfit themselves for school was really ludicrous. What you actually had were irate, frustrated mothers in department stores, trying to stuff their reluctant and often openly rebellious offspring into the dress slacks and pretty dresses that they would be forced to don for opening day but which no self-respecting youngster could be demoralized enough into wearing ever again.

It was with these thoughts in mind that I decided to try and make a last-minute attempt to salvage my final week of precious freedom by going to visit Arthur and Alissa. Since Marcie was vacationing in Lake George with her family, I really had nothing to lose and might even have a good time.

The first three days of my visit were exceedingly dull, and just when I was having second thoughts and looking for the most tactful way to depart early, Alissa decided to take over.

The original idea had been for me and Arthur, while he was also on vacation, to spend some time alone together. Alissa, who always regretted not having siblings of her own, thought that this would be a good opportunity for us, and since she claimed to have some research to do, she wouldn't feel left out.

My days alone with Arthur were a big disappointment although I think more for Alissa than for myself. The best thing that could be said for conversations with Arthur was that he never disagreed with you no matter what you said. He would never offer a definite opinion but would claim broad-mindedness rather than indecisiveness as he wavered from one side to another like an inebriated cat walking on a picket fence.

It was on the evening of my third day in Pine River Falls when all hell broke loose. Alissa had been spending every night deeply engrossed in her research locked behind the wrought iron gates of the library. On this particular night, she came into the parlor to offer us refreshments. Instead of the lively and intimate interchange of thoughts and ideas which she had been picturing us having, she saw Arthur asleep on the red velvet couch while I, in total boredom, thumbed through a very dull magazine.

"Don't tell me this has been going on for the past three days!" she exploded, gesturing toward Arthur. As she roughly shook him awake, I tried to make peace by claiming that it really didn't matter.

"Of course it matters. It's bad enough that he has no consideration for me, but to fall asleep when he's supposed to be entertaining his own brother is inexcusable."

"You know he always falls asleep," I said, illogically defending Arthur whom I felt was still too groggy to know what was going on.

"That's just the problem. He's so used to catering to his own desires that he has absolutely no consideration for anyone else. He's the only person I know who is so wrapped up in doing exactly as he pleases at any given moment that even the rules of normal courtesy are overlooked by him. I keep hoping that even if he refuses to change toward me that he will, at least, become conscious of other people and his obligations toward them. It's not just you, Edward. You've seen your brother fall asleep even in the midst of social engagements. I try to excuse him when he's working because I know that he works long hours, but what's his excuse now after having been on vacation for the last five days? Besides, other men work just as long and hard as he does, and they still manage to stay awake. I'm just sorry that I made you waste your last days of vacation in this way."

Turning to Arthur, who was fully awake by this time, she asked, "What have you been doing the last three days to entertain your brother? It's obvious that after dinner, you've been sleeping as usual, but what about during the daytime?"

"I don't know," Arthur answered vaguely. "Sitting on the hammocks, cutting the grass, listening to the radio, you know, the usual things."

"Haven't you even gone for a drive?"

"Sure! Just this morning, we took the lawn mower blade into town to be sharpened. Right, Edward?"

"Right!" I agreed with embarrassment.

"How very exciting!" Alissa dripped with sarcasm. "I just hope that all of this invigorating activity doesn't wear you out so that you're not too tired to go back to school on Monday, Edward."

"Oh no," Arthur protested in his density. "He's had plenty of time to rest at night."

Turning away in disgust from her husband, she then suggested that we take the ferry over to Fire Island the next day and combine some swimming with sightseeing. With a great feeling of relief, I readily agreed with Alissa's plans.

*****

Tantalizing aromas from the kitchen awoke me early the next morning, and while I ate a delicious breakfast of eggs, crisp bacon, and freshly baked blueberry muffins, Alissa packed a picnic basket for our lunch.

Since Arthur still wasn't awake, I offered to get him up.

"No, don't bother, Edward. He told me last night that he won't be coming with us."

Just as I was about to question her statement, Arthur walked in. "Good morning."

"Arthur, why aren't you coming with us to Fire Island?" I asked.

"I have some stuff to do around here," he lamely answered. "Besides, I really don't feel like going."

"And God forbid Arthur should do something that he doesn't feel like doing just to please someone else," Alissa added.

Seeing Arthur shrug aside his wife's statement and help himself to breakfast, I couldn't help but feel annoyed with him. After all, whereas I had come in part to try and get to know my brother better, so far, the traits I was seeing weren't too admirable. While it could have been argued that Alissa was wrong in being so openly critical of her husband, she certainly was justified in her complaints. Arthur was lazy and selfish, and who knew how many arguments they had had in the past over these same things when they were alone?

Heading into the nearby town of Sayville, Alissa was soon in high spirits and brimming with interesting facts of local information. "Just think, Edward. The two places that we'll be going to today both got their names due to mistakes."

"Mistakes?"

"Yes, Sayville was originally supposed to be Seaville, but the clerk, who was mostly illiterate, recorded the town as Sayville instead. The same thing happened with Fire Island, which was supposed to be called Five Islands because of its geographical configuration. Again, an error in recording was responsible for the name of Fire instead of Five."

Although Arthur always complained about Alissa's "little instructional lectures," I enjoyed them and so encouraged her. She also informed me that Montauk Highway, the road we were traveling on, had until eight years ago been called South Country Road since 1734 and that Sayville was such a large tourist center that it had about a thousand commuters daily during the summer.

She made many side trips before we reached Sayville and showed me such interesting sights as the South Side Sportsmen's Club which boasted such famous patrons as August Belmont, Bayard Cutting, Lorenzo Delmonico, J. P. Morgan Sr., and Charles Tiffany. We also saw Idle Hour, the Vanderbilt estate rented by the infamous rum-runner, Dutch Schultz. I was also very impressed by Frederick G. Bourne's mansion, Indian Neck Hall, which would in later years become La Salle Military Academy.

On the ferry to Fire Island, Alissa, at my urging, filled me in on some historical background.

"In the 1600s, pirates on Fire Island buried a considerable amount of treasure which wasn't discovered until the 1700s and 1800s. The first White man to live on the island was Jeremiah Smith, a pirate who, in 1795, built a cottage in what's now the Cherry Grove section. When ships got stuck on the sandbar, he'd kill the crew and loot the ship. As many as six hundred ships were buried on the Fire Island sandbar, which is why captains refer to it as the 'graveyard of the North Atlantic.'

"It was so bad that in 1805, the American Humane Society built and provisioned shacks with instructions posted on the doors for how to obtain help in case of shipwreck. Despite all of this, the first lighthouse wasn't built until 1824. In 1872, the US Life Saving Service was founded which has now become the Coast Guard which, as you probably know, was organized to try to prevent rum-running.

"In 1892, the governor of New York tried to use Fire Island as a checkpoint for immigrants from Southern Europe when a cholera scare broke out in New York City. This caused civil war to break out on Fire Island which had, by this time, become a small but thriving community. The residents armed themselves and drove off the ships which were attempting to land the suspect immigrants."

By this time, the ferry was pulling into Cherry Grove which, Alissa informed me, had been settled in 1869 by Archie Perkinson who bought the land from the pirate Jeremiah Smith. It's Archie's wife, Ma Perkinson, who was credited with making the first saltwater taffy on record and then bringing it over to Cape Cod.

We spent a very enjoyable day swimming in the clear waters of Fire Island. We also did a great deal of exploring and eventually came to one of the most incredible sights which I had ever seen—the famous Sunken Forest with its tropic-like sphagnum marsh. Although the climate was too sultry for extensive exploration in this area, we still covered a lot of ground.

We were both so exhausted by the time we got home that we happily flopped down on the patio with a frosty pitcher of lemonade. Arthur inquired about our day, and I was surprised to learn that he had never been to Fire Island although he admitted that Alissa had often offered to take him.

The next day, Alissa planned a trip to Montauk Point, and again, Arthur refused our invitation, explaining that sightseeing held no charms for him.

Seeing Alissa's disgusted expression, I began talking about my forthcoming senior year. Since my eighteenth birthday had just passed, Alissa asked me if I had started school late since she had already graduated high school at eighteen.

"Yes, I did start school late. The year that I should have been enrolled, Mother was visiting Uncle Teddy in England and Father didn't want to be bothered. Mother ended up staying in England longer than expected and didn't return until right before Christmas. Since I had already missed half of the school year, my parents decided to postpone my academic career until I was seven. If I ever do become a doctor, I'll be an old man before I can start practicing." I groaned.

"I never realized that your mother stayed away so long. I knew that she visited England frequently, but I presumed that her visits only lasted a few weeks. I'm surprised that she didn't mind being away from her children for so long."

Since I had also wondered about it, I couldn't answer Alissa. Of course, although I knew that it was the silly Somos-England feud that prevented us from traveling with our parents, I always did resent the fact that neither parent would agree to allow us to accompany the vacationing parent. While we certainly got away with a lot, especially when we were left with Father, we also couldn't help but feel neglected and inconsequential. I'd also always wondered if Mother doesn't now feel guilty about this neglect especially when it comes to John. Perhaps stricter supervision during his formative years might have prevented John from taking the criminal path that he had chosen.

*****

The last two days of my vacation were spent exploring the north and south forks of Long Island. I was amazed at the large potato farms which were so important to the economy of this part of Suffolk County. We also explored the old whaling town of Sag Harbor whose residents were only too happy to discuss the "good old days."

The scenery at Montauk Point was breathtaking with its blue skies and white-capped blue water. We spent several hours just sitting on the boulders around the lighthouse, watching the seagulls and enviously counting the distant white sails and masts of fishing boats and private yachts.

We stopped at various roadside farm stands, and Alissa purchased innumerable bushels of fresh produce and locally baked products to bring home to Arthur.

Despite the fact that Alissa had obviously done these same things countless times before, she never seemed to tire of walking along the beaches or exploring different roads to discover some new point of interest. She often had me laughing aloud because she traveled with a compass and map and insisted on creating her own roads only to have the car get stuck in a mudhole or ditch. Fortunately, the residents of Suffolk County were quite tolerant of her idiosyncrasies, and while rather taciturn on the whole, they were always more than willing to lend a hand when we were in trouble. Several farmers even offered to tow us out of the craters which Alissa could be depended upon to drive her car into.

In spite of the dubious start to my visit, I was really sorry to have to return to Queenstown and not only because of school on Monday. It was thanks to this loving effort on Alissa's part in showing me around Suffolk County that in later years, I would enjoy showing these same sights to my own family. This visit marked the beginning of many Andros family vacations spent on Long Island, and I, like Alissa, would always be gratified to hear one of my own children repeat to me the same words which I had spoken to Alissa: "Thank you. I never before realized how very beautiful Long Island could be."

CHAPTER 17

The Stock Market Crash

> When, in disgrace with fortune and men's eyes,
> I all alone beweep my outcast state,
> And trouble deaf heaven with my bootless cries,
> And look upon myself, and curse my fate.
> —Shakespeare, 1929

My senior year in high school was marked by the usual frantic pace with cramming both for finals and college entrance exams. It had finally been decided, after a major disagreement between Alissa and Mother, that I should start college in September. Mother tenaciously clung to her belief that it was too expensive and I was too slow-witted while Alissa, surprisingly backed up by Richard, argued that I would do well enough in my slow, plodding but determined way.

Although me not winning a scholarship to college was a disappointment, no one, least of all myself, was surprised. It was agreed upon that Alissa and Richard would finance my education. I would pay them back after I started practicing. While Alissa adamantly refused to even consider interest, I would pay Richard half of whatever the prevailing rate of interest was at that time. More generous terms could not have been asked for, especially after I told them I was so determined to be a doctor that I would have even agreed to Shylock's rates.

I spent the summer following my graduation by purchasing in advance all the books which I would be using in college in the fall and trying to get a well-needed head start.

While many girlfriends would have complained of my neglect, Marcie, to her credit, never uttered a word—she would simply sit in the room where I was trying to study and sigh and groan or else fan herself with Mother's old bamboo fan so diligently that she produced a sound like an overzealous bumblebee. When all these stratagems failed to distract me, she would stand looking over my shoulder, emit one last heartbreaking sigh, and finally walk out.

*****

Labor Day was celebrated in 1929 on September 2. Little did we realize as we gathered at my brother's for the official end of summer that we were also witnessing the beginning of the end of an era.

Since we were experiencing a severe heat wave, many families had the same idea of leaving the city for the holidays. The roads leading in and out of New York that night were so tied up that many motorists were forced to abandon their vehicles and look to public transportation if they hoped to be at work the following day. Fortunately, we stayed over in Pine River Falls that evening and departed for Queenstown on the third, which ended up being the hottest day of the year.

It was a holiday marked by many diverse events. The Graf Zeppelin was nearing the end of its first round of the world flight. Eight people had been killed in the crash of a Transcontinental Air Transport trimotor plane in a thunderstorm in New Mexico. Babe Ruth had, so far, hit forty home runs that season, *All Quiet on the Western Front* was the best-selling book, and... Edward Andros was beginning his college career.

September third and fourth showed a strong stock market while September fifth showed a slight break with a drop in some stocks. The drop on the fifth was attributed to the words of Roger Babson, a famous economic forecaster, who said in his speech before the Annual National Business Conference, "Sooner or later, a crash is coming, and it may be terrific." He then went on to predict that market averages would drop sixty to eighty points and concluded that "factories will shut down...men will be thrown out of work...

the vicious circle will get in full swing, and the result will be a serious business depression."

By the autumn of 1929, the United States economy was already well into a depression. Industrial and factory production was down. Steel production and home building were also showing definite downward trends.

It could be a little wonder that I left for college with an air of pessimism.

It had been said that J. Pierpont Morgan averted financial collapse in the panic of 1907 by keeping under lock and key in his library 125 leading New York financiers until they came up with the necessary capital to avert economic disaster. Unfortunately, in 1929 with the elder Morgan dead and his son in Europe, we had no one capable of such heroic efforts to prevent the present economic disaster.

Thus, on October 24, a day that would forever after be known as Black Tuesday, the Great Crash of '29, was heralded in when 12,894,650 shares changed hands at such low prices that eleven well-known stock market speculators committed suicide by noon of that same day. Although the next two days saw steady trading, many would consider the following Monday and Tuesday to be the worst days of the crash with far more severe losses than even those of Black Tuesday.

It was, however, the failure of the banks which brought the crash home to most people. One of the major weaknesses of the banking system of that time was the fact that there were a large number of independent units. When one bank failed, the assets of the others were frozen. Naturally, when word of a bank's failure spread, depositors elsewhere were given a warning, and they soon rushed to their own banks and demanded their money, thereby causing a domino effect. As more and more depositors withdrew their funds, more and more banks were forced to close. In the first six months of 1929 following the stock market crash, 346 banks failed, and over the next few years, many more were to follow.

As was understandable, I wasn't the only college student urgently called home the weekend of November second, following

Black Tuesday. As I packed my meager belongings, I tried to summon the necessary courage to face the impending conclusion of my college career.

Mother was hysterical, Richard resigned, and John indifferent as we sat around awaiting the arrival of Arthur and Alissa who were trying to determine the extent of their own solvency. While I had no idea how the Saronnas had made out, there was no mistaking the gravity of the Androses' financial situation. The bank where Mother and Richard kept their savings had closed down a few days before, and unfortunately, they weren't among the lucky first customers to storm its doors. We suddenly found ourselves fallen from the lofty heights of upper middle-class prosperity to the brink of lower-class poverty in less than one week.

Both Arthur and Alissa looked tired and upset when they entered Mother's house. After Alissa kissed us all hello and tried to console Mother, she took out of her shoulder bag a large sheaf of papers.

"Since I now know of your financial situation, I'll fill you in on ours, and then we can try to work out some sort of plan. Father's financial affairs are a lot more complicated than my own, so it will be some time before we really are certain where he stands. While his savings along with ours were wiped out when the banks closed, we really aren't as badly off as might be expected. Father, as you probably know, went into some extensive business expansion this past summer."

"Didn't he open some gas stations?" Richard asked.

"Right. He also opened several additional repair shops to increase Arthur's side of the business. Since he refused to touch our savings, he laid out the money himself. However, because he also kept more than a month's business expenses at all times in a private vault, he's not totally without cash.

"I'm afraid that Arthur was probably the biggest loser in our family. Since Arthur has always been reluctant to withdraw money from the bank and since he's seldom used any of his own capital for investments, he really has lost a very substantial amount of money. Luckily, Father was insistent that Arthur also keep at least a month's operating expenses available so we're not without some cash."

"What about yourself?" John tactlessly demanded. "I always thought that you had your own separate account. You always look like you're loaded."

"John," Mother admonished, "you have no right to question Alissa about such things."

"Why not? She's the one who called this family conference, and she's also the one who spoke about forming some plan, so why shouldn't I have the right to ask her?"

As Mother was again about to reprimand John, Alissa cut in. "It's all right, Eleanor. I was just about to go into my own financial situation when John interrupted me. And, John, as to any 'rights' that you think you might have, let me tell you now that you have none. The only people who have 'rights' to my money or any knowledge of it are my parents and your brother…and even they have been a great deal more circumspect than you."

"Well, if your parents have rights, I don't see why we don't also have them because of Arthur."

"My parents have 'rights,' as you insist on calling them, because basically every cent I have was given to me by them. My father paid for my education and your brother's employment. As to any 'rights' to your brother's money, I've already told you that his personal savings have been wiped out and his business capital will have to be used for just that, business. As to my personal money, my savings were also wiped out, but I have been more fortunate than most people."

"In what way, dear?" Mother inquired.

"Last summer when Teddy was visiting, I asked him about an investment that I was thinking of making. When I had mentioned it to my father and Arthur, they both brushed off my idea as a feminine fluke and didn't take it seriously. Unlike Arthur, I never really received much enjoyment from looking at my bankbook. Numbers on a page didn't hold much interest for me, and I wanted something more…tangible. That's what made me think of diamonds."

"Don't tell me those diamonds you wore to Uncle Theo's dinner party were real?" I asked in astonishment.

"Most of them were. The pendant and earrings, of course, were real along with the bracelet and rings."

Yes," I said, remembering. "Those looked real, but I never thought the large ones loosely scattered in your hair could possibly be."

"No, the ones in my hair were only copies."

"Do you mean to say that you actually own the originals?" Mother asked in awe.

"Yes, not only those but quite a few more."

"Do you keep all those diamonds in the house?" John asked with suspicious interest.

"Of course not! They are in several different absolutely safe places which I will not reveal. Needless to say, Father's and Arthur's financial needs will have to be considered first, but I'm sure I can eventually help Richard with the store. I've already written to your Uncle Teddy who has seen the diamonds and asked him to try and find some buyers. My own agent is also working on it, but he's swamped with problems at this time and really won't be able to devote much time to me. That, of course, is the trouble—a lack of ready cash when you make a move like I did. Teddy warned me about it, but I never thought I would need additional cash other than the emergency funds I left in the bank. Do you have a good accountant, Richard?"

"No, I've always done the books myself since it's just the one store."

"Fortunately, for me, Father and Arthur have an excellent man who I'm sure would be happy to go over your books with you and help you find ways to cut expenses. Do you have enough cash available for your immediate needs?"

"I don't really know. I suppose if Mother, John, and I pool whatever cash reserves we have, we might manage for a few weeks."

"Even though Father and Arthur are doing their best, I'm afraid that layoffs are going to be inevitable. While we've canceled all unnecessary orders and are going to try and make do with what we have in stock, I don't know how long we can meet the payroll… That's going to be the hardest thing of all, firing people whose financial situation is probably worse than our own."

As we all sat around looking gloomily at each other, the doorbell rang and in walked Uncle Theo.

"Why such long faces?" he inappropriately asked. As Mother, Richard, and John were just about to jump on him, he held up a restraining hand. "I know! I know! Things are not so good, but making yourselves sick will not help. Tell Uncle Theo your troubles, my children."

After Richard finished explaining to Uncle Theo where we all stood, Alissa asked him how he had weathered the storm. "That is what I have come to tell you. While business is certainly not booming, I still have my savings."

"You do?"

"Yes. I never did trust banks, and besides, they were only open at most inconvenient times. After all, most people are themselves at work between nine and three, so when is one supposed to go to the bank? If they were smart, they would be open in the evenings and on weekends when people need them. Bah! Who can be bothered with such hours as theirs? While I prefer not to reveal where my savings are hidden, I hope that none of you will take it personally," Uncle Theo stated, glaring at John. "Suffice it to say that except for loss of business, I still have all of my money and have come to help you if I can."

"That's very generous of you, Uncle Theo," I stated, thinking to myself how the family eccentrics, Uncle Theo and Alissa, had—due to their unconventionality—come out of this mess better than anyone else.

"Of course, money will still be tight, Uncle Theo," Alissa pointed out, "since you will have a severe loss of income."

"That is certainly true, Alissa. While there will not be enough money for luxuries, I doubt if any of us will go hungry, and I really would like to help my brother's emporium if I am allowed."

"Your offer will be kept in mind, Theo," Mother said. "But we are going to try and make it on our own. Naturally, John, Edward, and I will immediately begin working in the emporium to help out, and while I regret laying off three people, it will be necessary. The less expense we have, the better our chances will be of holding on to the store."

"I am sorry, Edward, that you'll have to leave college," Richard apologized. "While we could do without your help, I'm sure you realize that we couldn't possibly handle the expense."

"Of course, I understand," I assured Richard as I smiled stiffly at everyone.

"Edward, don't tell me I forgot to mention it! I thought you were aware that your tuition, books, and lab fees are paid up for the next two years," Alissa explained. "Of course, there won't be money for extras, and you won't be able to come home every weekend, but I'm sure that will only be for a while. After all, things can't go on like this forever."

Too astonished and relieved for words, I could only stare at Alissa in dumbfounded silence while her words echoed in my mind. It seemed incredible that I would be returning to college not only to complete the semester but to also actually be financially secure for the next two years. And as Alissa said, things couldn't go on like this forever—but who could have foreseen that they would actually get… worse?

CHAPTER 18

Depression in the Nation and at Home

> O yet we trust that somehow good
>   Will be the final goal of ill,
>   To pangs of nature, sins of will,
> Defects of doubt, and taints of blood.
> —Tennyson, 1933

My first years of college were extremely difficult ones, not just on an intellectual level but also on a national one. The Great Crash of '29 proved to be just the tip of the iceberg, and no one who had lived through them would ever forget the years of the Great Depression which followed.

In 1933, hourly wages had dropped 60 percent since 1929. White-collar workers had fared little better with salaries now 40 percent lower. Even the usually top-paid professions, such as the medical ones, suffered with doctors earning an average of $3,382 annually. Only pilots and US Congressmen earned more with salaries of $8,000 and $8,663 respectively. Farmers were getting about five cents a pound for cotton and less than fifty cents a bushel for wheat.

These were the lucky ones. Everywhere one turned, one came face-to-face with the huge numbers of unemployed. Apple sellers and food lines on every major street corner reminded us that 25 percent of the labor force was out of work with thirty million mouths to feed besides their own. It's no wonder that twenty thousand people committed suicide in 1931.

In cities all over US, Hoovervilles sprang up. These were shanty towns where the scores of homeless sheltered themselves in shacks made of scrap metal and discarded packing crates. New York City had several Hoovervilles with two of the largest located in Central Park and below Riverside Drive.

In one of our country's most shameful incidents, one of these wretched Hoovervilles became internationally known. In June of 1932, Bonus Expeditionary Forces of Veterans of World War I camped in Washington, DC, pleading for advance payment of war bonds which they were due to receive in 1945. Since money was so desperately needed, they pleaded with the leaders of the country they had fought for to pay them the funds ahead of time.

When the Senate voted against their proposal, they were ordered to leave the city. When by nightfall of July 28, 1932, Hooverville still hadn't been totally evacuated even though a steady stream of these ragged and hungry veterans and their families could be seen leaving, President Hoover ordered a military force to clear out the stragglers. A force of infantry and cavalry equipped with machine guns, tanks, tear gas bombs, and sabers led by Eisenhower and MacArthur pursued the fleeing women, children, and even some legless veterans and then proceeded to burn the shacks. It was also reported that in the last explosion of gas bombs, an eleven-month-old baby died.

Considering the sorry state of the economy, I was extremely surprised and gratified that even after the two years of college that Alissa paid for in advance had passed, I never had to consider dropping out due to lack of funds. Through a gargantuan effort on the part of the whole family, my bills were always promptly paid. This could not have been easy since every one of the family businesses suffered severe losses.

Andros's Emporium had been suffering setbacks since the growth of the chain stores in the late '20s. Not able to compete with the low prices which such stores as A&P, F. W. Woolworth, and Piggly Wiggly were offering due to lower costs from volume purchasing, Richard tried to hold on to his customers by extending credit to them. This was a standard practice in small neighborhood stores which, unlike chains, had personally known their customers for years.

When the Crash of '29 occurred, it was inevitable that these same small stores would get the hardest hit. With customers unable to pay their debts, the stores were, likewise, unable to pay theirs. Neighborhood stores, which had, at one time, gone far in promoting goodwill, suddenly found themselves cast in the roles of villains as they were forced to turn more and more of their old customers away empty-handed even during the hungry Depression years. Richard would often be heard asking, "How can I offer them goods which neither they nor myself can pay for?"

While people understood that their pockets were empty, they somehow failed to see that the cash registers of Andros's Emporium were in the same state. It was not unusual during those terrible years for either the store or ourselves to be the victims of some malicious form of attack or vandalism.

With so many unemployed, those who had jobs and especially those who owned businesses worked with herculean effort to try and retain their jobs and keep their businesses running. Many employers were forced to lay off their help and put family members in their places, who were willing to work long hours for just their room and board.

While Alissa was able to sell her diamonds, it was a very slow process, and she, naturally, had to settle for much lower prices since diamonds weren't exactly in peak demand. Mr. Saronna's cab business was a loss too. When people didn't have enough money to feed their families, they're hardly thinking of taking cabs. The newspaper even reported one Arkansas family who walked about nine hundred miles trying to find work in the Rio Grande cotton fields. They trod on undauntedly while the husband pushed a primitive wooden handcart containing their meager possessions. The wife followed behind with a baby carriage containing, what looked like from the picture, at least two infants while a child of about six years old helped her along.

One thing in which Gabrial Saronna's foresight paid off was in the expansion of his repair shops. Since people couldn't afford new cars, it automatically followed that they kept the ones they had longer and drove them harder, thereby needing more repairs. Arthur's end of the business went a long way in picking up the slack which the cab business had caused.

With money so tight, even they had to cut operating expenses to a minimum and Alissa and Josephine were put to work in the business offices just as Mother, John, and occasionally myself were put to work in the emporium.

The main reason that I worked there so seldom was the fact that I had decided to go away to college. While Mother had originally wanted me within daily commuting distance, Alissa, Richard, and Uncle Theo pointed out that I would probably do a lot better if I could devote all my time and energy to my studies. Since they were bearing the brunt of the financial burden, they finally won out.

Because I saw very little of Marcie anyway, she decided to go to nursing school so we could be a team when I eventually set up a practice. She came through her studies with flying colors and was already working in a local hospital. Although I had grave doubts about the wisdom of husbands and wives working together, I wasn't given much choice.

Our biggest worry during this time was Uncle Theo. Without us realizing it, he had become an old man overnight. He had opened Theo's Den of Delights in 1929 at sixty-three years of age, a time when most men are looking to retire, not embark on a new venture. It was only during the past year that the very fact of his mortality was brought home to us. Instead of the lively, robust giant that we were all used to, a thin sickly old man had taken his place.

It was during one of the now-all-too-rare family gatherings, a few months prior to my college graduation, that the subject of Uncle Theo's health was brought up.

"Have you noticed lately how skinny Uncle Theo is getting?" Alissa asked us in general as we all assembled for dinner one evening in March of 1933.

"Who could help but notice it? He looks like an old man," John confirmed.

"Who isn't getting old? After all, I'm sixty-three, and the rest of you, with the exceptions of Edward and Marcie, aren't exactly spring chickens," Mother added.

"Has Theo said anything to you, Eleanor, about not feeling well?"

"No, you know Theo. He'd probably consider it unmanly to talk about his health, but he certainly is losing weight, and I notice he's often short of breath."

"Do you think the nightclub is too much for him?"

"I doubt it. Theo's always thrived on work. Besides, business isn't what it used to be. If you ask me, the only reason he keeps the place open is to have something to occupy himself with."

"When was the last time you saw him, Edward?" Arthur asked.

"It was about a month ago, I guess. Wasn't it, Mother?"

"Yes. Now that we're all so busy, we seldom have family dinners. I usually just make something the night before, and then we all eat in shifts whenever we find the time. Don't you have the same problem, Alissa?"

"Yes, we very seldom eat together either. I'm lucky though because Mother has been doing all the cooking."

"I thought she helped out in the office," I said.

"Sometimes she does, but she really doesn't have the head for business, and Father makes her nervous. He's so convinced that she's going to make some dreadful mistake that he hangs all over her."

"And, therefore, causes her to make even more mistakes," I guessed.

"Right!"

"How do you like working with your father?" Richard asked Alissa.

"It's not too bad. He also makes me nervous, but he seems to have more faith in me, and besides, he's so busy with his own work and checking up on Mother that he doesn't have too much time left to bother me."

"Getting back to Theo," Mother said, "I invited him here tonight for dinner. He said he had some business to take care of but would probably be over later on."

"That was good of you, Eleanor," Alissa complimented.

"Well, he is Demetrius's brother after all, and some good roast beef and Yorkshire pudding might have helped build up his strength."

It wasn't until after 9:00 p.m. when Arthur and Alissa were debating whether or not to depart for home when Uncle Theo walked in. Since we hadn't heard the doorbell, he entered, as usual, unannounced and caught us off guard. His appearance was so altered that a stunned gasp escaped us before we could suppress it. Using his sudden entrance as an excuse, I tried to cover up our shock.

"You startled us, Uncle Theo. We didn't hear the doorbell."

"How can you hear anything with all that jabbering?"

"Can I get you some dessert, Uncle Theo? I baked your favorite fudge cake especially for you."

For a second, that old beloved look of gluttony came into Uncle Theo's eyes only to be just as quickly extinguished. "No, thank you, my dear Alissa. I shall just feast my eyes on you instead of feasting my stomach," Uncle Theo said, grimacing.

"You're not looking at all well, Theo."

"You are right, Eleanor. It is why I wanted to see you all tonight. I am getting old—"

"Who isn't?" Mother interrupted. "That's no reason to let yourself go. If your Den of Delights is too much for you, why not give it up or at least find yourself a good manager? God knows there are plenty of qualified men who could use the job."

"I was just getting to that if you had not so rudely interrupted me, Eleanor. As a matter of fact, I am giving up the nightclub."

"Giving it up!" I said incredulously. "What will you do with yourself?"

"I have decided to go home to Somos."

"Nonsense!" Mother exclaimed. "Who do you have on Somos? Your home should be where your family is, and like it or not, we're the only family you have."

"I agree with Eleanor, Uncle Theo. If you aren't feeling well, you should be among those who love you and can look after you."

"Right," Mother grudgingly admitted. "Why don't you move in with us?"

At our look of shocked surprise, Mother tried to cover up her kindness by making excuses. "Well, we certainly have the room, and we could use the money. It's bound to be cheaper for both of us than running two separate establishments…unless you don't think we'll take good enough care of you."

"No, no," Uncle Theo quickly protested. "I am more flattered than I can ever tell you by your offer, Eleanor. But you should understand how I feel about my native land. After all, I have often heard you recite that depressing poem about England. You know the one—"

"Oh, you must mean: 'If I should die, think only this of me, that there's some corner of a foreign field. That is forever England. There shall be in that rich earth a richer dust concealed.' Is that the one you mean? The poem by Rupert Brooke?"

"Yes, that's the one. No matter how much we love another country, we never really forget the land of our birth. It is always part of us and we part of it."

"But, Theo, what kind of medical help can you get on Somos? You know, as well as I, how primitive everything is over there. At least in America, we have the finest doctors and medical facilities… Have you even seen a doctor?"

Ignoring Mother's question, Uncle Theo went on to tell us that he would be leaving for Somos on the first of next month.

As Mother was again about to protest, Alissa cut in. "Uncle Theo, I hope you realize how much we will all miss you. Arthur and I would also love to have you stay with us, but if your mind is really made up, we won't try to stop you, but please consider what will be best for you. If you aren't well, it would be better for you to stay where those you love can help take care of you, and I hope you know how much we all love you…" she trailed off, her voice breaking.

"I am truly a fortunate man. How many men, with no wife or children of his own, are blessed with such a loving family?"

"If you really mean that, you'll stay with us," I added.

"Now, now, Edward, I have made up my mind. Somos is like a magnet drawing me to it. I am not getting any younger, and if I want to once more visit my little island, I must do it now."

Since it was obvious that Uncle Theo was going to keep up the pretense that everything was all right and that he was only going away for a visit, I decided to drop the argument. After all, it was apparent that Uncle Theo was dying, and he certainly had every right to decide where he wanted to do it.

It was probably one of the most difficult charades that any of us ever had to put on, when we saw Uncle Theo for the last time. We had all gathered for a bon voyage party in his stateroom aboard the luxury liner Olympia, and as we each tearfully bid Uncle Theo "au revoir" instead of "goodbye," I thought it ironically apropos that his departure date should be April first, April Fools' Day.

CHAPTER 19

Family Upheaval

> Sigh no more, ladies, sigh no more,
>   Men were deceivers ever;
> One foot in sea, and one on shore,
>   To one thing constant never.
>
> —Shakespeare, 1934

It was on a Friday afternoon late in October, as I entered my off-campus boarding house, that I received a surprise visit which was to alter forever the Andros family. When Mrs. O'Hara, my landlady, met me at the door and told me that a visitor was waiting for me in her drawing room, I had no idea whom it could be. My only clue that my visitor was probably a female was due to the fact that most of my fellow boarders were hanging around outside the drawing room door, trying to peek in. Since Marcie wasn't expected, I couldn't imagine what other female would be crazy enough to go out of her way in order to visit me.

Quietly opening the door, I was surprised to behold my elegantly clad sister-in-law Alissa. She was sitting in one of Mrs. O'Hara's uncomfortable straight-backed horsehair chairs while her white-knuckled hand tightly clasped what could only be Mrs. O'Hara's horrible homemade cranberry cordial. Clad in a fawn-colored suede suit and pink silk blouse, she was an incongruous sight in Mrs. O'Hara's shabby drawing room. She nervously tapped a suede-pumped foot while her free hand beat a tattoo with her long pink polished nails on her matching suede purse.

Catching sight of me, she got up so quickly that she dropped her purse and came close to spilling her cordial all over the rug which was, however, such a muddy color that I doubt if anyone would have noticed.

Since Marcie and I had decided to get married in January and since Alissa was giving the wedding, I was surprised but not alarmed at this unexpected visit.

Marcie's parents had suffered severe financial problems in the past few years. Her father, who was something of a gambler, had begun suffering setbacks in the mid-1920s when his Florida land investments fell through. Having spent several memorable summer vacations as a boy with his parents in Florida, he, like so many others, speculated on a large scale in the early 1920s. Without ever examining the land which was offered for sale, many purchasers snapped up large tracts of what was advertised as prime tropical real estate but only to discover that they owned worthless marshland or, in some extreme cases, the land didn't even exist. News of these swindles combined with a severe hurricane in 1926 which killed four hundred people and tore roofs off thousands of houses soon burst the lucrative Florida bubble.

Despite these losses, Marcie's father decided to recoup his money by heavily investing what capital he had left in the stock market. With stocks rising by leaps and bounds during 1927 and 1928, he almost did succeed, but despite the warnings of many notable financiers that as a simple matter of probability the boom could not last much longer, Marcie's father did not pull out in time, and by 1930, he was totally bankrupt.

When Marcie's father lost his job and the bank foreclosed on his mortgage, the Jennings family had no choice but to move to Arizona where Marcie's widowed grandfather owned his own hardware business and a large old house, which he happily offered to his son's destitute family.

Having won a scholarship to nursing school and having quickly found a job upon graduation, Marcie set up her own small apartment where we kept many a romantic but frustrating (at least for me) tryst. Marcie being something of a puritan, at least where her own life was concerned, our lovemaking never reached a point where I received any real satisfaction. Despite the fact that our medical backgrounds certainly made us knowledgeable enough to prevent an unwanted pregnancy, Marcie would not veer from her antiquated moral code, and I was left to sulk in the customary cold shower, which certainly was not all it was chalked up to be.

When Marcie was offered a nursing job to begin in January only two miles away from my medical school, we finally decided to get married. Planning only a small family dinner in Marcie's new apartment, which was all we could afford, our plans were soon upset by Alissa who offered to give us a traditional wedding in her home. Seeing Marcie's face light up at this suggestion, I didn't have the heart to turn down Alissa's generous offer.

Thinking that she and Marcie had again come upon one of their planning crises, I happily strode into the drawing room graciously prepared to give them my expert opinion.

"Alissa, how nice to see you although surely tomorrow would have been soon enough to seek my sage advice. Didn't Marcie tell you that I'm coming to Queenstown this weekend?" I asked condescendingly.

Noticing that my words failed to bring the accustomed smile or look of disdain to Alissa's face, I suddenly began to worry. "Alissa, what's wrong? Is it Mother or Marcie?"

"No, no," she quickly reassured me. "Everyone's fine. I'm the one with the problem."

"Are you ill?"

"No."

"Is it a problem with the wedding?"

"No…well, I guess indirectly."

Becoming totally frustrated by now, I forcibly restrained her pacing figure, sat her down, and refused to release my hold on her shoulders until she made some sense. "At this rate, maybe I should change my medical field," I complained.

"What do you mean?"

"Since obtaining information from you is like pulling teeth, I think I'll change to dentistry."

Feeling her finally begin to relax and noting a smile playing around her lips, I loosened my grasp and sat opposite her. "Now, dearest sister-in-law, please tell me what is troubling you," I said, practicing my best bedside manner. Confidently sitting back and benevolently waiting for Alissa to unburden herself, I was soon forced again to the edge of my seat as she suddenly burst into tears.

"What did I say?" I asked genuinely distressed and embarrassed as I noticed the drawing room door opening slightly, and I pictured the myriad pairs of eyes peering in. Edging my way over to it, I gave the door a forceful push, which caught at least one pair of prying fingers.

"It's what you called me." She sobbed.

"I called you 'sister-in-law.' You are my sister-in-law, aren't you?" I asked perplexedly.

"Not for much longer," she wailed.

Not knowing how to cope and remembering Mother's panacea of a cup of tea, I went to fetch Mrs. O'Hara who promptly fell into the room as I opened the door to summon her, leaving me with no doubt as to how she'd been spending the past few minutes. I only hoped that the pair of pinched fingers hadn't been Mrs. O'Hara's since I could hardly afford my rent as it was.

"Is the poor lady upset?" Mrs. O'Hara asked as Alissa's wails continued to reverberate throughout the entire house.

"A little, I'm afraid," I prevaricated as she shot me poisonous glances as if I were Jack the Ripper.

"Could you possibly bring us some tea?"

"Surely! Although some more of my cranberry cordial would probably be of more help."

"No! No!" I quickly protested. "You're too generous. The tea will be just fine."

Hesitating as to whether I could be trusted alone with Alissa or whether I would again perform some heinous act, she shot me a doubtful glance and walked out, muttering to herself.

Giving Alissa time to regain her self-control, I now began pacing up and down while I tried to sort out the problem. Obviously, it had to do with Arthur and Alissa's marriage, or the word *sister-in-law* wouldn't have been so calamitous.

When I finally got rid of Mrs. O'Hara who spent at least ten minutes arranging the tea tray while surreptitiously eyeing us, I got down to business.

"Are you ready to begin?" I gently inquired of Alissa.

"Yes," she said, squaring her shoulders and taking some papers out of her purse.

"This morning, I went into town to do some grocery shopping. As I was putting my groceries in the car, a man whom I recognized as an acquaintance of my father walked over to me. 'Mrs. Andros, isn't it?' he asked. 'You probably don't remember me, but my name is George Carwood, and we met about two years ago in your father's office.'

"It was then that I remembered he was a prominent executive with a major sewing machine company. Returning his greeting, I was surprised to notice that he looked decidedly uncomfortable.

"'Mrs. Andros, I can't tell you how much I appreciate your civility. I mean, after all, sometimes in cases like this, people can react so unreasonably, and I just want you to know that I am truly sorry to have to involve a fine and lovely lady like yourself in this whole sordid business. I also want to reassure you that I will do everything I can to keep this whole thing as quiet as possible, but considering the people involved and the size of the town, I'm afraid that this just might become a…cause célèbre.'

"Seeing my confusion, he looked shocked as he realized that I had no idea what he was talking about.

"'It isn't possible that you're actually unaware of what's been happening! It's the main topic of gossip around town.'

"'Mr. Carwood, I happen to live about ten miles outside of town and make it a point to ignore any gossip when I do come here, so I really don't have any idea what you're talking about. Since you seem to feel that whatever it is involves me in some way, please do enlighten me,' I said with annoyance as I felt my stomach sinking.

"'Please forgive me, Mrs. Andros, but I don't think that I should. After all, this is really your husband's responsibility. I don't wish to distress you.'

"'Well, since my husband obviously doesn't share your feelings and if you really don't wish to distress me, please tell me what's going on.'

"'Well, all right. I suppose it would be kinder, but we can't stand in the middle of the parking lot like this. Where can we talk privately? How about joining me for lunch at the Pine River Falls Inn?'

"Not really feeling like eating but wanting to get this ordeal over with, I agreed. After ordering our meal, Mr. Carwood told me the following story. It seems that Arthur has been having an affair with Mrs. Carwood for the past year, and Mr. Carwood finally has the proof he needs to file for a divorce on grounds of adultery. The case comes to court on Monday and names your brother as corespondent."

"Do you believe him?" I asked incredulously.

"Of course, I do. This isn't the first time that your damned brother has been unfaithful."

"It isn't?"

"No, there have been others. I'm not even mad about that. I'm just furious that he was so stupidly careless, and I was forced to find out in this way."

"Have you spoken to Arthur? What did he say?"

"That's the most incredible thing of all! When I asked him why he hadn't told me about the case on Monday, he said that he hadn't bothered because it didn't really involve me. It's between him and the Carwoods, and I'd probably read all about it in Monday's evening paper anyway."

Feeling both outraged at Arthur and at the same time stunned by his callousness, I didn't know what to say to Alissa. "What are you going to do?"

"What can I do? I'll have to divorce him, of course. Once this thing gets out, I'll have no choice."

"Have you told Arthur?"

"Yes, and he's overjoyed. He can't wait to move in with his little slut," she said venomously.

Seeing that she was really in no shape to continue this discussion and needing time alone to think, I asked Alissa to stay overnight in town, and I would drive into Queenstown with her tomorrow, and then we could continue our discussion.

*****

Setting out early the next morning, I could see that Alissa was in a better frame of mind.

"Can we talk while you're driving?"

"Of course," she said determinedly.

"There's one thing I don't understand. If this Carwood is such a nice guy and wants to make this as easy as possible, can't he use other grounds to file for divorce?"

"I guess he could, but there are two children involved, and he wants to try and get custody although it's doubtful since he admits that his wife could probably counter-file with adultery charges."

"You mean they're both adulterers?"

"Of course."

Not wanting to delve deeper into that or Alissa's matter-of-fact tone, I quickly asked another question. "I thought Arthur dislikes children? Does he realize if he marries this woman, he might get stuck with two of them after all?"

"Of course, he realizes it. That's another thing that infuriates me," she said, swerving off the road. Straightening the wheel again, she continued, "All these years, he never wanted any children of our own. Now that I'm almost thirty-seven years old, that miserable bastard is leaving me to live with that adulteress and her two brats!"

"Speaking of the two children, by the way, what are they?"

"What are they? They're two lumps, that's what they are!"

"I'm talking about their sex, not their shapes. Are they boys or girls?"

"One of each, a boy lump and a girl lump."

"How old are they, and why do you call them 'lumps'?"

"As to their ages, I think the girl is around thirteen and the boy fifteen. Arthur wasn't sure, but he thought my guesses were fairly accurate. And as to why they're lumps, they just look like lumps."

"You've seen them?"

"Of course. Yesterday morning, I drove by their house and waited for them to leave for school so I could get a look at them, and they both look like lumps just as I've said."

"What about Mrs. Carwood? Have you also seen her?"

"Yes."

"And?"

"Well, you can't really expect me to be very objective about her, can you?"

"No, I guess not."

"Besides, you'll be able to see for yourself soon enough."

"What do you mean?"

"You'll be able to judge what she looks like for yourself when you see her at your wedding."

"You're inviting her?" I asked incredulously.

"I really don't have a choice. After all, she'll be the groom's sister-in-law, and if I don't invite her, it will really set tongues wagging. You do see that, don't you?"

Not really knowing the "ins and outs" of social conventions, I didn't understand why Mrs. Carwood had to be invited. Surely, she wouldn't be married to Arthur already in just three months, but Alissa soon set me straight.

"I'm afraid that she'll be an Andros before Christmas. Mr. Carwood will have no trouble getting a divorce decree with the proof he has," she said, handing me a copy of the detective's report that she had brought with her yesterday but hadn't remembered to show me. "He knows people in high places and won't have to wait."

As I perused the long report, I couldn't help but feel very sad for all the people involved, especially Alissa and the Carwood children who really seemed to be the pawns in this dirty domestic disaster.

"Alissa, if you've known about Arthur's infidelities for so long, how come you didn't get a divorce years ago?"

"I don't know. I suppose I always hoped that things would get better. Remember, I've been with Arthur since I'm sixteen, and it's awfully hard to break a tie that's over twenty years old."

"What about Arthur? You said he's glad about the divorce. Why did he stay with you for so long?"

"I guess he also found it easier to just stick with what was for him a pretty cushy situation, and I guess too that he never before found someone whom he wanted to marry."

As I reflected on all the reasons Alissa had given for them staying together and upon our entire discussion of the last two days, it suddenly struck me as very sad that in dissecting a relationship of over twenty years duration, the word *love* had never been mentioned by anyone even once.

Chapter 20

Hell Hath No Fury

> Then sigh not so,
> But let them go,
> And be you blithe and bonny;
> Converting all your sounds of woe
> Into. Hey nonny, nonny.
>
> —Shakespeare

While Alissa and I lunched in Queenstown, I decided that the only fair course of action left was for me to arrange a meeting with Arthur. Phoning Mother from the restaurant, I again conveniently used the wedding arrangements as an excuse as to why I would be late, and then we proceeded to Pine River Falls. After dropping Alissa home, I borrowed her car and tried to track down my brother. Fortunately, he was in the local office, and since it was already late in the afternoon, I asked him to leave work early and join me at the inn for cocktails.

Despite my high hopes, my discussion with Arthur was far from satisfying. He was as uncommunicative as ever, and I felt totally disheartened when our interview was over. Arthur's and Alissa's stories were very similar. Arthur readily admitted to his infidelities, but to his credit, he offered no excuses for them and in no way blamed Alissa. He was infuriatingly complacent over the whole affair and didn't seem concerned about how many lives his actions would affect. The only worry he did have was over his job. Mr. Saronna couldn't be expected to look kindly upon Arthur after the case became public on Monday.

Arthur remained visibly unruffled when I explained all the changes in everyone's lives his separation from Alissa would precipitate; and except for shrugs, yesses, and noes, he, not surprisingly, refused to discuss his private life with me. It was only when I mentioned Mother that a noticeable change in his demeanor occurred.

"Mother! What does this have to do with her?"

"Arthur, don't be so dense. It would be very dangerous for her health if she read about it in the newspapers. She has to be told, and you're the one to do it."

"I'm not doing any such thing! You're the doctor. If you really think it's necessary, do it yourself...or have Alissa do it."

"You'd really expect Alissa to tell Mother?" I asked in surprise.

"Why not? She's probably dying to cry on Mother's shoulder. Look how she couldn't wait to run to you."

"Arthur, that's not fair. Alissa came to me because she was concerned about what the shock could do to Mother and because your situation will create no small amount of awkwardness at my wedding. You do see that?"

"No, I don't. Alissa can still give the wedding. As for us continuing to be the best man and matron of honor, we don't have to be married to each other anyway. So what's the problem?"

Not believing the extent of his insensitivity and not wanting to get into an argument, I explained that I was borrowing Alissa's car for the weekend and had to set out for Queenstown before it grew any later.

*****

The whole family including Marcie were eating dinner when I arrived at Mother's. When dessert was finished and everyone was about to disperse in pursuit of their own activities, I asked them to please gather in the parlor because I had something important to discuss.

"You two haven't decided to call off the wedding?" Mother asked nervously.

"No, no, Mother. It has nothing to do with Marcie and me... well, perhaps it does indirectly involve the wedding."

"Don't be so mysterious, Edward," John complained. "And snap it up! I have a date tonight."

Everyone sat in stunned silence while I related what I had learned from Alissa.

"But this is incredible," Mother stated. "Who would want to marry Arthur? Well, I mean, after all, he's my son and I love him, but Arthur is one of the most boring people I have ever known. He is never awake long enough to have an affair! It all has to be a mistake. Yes, that's it. Alissa has been under too much strain lately, and she misunderstood Mr. Cartwood."

"Carwood."

"Yes, Carwood."

"I'm sorry, Mother, but it's not a mistake. I also spoke to Arthur today, and he admits the whole thing."

"But where would he meet another woman? He never goes anywhere except to work."

"And that's exactly where he met her."

"At work?"

"Yes, it seems Mrs. Carwood was having some problems with her car's repairs, and as the general manager of Saronna's Auto Repair Shop, Arthur met her, and…well, I guess one thing led to another."

"At work! In the very business that his father-in-law was good enough to establish for him. I can't believe that any son of mine would act in such 'bad form.'"

"The only 'form' Arthur was probably interested in was this Mrs. Carwood. Have you seen her, Edward?"

"No, John, Arthur didn't describe her, and Alissa, claiming prejudice, refused to."

"Dear Alissa!" Mother wailed.

"Edward, we can't allow Alissa to go through with giving us the wedding. It will be too awkward for her."

"I've already said the same thing to Alissa, but she insists on it. Some very painful times are ahead for her, and it just might help if she has something to keep her busy."

"What is this woman's first name?" Richard asked.

"I think Arthur called her Dee Dee."

"Dee Dee! What kind of name is that?" Mother asked in her most outraged voice.

"I think it's probably the nickname she uses for Diana."

"Well, it seems to me that Diana's a perfectly good name. Dee Dee, indeed! Only a dumb-dumb would change a normal name like Diana into Dee Dee. I hate nicknames. They're so vulgar! She must be of very common stock," Mother declared in her most haughty English accent.

I couldn't help but laugh to myself whenever Mother climbed on her British high horse. While I certainly didn't feel like defending this Dee Dee Dumb-Dumb, I could see the unfairness of Mother's statement. After all, although Mother never used them herself, she was from a country in which such nicknames as Caro, Sugey, Prinnie, and Bertie were legion. What about her own stepbrother Teddy?

"Do calm down, Mother. There's really nothing we can do to change things. It is Arthur's life, and we'll just have to make the best of it."

"Make the best of it! I most certainly will do no such thing. You may tell your brother Arthur that if he goes through with divorcing Alissa and marrying this dumb-dumb, I will never speak to him again!"

"Mother, don't be ridiculous. I love Alissa as much as you, but we've been through this same type of situation once before. You saw then that refusing to speak to Arthur was no answer. You've often said yourself that you regret those lost years."

"That was different, Edward. Alissa turned out to be a darling young woman. This Dee Dee person is an adulteress and homewrecker. I would never even associate with such a person, let alone welcome one into my family."

"Maybe she won't be so bad, and she has two children. You know you'd like grandchildren. You'll have a ready-made granddaughter and grandson."

"That's even worse! Not only is she interfering in the lives of adults, but she's wrecking the lives of her own children. What kind of woman can be so selfish and still call herself a mother?"

*****

When the divorce case hit the newspapers on Monday, they did everything possible to play up the affair's seamy side. While Mr. Carwood won the divorce, the adultery charges didn't prevent Mrs. Carwood from being given custody of the children. I supposed the fact that Arthur and Dee Dee had every intention of marrying as soon as possible didn't do her any harm and despite Mr. Carwood's protests, he failed to prove that his wife couldn't provide a decent home and moral environment for their offspring…or maybe he just failed to prove that he could do better. With so many people out of work, the fact that Arthur was employed also was a factor in giving Mrs. Carwood custody.

I discussed my surmises with Alissa the next time I saw her, and her explanation left me in no doubt as to the validity of the statement "Hell hath no fury like a woman scorned."

Alissa visited us the weekend after the divorce case was settled. The more boring arrangements of the wedding such as the date, caterers, band, and number of guests had all been settled, and now we could get down to what Alissa described as the more enjoyable (at least to her) arrangements. Before she could get started talking about her wedding plans, I expressed my surprise over the fact that Arthur was still in the Saronna employ. Her answer was a Machiavellian masterpiece.

It seemed that the only thorn in Arthur's side about marrying Dee Dee was the possibility of getting custody of the Carwood children. Disliking children as he did, he, needless to say, didn't want them, and though he never expressed his feelings to Dee Dee, he had made the mistake of admitting this to Alissa. Since the facts of Arthur's impending marriage to Mrs. Carwood and him being employed were all major considerations in the judge's decision, Alissa decided to help him along. She told the judge that she was also immediately filing for a divorce of her own and that Arthur would continue to be employed by her father. Always as good as her word, she did file for divorce, and Arthur, while still working for Mr. Saronna, soon found his position somewhat altered. Instead of general manager, he found himself demoted to local manager with all his special privileges taken away in addition to a drastically reduced salary. With employment opportunities just about nil, he had no choice but to accept whatever was dished out to him, and knowing Big Al, I had no doubt that plenty was dished out and all of it unpalatable.

Alissa also had their wedding on tenterhooks. She kept stalling the final meeting with her lawyer. While she claimed that it might be easier to just wait until after our wedding, I had no doubt that she also enjoyed thwarting them. The division of property was fairly easy since both Arthur and Alissa had kept separate savings accounts. The house, which was bought and furnished by the Saronnas, was under Alissa's name. Except for personal possessions, Arthur would be practically destitute. The judge, who was something of a Victorian, was extremely hard on Arthur and Dee Dee, and it was only thanks to what the judge referred to as Alissa's "kind Christian intervention" that he overturned his original decision and gave Mrs. Carwood custody of her children.

As Alissa eloquently pleaded, "Children belong with their mother. It has always been my profoundest desire that God would have blessed me with children, but since he has decided otherwise, I can only beg that you do not deprive another woman of her beloved offspring." The newspapers reported that her speech was so touching that most of the spectators were moved to tears. This included Arthur whose tears, I was quite sure, were for a different reason.

Alissa's stand helped her in two ways. She not only got her revenge on her erring husband, but she was also declared to be a saint by Pine River Falls society. Her unselfish generosity was the talk on everyone's lips.

When Alissa related these things to me, I had mixed feelings. There was no doubt that Arthur's own actions had caused him to be a loser in a very big way. However, he was my brother, and I didn't enjoy seeing him brought so low. Then again, what person with such an opportunity for revenge handed to them like that wouldn't take advantage of it for "revenge is sweet" despite what the moralists preach.

It was very difficult for me to remain annoyed with Alissa. She had been wonderful to my family over the years, and even now, she was being more than generous with her plans for our wedding. She was still determined to give it even though she knew that it would draw many of the curious who would want to be present at the first social occasion at which Arthur, Alissa, and possibly even Dee Dee would all meet face-to-face.

"Enough talk about all of that. Let's get down to the real reason why I've come here tonight. What are you wearing to your wedding, Marcie?"

"I'm not sure, but I'm going to try and find a reasonably priced ready-made long white gown. If you wouldn't mind, I was hoping that you would let me alter one of the lovely evening gowns that you own. You seem to wear a lot of white, and even one of your oldest would be more elegant and fashionable than anything I could afford," Marcie tentatively suggested.

"Great! I have an even better idea. Why don't you wear my wedding gown and veil? They're really exquisite, and no one who will be at your wedding have seen them before," Alissa said, looking embarrassed as she realized the tactlessness of her last sentence.

"Could I really?" Marcie asked in awe, for once not answering her own question.

"Of course. The gown will have to be shortened and taken in a bit, but that's no problem. I even brought them with me just in case you agreed," she said, running back out to the car.

While the three women went upstairs to help Marcie try on the bridal finery, which I wasn't allowed to see ahead of time, I waited downstairs and pondered the sad irony of the situation.

Here were Marcie and I being given a wedding by the munificence of a young woman whom my family had refused to speak to for thirteen years and who would now soon be my former sister-in-law. We were to celebrate in a pseudo-Elizabethan, pseudo-medieval manor built by Alissa's father for the marital bliss of his daughter and my brother. My future wife was even to be married in the gown and veil that had been the talk of the society columns for weeks after Alissa wore them. Despite all the trappings and all the effort that Big Al had gone through to try and insure his little girl's conjugal bliss, Alissa had ended up a bitter childless divorcee whose only salvation at this time was in reusing these splendid accoutrements to provide a setting for Arthur's brother and his bride-to-be.

The final and biggest irony of all was that, despite my earlier fears, neither Richard nor Roderick had ended up being Mordred after all. In the end, it was Arthur himself who finally succeeded in destroying Camelot.

Chapter 21

Nuptials at Joyeuse Garde

> O my luve is like a red, red rose,
>   That's newly sprung in June.
> O my luve is like the melodie,
>   That's sweetly played in tune.
> —Burns, 1935

By the time my wedding day rolled around, a great many other important things had occurred. Alissa obtained her divorce from Arthur, and he and Dee Dee were ensconced in a seedy little house about fifteen miles outside of Pine River Falls in the opposite direction from where Alissa's home was. Arthur couldn't afford a home in town and yet had to be within commuting distance since he still hadn't found a new job. He was, therefore, forced to live in the outlying commercial section to the west of his former home.

While we didn't see much of Arthur anymore since Mother refused to acknowledge his new wife and her offspring, Arthur did stop by during the holidays in order to deliver Christmas presents. Although he tactfully arrived without Dee Dee, Mother, after opening her gifts, claimed a bad headache and retired to her room. Seeing Arthur's humiliation, I offered him a drink and tried to be as pleasant as possible although we were both stiff with each other.

It was then I learned about Arthur's new living conditions. The four of them were inhabiting a one-bedroom, three-room bungalow with the two adolescents sleeping on daybeds in the living room.

Arthur was optimistic, however, that a small screened porch could be enlarged and converted into bedrooms for the two young people.

After Arthur departed, my thoughts naturally drifted to Alissa who was spending the holidays with her parents. This would probably prove a most disagreeable occasion for her since with age, Mr. Saronna seemed to have increased his sadistic tendencies and would very likely spend the entire day picking on and humiliating his increasingly cowed wife. While these family gatherings literally sickened Alissa, she didn't have the heart to refuse their invitations. In truth, she knew the gentle Josephine would suffer even more from her daughter's absence.

Despite her father's protests, Alissa had refused to move back in with her family and instead remained in her own home. There she lived in solitary splendor in the house, which she went back to calling Joyeuse Garde, her original name for it which she had dropped when Arthur complained about it being affectatious. After being told that Joyeuse Garde had been named after Lancelot's French castle, I decided it was as good a name as any. I only hoped that Alissa would find a Sir Lancelot to install in it before it ended up becoming another convent like the one at Amesbury where Guinevere was reputed to have spent her final days in chaste sanctuary.

On January 18, we were to meet at the Saronnas' since Alissa's house was in a turmoil of last-minute preparations and then proceed to St. Anthony's Church for the wedding rehearsal. Independently of each other, Arthur and Alissa had both begged off as best man and matron of honor. Alissa claimed that she would have too much to supervise at the house, and Arthur gave no reason, but realizing how painful their second walk down the aisle together would be, we asked no questions. Two of our friends were substituted in their places. It had been decided that since Marcie's parents wouldn't be present for the wedding that Richard would give the bride away.

It was, therefore, with great consternation that we heard Alissa's announcement right before we were to leave for church.

"Edward, Marcie, I have some bad news for you."

"What now?" I groaned since our new best man had already phoned that he'd be late due to a flat tire.

"I'm afraid that Richard won't be able to make the rehearsal."

"But if he's not here, how will he know what to do tomorrow?" I complained.

"Well, the worst part is that he won't be here tomorrow either. He just phoned to say that he's come down with the flu."

"Do something, Edward." Marcie sobbed. "Now I'll have no one to give me away."

"Will I do?" came a voice from behind us.

"Father! Mother!" cried an ecstatic Marcie as she raced into her parents' arms.

Glancing in astonishment at Alissa, I caught her surreptitiously wiping her own tears as catching my eye, she merely shrugged her shoulders and assumed an angelic expression.

Alissa had, from the start, offered to pay the Jenningses' fare from Phoenix for the wedding. Feeling that they were already greatly in Alissa's debt for the financial burden of the wedding, they stubbornly refused all her entreaties.

It was Alissa's final plea that finally moved them. While Richard was to give the bride away and assume Mr. Jennings's role, Alissa was to assume Marcie's mother's role by signaling the approach of the bride with her own entrance. Explaining the past months' events to the Jenningses, she finally convinced them that they would be doing her a big favor by coming. Besides, removing the cloud that their absence threatened to cast over their daughter's wedding day, the Jenningses would also free Alissa and Richard for other last-minute chores. Alissa also explained how viewing a wedding at which her ex-husband and his new wife would be present would be extremely difficult for her with the eyes of curious Pine River Falls residents looking. If the Jenningses would attend, they could spare Alissa this ordeal.

After the rehearsal, we returned to the Saronnas for the customary rehearsal dinner. When this was over, Alissa, Marcie, and her parents would retire to Joyeuse Garde for the night while I, in keeping with tradition, would spend the night at the Saronnas. The next time I saw Marcie, she would be walking down the aisle on her father's arm about to become Mrs. Edward Andros.

While things should have been relatively peaceful the next day at the Saronnas, Big Al's constant harping on his wife soon reduced me to a quivering bunch of nerves. I wondered how Alissa could stand visiting them, let alone poor Mrs. Saronna who had to live with the man.

I learned afterward that although the problems came from a different source at Joyeuse Garde, they, nevertheless, were abundant. Alissa, realizing that many people would be critical of the lavish expenditure of money during such hard times, tried to alleviate the criticism as much as possible by hiring as many ex-Saronna employees for the day as she could. She hired several professional waiters and a head chef but insisted that the caterers train her father's former employees to work as waiters, kitchen helpers, coat checkers, and various other jobs required for the reception. Although this met with a great deal of opposition from the professionals because of the large extra amount of money Alissa was willing to pay and because of the lack of unions at the time, Alissa's wishes were carried out, but problems did ensue.

Like most people, my wedding day was something of a blur. The one thing that I shall never forget was the breathtaking vision of beauty that was Marcie as she glided gracefully down the aisle. Arrayed in Alissa's pearl-studded antique satin gown and Chantilly lace veil, a more lovely bride had never existed. I only wished that Alissa had been able to come to the church.

It was while we were heading back to Alissa's for the reception that I realized that I hadn't seen Arthur. When I questioned Marcie, she hadn't seen him either and wasn't even sure if he had ever answered the invitation.

As we were riding in the limousine, I noticed that Marcie, who was usually such a modest young woman, kept glancing worriedly at herself in a little mirror which she carried in a tiny satin reticule which hung from her wrist. When I assured her that she looked just perfect, she appeared confused at my reassurances. When I explained that I was only trying to reassure her because she kept looking at herself, she explained that she was checking the tiara. I then told her not to worry because it was on straight.

"I'm not worried about if it's on straight or not," she said with some exasperation. "I'm just afraid of losing the stones."

"Don't tell me they're real!" I gasped as I looked incredulously at the full crowned diamond and pearl-studded tiara which held the yards of precious French lace.

"Do you really think Mr. Saronna would have purchased paste and glass for his daughter? Of course not," Marcie asked and answered.

As I digested the information, I accustomed myself to the fact that everyone would just have to think Marcie was vain since I couldn't blame her for checking on the jewels. I only hoped that I could prevent myself from also glancing at and counting them too often.

A butler whom I recognized as Jim, who had retired several years ago from the Saronnas, ushered us into the foyer. Marcie and I gasped in wonder as we observed the garlands of pink roses, phlox, and baby's breath which wound around the bannisters leading to the upstairs landing. Huge hanging baskets of flowers were suspended everywhere interspersed with the traditional wedding bells.

"Alissa, how did you get all of this done while we were at church?" Marcie's mother asked in awe.

"All the other rooms were already decorated which is why I led you straight to your rooms last night, so all I had to do were the foyer and landing after you left. Besides, I had plenty of help."

Going over to thank her, I was struck anew by Alissa's beauty. She was wearing a pale gold satin strapless gown, the skirt of which was embroidered with metallic gold thread and seed pearls forming an intricate floral design. Her dark auburn curls were held back à la Greek by a wide gold mesh band which was also studded with seed pearls and exactly matched her gold choker and bracelet. While the events of the past few months had left a visible mark on her, it only served to make her even more lovely. The underlying sorrow in her large green eyes managed to transform her from a beautiful young lady into a fascinating and desirable woman.

"Hurry into the drawing room so I can show you around before the other guests arrive."

The drawing room was also a beautiful bower of flowers. Alissa had coordinated the flowers with the dominant reds, golds, and greens of the room. Garlands of clustered red-and-gold roses, phlox, and baby's breath were everywhere. In Alissa's library, the band was tuning up, and even the wrought iron gates, which separated them from the rest of the room, were so beflowered that I wondered if the music would be muffled.

Crossing over into the moss-green dining room, all the traditional white flowers associated with weddings were in evidence—orange blossoms, white roses, gardenias, myrtles, veronicas, lilies of the valley, plus a great many more whose names eluded me.

The buffet was the masterpiece I would have expected from Alissa. There were beluga caviar, pâtés, ham, turkey, beef Wellington, and mountains of fresh vegetables both in season and out to just name a few dishes.

As we were admiring all these things, the doorbell rang, heralding the arrival of our first guests. As we formed a receiving line in the foyer, I looked up and saw Alissa's anxious expression and realized that I had forgotten to tell her of Arthur's absence from church. Thinking better of it, I held my tongue since there was no guarantee that he wouldn't be attending the reception, and this, in fact, might even be him.

Since the invitations had announced that the reception was to begin at 7:00 p.m., at 7:45 p.m., we decided that all the guests who were coming had probably arrived, and we could disperse and mix with the guests who were freely partaking in champagne and hors d'oeuvres being passed around.

After dinner, we returned to the drawing room where dancing was in progress. While we had been eating, silver fountains that gaily spewed wine and champagne had been placed around the perimeter of the room. Alissa explained that this was a precaution taken to prevent the inexperienced waiters and waitresses from colliding with the dancers and spilling drinks on our elegantly clad guests.

The dessert buffet did not prove as huge as I had feared due to Alissa's sweet tooth. Since most people would probably just eat the wedding cake, she had stuck to simple alternatives. There were fancy bombes and ice cream molds in the shapes of bells, wedding rings, cupids, flowers, and the ever-present unicorn.

Seeing my admiration of the heraldic beast, Alissa merely shrugged and, with a glint in her eyes, said, "I couldn't resist."

There were flaming jubilee, rum raisin, and hot fudge sauces to accompany the ice cream and cake. Despite all these things, the real pièce de résistance was the wedding cake. It had seven tiers and was elegantly decorated with real crystallized flowers. Besides being beautiful, the cake was also delicious. Unlike the traditional cake, this one was of our favorite chocolate and filled with brandied cherries between the whipped cream-coated layers.

As I took a closer look preparatory to helping Marcie cut it, we had another surprise. The cake's centerpiece was an exact replica of Marcie and me. Alissa had found a local unemployed artist who had worked from photos in sculpting dolls so exactly like us that we kept gaping at them in wide-eyed disbelief. They were our mirror images in every detail, from the tops of their heads to the tips of their tiny satin and leather-shod feet. Marcie's doll was even clad in an exact replica of her bridal outfit, and mine wore a miniature cutaway.

When John heard that even the dolls' hair were swatches of our own which Alissa had made deals with our haircutters to collect, he jokingly warned us not to use them as voodoo dolls when we had the inevitable marital spats.

With the evening's progression, I noticed Alissa's discomfort every time the doorbell rang and some straggler was announced. Unfortunately, Mother's little remark about Dee Dee's name had stuck, and all night, everyone in my family kept referring to her as Dumb-Dumb.

"Do you think Arthur and Dumb-Dumb will show?"

"Have Arthur and Dumb-Dumb arrived yet?"

"I wonder why Arthur and Dumb-Dumb weren't at the church."

"That Dumb-Dumb better not show her face here!" This was from Mother.

We mingled for a while longer with our guests, and then Marcie hurried upstairs with Alissa and Mrs. Jennings to change so we could depart for our honeymoon. As I waited for Marcie to reappear, I stood in the foyer talking to John and Richard.

"I'm surprised that Arthur never showed," John said.

"I'm not. We aren't all as thick-skinned as you," Richard retorted. "I can't imagine even Arthur being tactless enough to show up at Alissa's house with his new wife, Dee Dee Dumb-Dumb."

Just then, Marcie appeared at the top of the stairs dressed in her navy-blue traveling suit. While Alissa went to fetch the guests so Marcie could throw her bouquet and we could make our getaway, the doorbell rang. Since old Jim was helping pass out the packets of rice and since I was standing next to the door, I opened it.

I would never understand if it was nervousness due to the wedding, too much champagne, or conditioning due to repetition which caused me to blurt out just as everyone was assembled in the foyer: "Look who's here, Arthur and his wife, Dumb-Dumb!"

Chapter 22

Medical School

> There was an Oxford student too, it chanced,
> Already in his logic well advanced...
> Whatever he got by touching up a friend
> On books and learning he would spend.
>
> —Chaucer

Although most people felt that I was crazy getting married the same year I was to enter medical school, I discovered that Marcie's unwavering support, good humor, and faith in me were the very factors which made it possible for me to survive the grueling routine that I was about to embark upon. While I had found college and premed school difficult, I was ill-prepared for what was to follow.

Having already experienced the frustrations of registration, I resignedly stood on long lines for each class, trying to organize some kind of workable schedule. This was no different than college. With the thick school catalog in hand, you tried to select the courses you preferred only to discover that you hadn't taken the necessary prerequisites. While originally, your selection seemed tremendous, when you finally determined which courses you were qualified to take, you were down to about a half a dozen.

Since each course had a separate line to wait on, it was not unusual to discover that just when your schedule had started to take shape, you were closed out on one of the courses you had slotted yourself in for, and the only other open courses conflicted with one that you had already enrolled in. This, in turn, meant dropping something and usually trying to reslot several other courses. After hours of frustrated juggling, you hopefully emerged with a full and satisfying number of required courses.

Naturally, there were bound to be some differences between undergraduate registration and medical school registration. This one was conducted in a much more somber and mature way. While it was not unusual to see a college freshman actually burst into tears of rage and frustration upon discovering that his ninth or tenth schedule hadn't worked out, this would have been unthinkable in med school. After all, discipline was to be the key word for the coming years, and such unseemly lack of control would have been out of the question.

There was another difference I think worth mentioning. In the vast hall that was being used for registration, several skeletons were dangling from the ceiling. I personally wondered if they were specimens for study or former students who were still trying to arrange their schedules. In any case, they left no doubt in any medical student's mind that he might have been in the wrong place.

Several days after registration, we had orientation. As I glanced around at the other students, I wondered if I looked as bright and eager as they did. Somehow I doubted it and was certain that I stuck out because of my look of baffled anxiety.

The general excitement that accompanies such occasions made conversation among these strangers very easy. United by common goals and experiences, we were also united by common complaints. Among these were the inevitable Saturday morning classes and lecture hours.

Orientation proved to be the expected day of long-winded speeches given by men whose names and titles we wouldn't remember anyway. During one of these speeches, we were informed that while everything was now very new to us and might seem impersonal, each of us would be assigned an adviser who would help us with any personal or academic problems which we might encounter. In fact, this person whom we were all beginning to visualize as the second savior was said to be so anxious to meet and assist us that we were urged to make an appointment with him as soon as we learned his name. In this way, he would get to know us and could head off any possible future problems which during our initial discussion might surface. Feeling greatly encouraged by this, I was determined to do just what he suggested. I was going to start off on the right foot.

Returning to the loving arms of my wife in the evening, I bent her ears, relating the day's happenings. After a late dinner, we scanned the booklists of the classes I had registered for.

"Oh, Edward, there are so many!"

"Didn't you expect there would be? After all, you're a nurse. You must have had to buy a lot of books too."

"Yes, but nothing like this. Besides, we could purchase most of them secondhand. Do you think you can too?"

"Probably. I'll have to check with the bookstores. As a matter of fact, there's one right on campus which, if it's anything like the undergraduate bookstore, probably deals in used books. I'll have to get there really early though. Do you remember how many times the other one used to be sold out?"

"Yes. I suppose a lot of other undergraduates weren't rich either, but your medical school is a pretty posh place. Somehow I can't see very many of your fellow students scrounging around for used books."

"At one time, that might have been true. But remember, Marcie, this is the Depression, and almost everyone has been hit by hard times—especially the rich."

This proved to be the case. Leaving home at 6:00 a.m., I was shocked by the queue that had already formed outside the campus bookstore. There was a lot of good-natured ribbing about this, and soon everyone lost their self-consciousness over having to purchase secondhand goods.

While my book allowance from the family was generous, I was shocked by the total when my used purchases were rung up. Though I had enough money, even if just barely, I knew that many other expenses for supplies would crop up during the year. This left no doubt in my mind as to what I would be wanting as gifts during the next six years.

*****

While prerequisites had prevented me enrolling in courses with such forbidding names as major histocompatibility systems and synaptogenesis, I did get other beauties.

Physiology was my first course of the day. This had to do with the body's major support systems. It included such functions as breathing, eating, eliminating wastes, etc. I thought that almost everyone would agree that this was heady stuff for 8:00 a.m.—everyone, that was, except our teachers.

Despite the various personalities and teaching methods that our educators used, they all had one thing in common. Since all the classes were large, there were usually two doors to every room. One was located in the back of the room for students to enter by and one in the front for teachers. All my teachers arrived exactly on the stroke of the hour when their class was scheduled to begin and not one minute sooner.

Since we took notes during lectures, I was always surprised, when upon raising my head, to discover that some time while I was writing my last word, my wily lecturer had snatched up his notes and departed. Since every class left me bewildered, I would have often liked to ask the lecturer to clarify a point. Not wanting to make a fool of myself in front of the whole class by perhaps asking a dumb question, I would have found one-to-one confrontations easier to handle. I did find a large number of my classes incomprehensible and was forced to relearn on my own everything that I felt had been covered in class. This, needless to say, placed a double burden on me.

Weeks later, some brave soul brought this up in class after some of us had gotten together to discuss it. The lecturer whom he confronted with this problem merely looked at us disbelievingly as if we were the biggest bunch of morons. He then suggested that if some of us were having difficulties that we discuss them with our advisers—after all, that's what they were there for.

As he grabbed his notes and ran out, a collective groan greeted his suggestion. Most students had had the same discouraging results as I did. This was already November, and few, if any of us, had as yet obtained the promised meeting with our advisers.

Having inquired as to his name the first week of classes, I enthusiastically sought him out. I soon discovered that no one seemed to know which department he was connected with or where his office was located. After several weeks of this run around, I finally discovered someone who had actually heard of him and could even tell me his building's name and room number. While finding the building was easy enough, no one knew where office number 219 was. Since the doors in the building had no numbers on them, this wasn't very surprising.

By late October, I finally located his office but was told by his secretary that he had been available all this time but had just left town that morning. No, she didn't know how long he'd be gone. No, of course, she couldn't schedule an appointment for me without the former knowledge. Yes, I was welcome to keep in touch, and she would be happy to arrange a meeting for me at the earliest possible opportunity after my adviser's return. This was late in November, and still he wasn't back. In truth, I was having a very difficult time in accepting the fact that a Dr. Horace Felderman actually existed and was my adviser. What would I do if I really did develop a serious problem? I supposed you were expected to solve it yourself in the same way you were expected to teach yourself anything that your classes did not clarify for you—and that was a great deal.

*****

I had many memorable experiences my first year at medical school—most of which I would prefer to forget. My first forgettable experience was my initial lab class. Although I had previously handled microscopes in both college and premed, the one in medical school was a completely different type. After I had spent the first half hour of my two-hour class struggling to adjust it, the guy next to me casually leaned over and removed my finger from under the lens. No wonder every slide that I tried focusing on resembled a fingertip. Once I learned how to use the microscope, I found the rest of the class very interesting. I tried not to think of the people whose salivary glands, pieces of tongues, testicles, and intestines were ensconced between two slides.

One of my worst experiences occurred in the animal lab. Here, live animals were operated on. I would never forget one day when a dog was being operated on. Agonizing howls were suddenly emitted by the poor creature in the middle of the operation. While the instructor tried to calm everyone down by assuring us that this was just a reflex and the animal wasn't feeling any pain, I had never believed it. If this were true, he wouldn't have frantically ordered that the anesthesia be increased. When I brought this up, he again laughingly protested any negligence, saying that this happened all the time even in human operations and the patients never remember the incidents when they awaken so they couldn't have felt any pain.

In my over thirty-five years of practice, I had never come across such a thing and neither had any of my colleagues. Too bad that dog couldn't talk although looking back, it wouldn't have helped since the poor creature never did survive the operation.

I'd never told anyone of this experience before. I guess I'd always been too ashamed. Even the students who had been present never again referred to the incident, but I knew twenty-six men who had probably never forgotten that horrible sound.

While almost anyone would have been horrified by this story, Alissa especially would have been shocked. She had always opposed animal experimentation and felt, not without some justification, that animals should not be made to suffer for diseases such as VD and lung cancer due to cigarette smoking, which in the natural course of events, they would never even contract. In later years, she would be very instrumental in having laws passed to carefully screen these experiments and to insure that every effort was made to prevent pain. While she never could have completely banned the experiments, she did help in her own way to ensure them being conducted as humanely as possible.

Another class which takes some getting used to was anatomy. I could still see myself the first day dressed in my pristine white lab coat, armed with a copy of *Gray's Anatomy*, scalpel, scissors, tweezers, and a probe. The first thing I noticed was the sickeningly sweet smell of formalin. We were told to form teams and then move up to one of the cadavers that were lined up on rolling tables and covered with sheets.

I was assigned to an old man in his eighties who had died of cardiac arrest six months ago. As I removed the sheet, I noticed the small puddles of embalming fluid which had accumulated in the body crevices. A cloth soaked in formalin was wrapped around the face, giving the gentleman some degree of anonymity. I would be especially grateful for this when I realized the extent of the indignities which I would be forced to perform on him. While the experience was painful enough, it would have been even worse with him staring at me.

Our first assignment was to open up the bloodless chest cavity. My gentleman had been obese, and we had to spend several minutes just scraping off the yellow fat globules. We flayed back the skin and cut the intercostal muscles from the upper ribs. The difficult job was pulling the ribs apart to get the lungs, which had been the whole point of the exercise. By the time we got this far, it was lunch time, and we were told to pour formalin all over the body and to fill the cavities with formalin-soaked rags. This was to prevent mold from forming. Since this was to be our body for the whole term, we were admonished to take good care of it.

Before the term was over, we would have dissected, in turn, the pelvic cavity, legs, arms, neck, and finally the head. In the last class, each skull would be severed from the body and split in half. In this way, we would be able to remove and study our corpse's brain.

This was the most awe-inspiring moment for me. As I handled this man's brain, I couldn't help but treat it with reverence. Here I was with the very thing that had controlled all the physical functions and even the emotions and identity of this human being. Who was he? Had he loved and been loved? What beautiful or evil thoughts had been formed in this organ? How I wished I could know.

When these thoroughly dissected corpses had served their purposes, they were dispersed to various funeral directors who would see to their burials with their brains usually tucked under their arm muscles—the corpses' brains that was, not the directors'.

The one class that I especially enjoyed was bacteriology. This to me was real medicine and more like what I had been looking forward to. We learned about symptoms, causes of illnesses, and their treatments. I also learned the disturbing fact that we were literally covered from head to toe with bacteria, and this was regardless of how clean we were. One redeeming fact was that some bacteria, such as the ones which manufacture vitamin K in the gastrointestinal tract, were actually beneficial. Only the blood and lungs were sterile which was why the bacteria play such havoc with them.

I think a word about tests was appropriate. Those in medical school were no different than any others. The minute I scanned them, no matter how long I had spent studying, I panicked. My first reaction was always the same: "My god, I don't know any of this stuff. I studied everything but this!" Fortunately, once my equilibrium was restored, the material began to take on a semblance of familiarity. While I was never the top in my class, I was usually in the top half, and that was good enough for me.

My only big disappointment was that we received no practical experience during our first year. In European medical schools, you learned less theory but more practical skills. In Europe, you were immediately assigned to a hospital where you work through all the phases of hospital service. You were given specific responsibilities which you were paid for. Of course, if you were negligent, they fired you.

Besides, the practical aspects of such a course of study, the pay would have been a godsend. Almost all medical students were financially destitute because of the astronomical cost of their education. Since few of us could even afford the small pleasures of life such as a movie or dinner out, it's no wonder that most of us felt deprived. I also wouldn't doubt if this was the reason why so many doctors in later years were so money-hungry.

Because of all the classes, lecture halls, labs, and library sessions, it's almost impossible to remember that there was actually another world off campus. It was only the remembrance of Marcie's warmth and love which prompted me to recall my real home. While these years were difficult ones for me, they must have been almost impossible for Marcie, but she never complained. She was always the driving force behind me. While some people might scorn the old adage that "behind every successful man, there's a good woman," in my case, it was indisputable.

By the way, I finally did hear from my adviser. At the end of the term, I received a card from him congratulating me on passing all my courses. It also included the name of my next year's adviser with the usual assurance of how he was looking forward to making my acquaintance so that he could help me with any problems which I might encounter.

Chapter 23

Bearding the Lion in Her Den

> Ring out the old, ring in the new,
> Ring, happy bells, across the snow.
> The year is going, let him go;
> Ring out the false, ring in the true.
> —Tennyson, 1936

I supposed it was the combined pressures of my marriage, the shock of Arthur's divorce, and most of all, the news of Uncle Theo's death which played a part in causing Mother's heart attack in November of 1936. Although a minor one, it was a warning that no future pressures must be brought to bear on her. She was, after all, sixty-six years of age, and while seemingly still feisty, she had sustained several major emotional blows within the past few years.

It was with the intention of informing Arthur of this fact that I ventured into Pine River Falls on a brisk windy Sunday morning less than two weeks before Thanksgiving. While Arthur and Dee Dee had extended several invitations to us, Marcie had always categorically refused them. It was only the prospect of seeing Alissa, whom I had also promised Marcie I would visit, which finally put in a chink in her armor.

I was pleased to discover that Arthur's bungalow was attractive and not at all the run-down shack I had been imagining. While certainly no Joyeuse Garde, it was neatly painted and looked cozy and inviting. As we stepped out of the car, the front door of the house was thrown open by a big boned smiling woman whom I recognized from the wedding as Dee Dee.

Despite my gaffe at the wedding, which I had tried to cover up by changing "his wife Dumb-Dumb" into "his wife dumb-dumb-de-dumb and new bride Dee Dee" by humming the bridal march, Dee Dee and Arthur never caught on that anything was amiss though I was sure that no one else had been fooled by my desperate ruse.

Even upon my second meeting with her, Dee Dee's appearance was still a shock. She was a large, overweight woman with coarse features whose only redeeming quality was her guilelessness. As she enveloped first Marcie and then myself in a crushing bear hug, I was again reminded of the fact that she was shorter than my brother's 5'11" frame by only an inch or two and easily outweighed him by fifteen or twenty pounds.

Looking quickly at Marcie, I was not surprised to see the look of outrage at the sheer audacity of Dee Dee hugging one of Alissa's staunchest supporters. This was accompanied by a groan of pain as my delicate wife angrily rubbed her undoubtedly bruised shoulders.

Not bothering to notice our negative reactions to her overexuberance, Dee Dee propelled us into her living room where we were confronted by my brother's recumbent form snoring in front of the radio, proving the old adage that "some things never change."

As Dee Dee attempted to awaken Arthur, I took a good look around the room. Although small, it was comfortably furnished and wouldn't have been too bad if it weren't such a mess. Assorted clothing, newspapers, magazines, used plates, and cups were strewn everywhere. Housekeeping obviously was not one of Dee Dee's fortes. As I tried to clear two chairs of their assorted debris, Dee Dee, abandoning Arthur for the moment, cleared the sofa with a sweep of her arm and led us to it. After we were seated, Dee Dee suddenly wedged herself between us, sitting half on my right thigh and half on Marcie's left thigh.

Just as Arthur awakened, the two Carwood youngsters joined us. Seventeen-year-old Patrick was an almost exact replica of his mother. Big-boned and overweight, he was as dull of feature as he was of wit. Except for a perfunctory nod in our direction, he gravitated toward the radio like a needle to a magnet. Any attempt at conversation with him was met by either a guttural grunt or an equally rude "Wait a minute, this is the best part," as he remained transfixed by the radio after which he would forget the question or remark anyway. Catheleen came out the better of the Carwood offspring, at least in this respect. She was much sharper of intellect and had a caustic wit.

After explaining Mother's health problems to Arthur, I spent over forty-five agonizing minutes trying to introduce a topic of conversation during which Marcie sulked, Dee Dee giggled (she giggled at everything), Patrick grunted and listened to the radio along with Arthur, and Catheleen was sarcastic before I hit on a subject of mutual interest.

This came about when Marcie, who had been trying all this time to pull her thigh out from under Dee Dee, said that we had better be going because we had another visit to make.

"Are you going to Joyeuse Garde?" Catheleen snidely asked. "Because if you are, you can say hello to my father for me."

Catheleen's little bomb had the expected result. I was too stunned for words, but Marcie had no such problem. "Just what do you mean by that? I would think that your father had bothered Alissa enough."

"Oh, he's hardly bothering her. I think she must enjoy it…at least, it looks that way from the pictures."

"Pictures! What pictures?" I asked in astonishment.

"Do you mean that you haven't seen them? Well, I guess the Queenstown papers wouldn't bother with our local news," Catheleen continued with feigned innocence. "The Pine River Falls society pages are just plastered with pictures of Father squiring Alissa around to all the local society functions."

"I never knew Alissa would go in for that sort of thing. Did you, Arthur?"

"No, Edward. While Mr. and Mrs. Saronna belong to the country club, Alissa's always been a loner and never wanted to be involved in the social obligations that sort of thing entails. I certainly wasn't interested in any of that," he needlessly added.

"Would you like Catheleen to show you some of the pictures?" Dee Dee asked, giggling.

Before I could answer, Catheleen was racing back from another part of the house with what proved to be a scrapbook.

In her enthusiasm at seeing the pictures again, Dee Dee had risen from the sofa, finally relieving our numb thighs. I moved closer to Marcie and protectively put my arm around her. Such paltry defenses did nothing to deter Dee Dee from her Sherman tank tactics as she backed onto the sofa, now wedging herself between the arm and my now partially squashed left thigh. She also had the disconcerting habit of positioning her face about an inch from yours while she spoke to you. Whether she did this out of nearsightedness or over-attentiveness, I never discovered. Worse was yet to come. It seemed that her usually lethargic mass could actually become enthusiastic, and then she would bounce up and down on your thigh in her excitement.

"Just look at these [tee-hee, bounce, bounce]! Don't they look wonderful?"

As I painfully tried to focus on the bouncing pictures she held, more surprises were in store. If Dee Dee's appearance was a surprise to me, her ex-husband's was a definite shock. Before me was a picture of a tall well-built handsome man with wavy black hair and moustache. He had the kind of glossy good looks and porcelain smile which was usually associated with Hollywood. In fact, he bore a distinct resemblance to Tyrone Power, and I could definitely visualize that actor looking like this when he reached his midforties. George Carwood was a definite ladies' man—the type men hate and women adore.

In the first picture, he looked as comfortable in his tuxedo as most men look in a favorite tattered shirt and slippers. He was also probably the type who could wear a satin smoking jacket and ascot without appearing a damned fool like the rest of us would.

Another picture showed a beaming Alissa in a white sequined gown and white fox jacket attending a charity ball with her impeccably tailored escort. In another, Alissa in white pleated skirt and navy blazer boarded somebody's yacht accompanied by the grinning popinjay.

"Whose boat is that?" I asked.

"It's called a ship when it's that size, and it's my great uncle's," Catheleen proudly informed me.

"That's right [tee-hee!]. The ship is my Uncle Victor's. You must have heard of him, Victor Barnett, the president of the Victory Sewing Machine Company [bounce, bounce, bounce]," Dee Dee added, getting up to show the pictures to Marcie who belatedly tried to sprawl herself out as Dee Dee now proceeded to destroy Marcie's right thigh.

The other pictures showed more of the same. In each, both Alissa and George Carwood were fashionably attired as they made the social scene together.

As I was wondering how George and Dee Dee had ever gotten married, she and Catheleen took turns enlightening me.

"Uncle Victor introduced our mother and father."

"Yes, I was the proverbial poor relation whom Uncle Victor felt responsible for, and George was my uncle's rising star in the company."

And so the star decided to rise even faster by hitching its tail to the boss's homely niece, I finished to myself.

"It couldn't have been easy for George. He could have had his pick of any number of beautiful women…"

But none, I was sure, with the prospect of such a lucrative future built-in. It wouldn't be the first time that dollar signs in front of the eyes blinded a person.

"The kind of prominent social life that my uncle desired for us came naturally to George. His family were well-to-do, and country clubs were a second home to him. My family was lower middle class. Whenever some social function required me meeting George's friends and associates, I would be a nervous wreck. When I'm nervous, I keep eating, and…well, you can see the results. It soon got to a point where I was so overweight that I no longer had to furnish excuses for not socializing, George made them for me. Since George's presence is always an asset, hostesses began urging him to attend parties without me, and he was only too happy to oblige. Soon, our paths diverged so much that they seldom met."

Making our final farewells to Dee Dee and her family, we stiffly made our way to the car accompanied by Arthur.

"I know what you're probably thinking. I guess it's hard for you and Marcie to understand how I could give up Joyeuse Garde and Alissa for this," Arthur said, pointing to the bungalow.

"It's really a nice little house," I lamely protested.

"Oh, I like it well enough, but I'm not blind to its faults. I'm also not blind to Dee Dee's. She hasn't Alissa's glamour, style, or education, and I guess she's not much of a housekeeper, but I'm comfortable with her. With Alissa I was always on edge. Nothing satisfied her. Whenever I fell asleep in front of the radio, I'd actually feel guilty as if I'd committed a crime by falling asleep in my own house. Maybe even the house was a problem. It was never really mine. It's a product of Alissa's and the Saronnas' fantasies. Instead of Sir Lancelot, I always felt more like Ichabod Crane caught in a time tunnel. This George Carwood is more of Alissa's type. They both like to dance and go out so maybe things have turned out for the best after all," he finished, shrugging.

★★★★★

As we pulled up to Joyeuse Garde, a sleek black low-slung car that resembled a panther stood in front of the door. Since Alissa's Bentley was also in the driveway, I hesitated about calling unexpectedly while she had company.

"Do you think we should go in, Marcie?"

"Why not? It's probably only the Saronnas visiting their daughter."

"You don't think it could be George Carwood?"

"So what if it is? I'm sure Alissa won't mind."

Not being quite so sure of Marcie's last statement, I nonetheless banged the door knocker.

Alissa clad in salmon-colored silk slacks and a short quilted brocade salmon and gold kimono, which Marcie later informed me were lounging pajamas and all the rage, answered the door.

Looking genuinely delighted to see us, she also exuberantly hugged and kissed us, leaving me to reflect on the injustice of the different reactions produced by a beautiful woman and a homely one like Dee Dee when performing the same action.

Standing in the doorway to Alissa's library was George Carwood himself. In a blue cashmere sweater which naturally matched his eyes and pearl-gray flannel slacks, he was even better looking than his pictures.

"Marcie, Edward, I'd like you to meet George Carwood. George, this is Dr. Edward Andros and his lovely wife, Marcie."

"A pleasure," George said, continentally kissing Marcie's hand and giving her one of those intimate looks which men like him always cultivate.

As George shook my hand, I glanced at Marcie who was still slobbering over George and had to be literally propelled by Alissa to a chair.

"You can't imagine how happy I am to see the two of you, but why didn't you phone first so I could have prepared something special for you?"

"Oh, we're not staying long, Alissa. We just dropped in on our way from Arthur's."

"No kidding! How do your thighs feel?" George laughed.

"Is it really true that Dee Dee sits on peoples' thighs?" Alissa asked skeptically. "George says she does, but I don't know if I believe it."

"It's true!" Marcie and I said in unison.

"And she always stares right in your face and stuffs her pockets with any food you might put out," George added. "Although you wouldn't have noticed that in her own home, of course. Tell me, Doctor, after meeting Dee Dee, are you starting to wonder if insanity runs in your family? To leave all of this," he said, gesturing around the room, "is bad enough, but to leave Alissa in exchange for Dee Dee the Dumpling is totally incomprehensible. And his job! Everyone's still amazed that he even has one with the Saronna company. Any other Victorian father of an adored only child would have fired him on the spot. Divorce is unheard of to people like Big Al!"

"Well, you're really more responsible for the divorce than Arthur," I remonstrated. "After all, it was your divorce suit that originally started all the trouble. How did your boss, Dee Dee's uncle, feel about that?"

"Oh, you're wrong, Doctor. Arthur and Dee Dee were responsible for the divorce. I was, like Alissa, an innocent, injured party. As to Victor Barnett, I had no problems there. Dee Dee, as you can imagine, was a hindrance rather than a help to the company. While explaining her absences from social functions was embarrassing, the possibility that she might actually attend was downright disastrous. Victor himself was only too happy for us to break our bond. It's not easy having a niece or a wife who can transform a Paris gown into a lumpy gunnysack just by wearing it."

"I don't see why he advocated the marriage from the beginning then," Marcie stated.

"It's the old Pandora's box again. Man always has hope. We both thought that her gaucherie and stylelessness would disappear. After all, she would be associating with the crème de la crème. While she could never be beautiful, style can serve just as well. If she could have developed other qualities such as wit, poise, grace…but this, we soon realized, was asking the impossible. How socially successful can someone be who giggles, stares in your face, and sits on your thighs?"

*****

Returning home, Marcie and I had mixed feelings about the afternoon. While we were both happy that Alissa was looking so well and enjoying herself, we disagreed on our reactions to George Carwood.

Marcie was still drooling over him and thought that he and Alissa were the most beautiful couple that she had ever seen. I, on the other hand, felt Carwood was a cad and an opportunist. No true gentleman would expose his wife to the kind of ugly publicity that the adultery charges had brought about. Since his gay blade lifestyle hardly seemed conducive to child-rearing, I suspected that he had a nasty streak and never really wanted his kids anyway. After all, having a sullen male "lump" and a sarcastic female "lump" around could not add much prestige to your social standing.

As to Dee Dee, my feelings were more complex. While her slovenly ways and annoying physical habits could not be overlooked, I tried to probe deeper. She did have some good qualities. Her honesty about herself greatly reminded me of Alissa's. She was friendly and certainly tried to make her guests feel welcome even if she did get carried away. While I could almost guarantee that she would never be a favorite of the Andros family, I could see where she and Arthur might very well be happy together.

Dee Dee was a very undemanding person, and Arthur was not an obliging one. She and Arthur both disliked socializing: Dee Dee because she was insecure and Arthur because he was too lazy. Both were even-tempered and neither seemed prone to any excesses of mood or passion. Their mutual lethargy made it possible for them to be able to spend many happy years together contentedly stretched out and snoring harmoniously together before the radio. All in all, I could see where Arthur's life with Dee Dee would be a very comfortable one—after all, dumplings were very comfortable things; they had no sharp edges.

Chapter 24

From Criminal to Hero

> God rest you, happy gentlemen,
> Who laid your good lives down,
> Who took the khaki and the gun,
> Instead of cap and gown.
>
> —Winifred Letts

The later Depression years were no better than the first. If anything, they were a great deal worse as even the staunchest optimists began to realize that the only lining this cloud would ever have would be the gray of despair. With honest means of earning a living so difficult to come by, more and more people were desperately turning to means outside the law. According to the Justice Department by 1935, crooks outnumbered carpenters four to six, grocers six to one, and doctors twenty to one. Instead of being condemned for their activities, criminals began being looked upon as a new type of folk hero. After all, they were the only ones with any real money who were steadily and gainfully employed. And to add to their appeal even more, they usually came from humble backgrounds.

Names such as John Dillinger, Baby Face Nelson, Machine Gun Kelly, Pretty Boy Floyd, Bonnie Parker, and Clyde Barrow were on everyone's lips. People followed their real-life exploits with the same interest that they listened to the popular radio program *Gangbusters*, which vied with such innocent fare as *Amos 'n' Andy* and *Our Gal Sunday* for popularity. The only "good guy" who seemed equally popular was J. Edgar Hoover, the director of the FBI, and I personally still feel that the gangsters had the edge in the hearts of the public.

No matter how bad things looked, as George Carwood had pointed out, man never loses hope and people looked to Franklin D. Roosevelt to be the new savior. From the very morning of his inauguration, he swept the country with reforms. When one plan failed, he merely scrapped it with never a backward glance and unflaggingly strode ahead, introducing a new one.

In his quest to provide employment, he inundated the country with the alphabet. His NRA and PWA took on such massive construction projects as dams and hospitals. He even remembered the arts and such people as Jackson Pollock and Willem de Kooning got their start through his WPA. Even John Steinbeck whose *Grapes of Wrath* would cause such a sensation in 1939 worked for the WPA. His job was to take a census of dogs in California's Monterey Peninsula. Old FDR would stop at nothing in his determination to create new jobs!

The repeal of prohibition in 1933 left such young hoodlums as my brother John and his friends with nothing to do. Mother was so proud of him when he announced that he and several buddies were off to Fort Dix to join the Civilian Conservation Corp. At last, her favorite son was on the right side of the law! The CCC would eventually be responsible for planting over two hundred million trees. This new breed of Johnny Appleseed would travel around the country fighting pine twig blight and Dutch elm disease. They would also dig drainage ditches and fishponds, build firebreaks and reservoirs, and even restore historic battlefields.

Unfortunately, the discipline demanded by the Army and Forest Service who jointly supervised the CCC soon had John hightailing it back to the safety and comfort of Queenstown and Mother. I could still remember Mother's exclamations of horror as John regaled her with tales of his hardships. Most of all, I remembered the disgust Richard and I felt when she actually cried over his blistered hands and went so far as to soothe them with expensive unguents and then bandage them while she lovingly waited on him hand and foot and actually became angry with the rest of us when we refused to follow her nauseating example.

Life for the other Androses followed a more or less normal pattern. Richard still struggled to hold on to the emporium although it became more and more obvious that he would soon have to capitulate and sell out to one of the chains who were offering to purchase it. He worked longer and longer hours for less and less profit. Prices were absurdly low, and still people couldn't afford to shop. Sirloin steak was being sold for twenty-nine cents a pound and milk for ten cents a quart.

For Marcie and me, since we did have a little money with both of us working and Alissa's eternal help, these low prices were wonderful. We had luxuriously furnished our apartment with a nine-by-twelve rug which cost us $5.85. Among our other purchases were an electric iron for $2.00, an eight-piece dining room set for $46.50, and a double bed and spring mattress for $14.95. I was even the envy of our friends, who were also struggling for their medical degrees, when I purchased a 1929 Ford for $57.50—an unheard of extravagance in our set!

*****

Thanksgiving Day of 1936 was a glum affair. We were all worried about Mother's health, and Mother was miserable at the prospect of spending another holiday without Alissa's elating presence. While I had tried to reconcile Mother to accepting our altered situation, she wholeheartedly refused. Arthur's tentative suggestion that he and Dee Dee stop by for a visit on Thanksgiving Day was met with such frigid disapproval by Mother that even a stouter heart than Arthur's would have been discouraged.

As we were grimly finishing our Thanksgiving dinner, the doorbell rang. John, who had been looking for any excuse to leave the table, quickly jumped to answer it. The long wolf whistle which we heard from the dining room transformed Mother's look of dour resignation into one of ecstasy. It was the whistle that John only used at home for Alissa. Mother's joyful reunion with this daughter of her heart suddenly died as she glanced behind Alissa. Standing with his arms loaded with gifts was George Carwood.

"George, let me take those packages and introduce you to my second mother, Eleanor Andros, and her sons Richard and John. Of course, you remember Edward and Marcie."

Even Mother's stern disapproval evaporated somewhat under Carwood's calculated charm. "Alissa dear, what in the world are all of these packages?"

"Thanksgiving gifts," Alissa said, handing Mother an enormous basket of fruit and several bottles of wine, "and premature Christmas gifts."

"Christmas gifts! But it's still a month till Christmas."

"I know, but I'm going to be very busy before the holidays, and naturally, I'll be spending Christmas Day with my parents."

"Why will you be too busy to visit us?" Mother asked, hurt and indignant.

"Oh, Eleanor, it's not just you. I'll be too busy to visit anyone."

"What's up, Alissa?" John asked.

"I'm sponsoring a benefit affair to aid the Republic of Spain."

"The Republic of Spain!" Richard said in astonishment. "With so many problems in the USA, I would think that you'd have enough charity work to do in your own backyard."

"That's not fair, Richard. Alissa has done a great deal of national charity work. Despite what some people may think, the wealthy don't all sit idly around. Millions of dollars have been raised by just the sort of benefit that Alissa is sponsoring," George defended.

"Just what is this business in Spain all about?" I asked.

"You can't be serious, Edward," George Carwood answered. "As a young doctor, I would have thought that the loss of thousands of lives would interest you."

"Of course, he's interested!" Marcie said in my defense.

"I have read the newspaper reports, but I admit to being more interested at this time in starving American lives."

"Edward, I agree with you but the plight of those poor Spaniards is really pathetic."

"This is the first cause other than national poverty or animal protection that has been able to stir any interest in Alissa," George said, fondly gazing at her.

"Well, my first love is still animals, but my heart goes out to anyone's suffering regardless of nationality."

"Refresh us on the facts," Richard requested.

"I'm sure you know the basics. In July, Fascist rebel forces led by General Francisco Franco supported by Hitler and Mussolini began an insurrection against the Republic of Spain."

"Why should we get involved in someone else's civil war?" I asked.

"Because, as I said, Franco is being backed by Hitler and Mussolini, which constitutes a threat to the whole free world."

"Why does this threaten anyone other than Spain?"

"Haven't you ever heard that lunatic Hitler's slogan of 'Today we rule Germany, tomorrow the world'?"

"He's probably only boasting, Alissa. He can't really mean it. After all, look what happened to Germany during World War I. I really don't see where the Spanish problem constitutes a world problem."

"Eleanor, many people would disagree with you. At this very moment, volunteers from all over the world are pouring into Spain to help the republic."

"Wouldn't our government take some kind of action if Hitler really was a threat to us through Spain?" Richard inquired.

"That's what's so ironic! President Roosevelt just put an embargo on arms to Spain. Since we still sell to Germany and Italy, naturally, these armaments are finding their way to Franco's forces."

This seemed to trouble Mother's sense of fair play. "That's not cricket then, is it? Doesn't that really mean that the US government is supporting the rebels?"

"Exactly, Eleanor. The only government that is doing anything to support the elected Republican government of Spain is Russia. Since they aren't a republic and we are, you can see the further irony of the situation."

"But if we support the Republic of Spain, aren't we really supporting the Communists since they're in favor of the Republic?" Richard asked in confusion.

"I certainly have no Communist sympathies, but when you hear how valiantly these badly armed and untrained Spaniards are fighting to preserve their elected government, you can't help but sympathize. These poor people are pitting themselves against the armed might of Spain's regular army who went over to the rebels, trained Moorish troops, and even the Foreign Legion."

"The Foreign Legion? What do they have to do with it?"

"Well, Franco began his attack from the south in Morocco where Foreign Legion troops are located. Since they are really mercenaries and don't care for whom they fight, they were just as happy to fight for Franco when he landed in Morocco. Did you know that their motto is 'Long Live Death'? The Regulares, who were also hired to fight, felt the same way. They didn't care whose side they fought on either, just so long as they were supplied with money, wine, and the spoils of war."

"Exactly what is your benefit for?"

"We want to raise money for arms and supplies for the Spanish people. When it comes right down to it, no amount of bravery will win a war if there are no ammunition, food, or medical supplies. It's the lack of these very things that usually decides the losing side. In every war, more people die from hunger, cold, and disease than actual combat fatalities."

As we further discussed these things, I was impressed by John's knowledge of the Spanish Civil War. He had never before seemed especially interested in anything that didn't directly affect his creature comforts. His extensive interest in this subject would become clear to us before the year was over.

*****

The *SS Normandie* left New York for France on Saturday, December 26, 1936. Since this was off-season, there weren't many passengers. First class was almost empty, tourist half full, and third class three-quarters full. Among the third-class passengers were ninety-six young men from all classes of society. They came from all over the US and were of various origins, religions, and political affiliations. The one common factor was a hatred of Fascism. Among this diverse group of future fighters for the Spanish Republic was one John Andros.

These young men had all met a week earlier in Manhattan. They spent the week shopping in local Army-Navy stores for clothing, ammunition, and knives. Even to the shopkeepers, they didn't reveal their true purpose but claimed to be members of a large hunting group. Even their immediate families were unaware of their intentions. Most of these poor people learned of their loved ones' departure for Spain in the same way that Mother did—through a letter.

It was, in fact, many months after his departure before we could begin to piece the whole story together. These ninety-six enthusiastic young men all appeared to find the five-day passage enjoyable. They were seen lounging in the salon and playing cards, chess, and shuffleboard like any other tourists. The one thing which separated them, however, from their fellow passengers was their choice of reading material. Instead of popular novels and travel brochures, they untiringly read US Army manuals on all phases of military life from weapons and drills to military courtesy.

These young US citizens were the forerunners of the over three thousand Americans who would eventually fight in Spain. Americans would one day form parts of the XV International Brigade, the Abe Lincoln Battalion and the George Washington Battalion, which would, in turn, become the Lincoln-Washington Battalion when the parent outfits were wiped out. Young Americans whose only prior knowledge of war came from such novels as *All Quiet on the Western Front* would serve almost constantly in the line of fire from February 1937 till September 1938.

It was the defense of Madrid which was to have such catastrophic effect on our troops. It was in February that the ninety-six Americans from the *SS Normandie* accompanied by four hundred other Americans went into action for the first time. They formed the Abraham Lincoln Battalion of the International Brigade. It was in Villanueva de la Jara that they received a very insufficient basic training course. Each man was issued a 1914 Remington rifle that had been manufactured by the US for the armies of czarist Russia. They also received 150 rounds of ammunition per man and a bayonet. After a pep talk in a bullring, they moved out by truck and traveled north under the command of Captain Robert Merriman, a twenty-eight-year-old graduate of the University of Nevada who had played college football and taken ROTC training.

Their destination was a sector near San Martin in Jarama Valley south of Madrid. From February 23 through the 27, they launched attacks against the Foreign Legion whose mission was to cut off the vital Madrid-Valencia Highway. Even handicapped by a lack of artillery, they conducted themselves admirably. They stopped the rebels, and the campaign was reduced to WWI type of trench warfare. It resulted to heavy casualties, and out of the nearly 500 Americans who took part in the operation, 120 were killed and 175 more wounded. It was a struggle that so impressed itself on the minds of the men who took part in it that they made up a song which they sang to the tune of "Red River Valley" to commemorate it:

> There's a valley in Spain called Jarama.
> It's a place that we all know too well,
> For 'tis there that we wasted our manhood,
> And most of our old age as well.

The Spanish Civil War directly touched the lives of thousands of American families. All in all, almost one million lives would be lost before the war came to an end in March of 1939. After three years of valiant struggle, the brave defenders of the Spanish Republic would be defeated by the very things that Alissa and others like her had feared—lack of armaments and supplies. More importantly, another fact which she had foresightedly feared came to pass—the Spanish Civil War proved to be a dress rehearsal in Hitler's bid for world domination.

The American volunteers who fought in Spain were repatriated at the end of 1938. This was a vain attempt by the Republican government to try and equalize the number of men fighting on both sides. By dismissing all their foreign troops, they foolishly hoped that Franco would do likewise and dismiss his fifty thousand Italian volunteers, sixteen thousand Germans, and twenty thousand Portuguese. Instead, this move was suicidal and guaranteed a victory for Franco and, therefore, an equal victory for Hitler and Mussolini.

Americans, likewise, had a dress rehearsal for the big battle still to come. More than nine hundred American veterans of the Spanish Civil War would see active service in US Forces during WWII. This would be a very commendable number since of the more than three thousand Americans in Spain, about one thousand were killed and an equal number seriously wounded. Among the number killed was one soldier from New York, John Andros. In World War II, four hundred more veterans of the Abraham Lincoln Battalion would become casualties. Like John, these men strongly believed in the words of Dolores Ibárruri, also known as La Pasionaria, in her message to the Spanish people in July of 1936: "It is better to die on your feet than to live on your knees."

CHAPTER 25

An Unexpected Visitor

> They throw in Drummer Hodge, to rest
>   Uncoffined—just as found:
> His landmark is a jopje crest
>   That breaks the veldt around.
>   —Thomas Hardy, 1937

Although I feared that the telegram announcing John's death would also be Mother's death warrant, she pulled through better than expected. While the news did cause a mild heart seizure, it did not precipitate the massive coronary that I had feared.

In order to facilitate Mother's recovery, Alissa agreed to accompany her to England. Aunt Henrietta had passed away some time in February around the same time that John had been killed. While her death wasn't as heroic, it was just as dramatic. When not quite sober, she had decided to milk the cows. Carelessly grabbing a sensitive udder, Aunt Henrietta was kicked in the head by the outraged cow. After spending three weeks in a coma, she quietly died. If anyone could console the stricken widower, I was sure that Mother and Alissa could.

Marcie, who still had visions of Alissa standing on the deck of the *Queen Beatrice* while she and Uncle Teddy gazed longingly into each other's eyes, was hoping for more than simple consolation on Alissa's part. While Marcie was still infatuated with the debonair George Carwood, like all the Andros family, she had a special place in her heart for Uncle Teddy.

It was on a Saturday evening in late June while Mother and Alissa were in England that Richard received a surprise visitor. Marcie and I, who had stopped by to see how Richard was managing on his own, were equally surprised when he ushered in a strange young man in an equally strange uniform.

"Marcie, Edward, I'd like you to meet Lieutenant Frederick Mannelli. He was part of the Abraham Lincoln Battalion in Spain."

"Wasn't that John's battalion?" Marcie asked.

"Yes, ma'am, that's why I'm here. I knew your brother-in-law really well, and I had promised him that if I was ever out this way, I'd look his family up," the lieutenant said, gasping.

"Were you wounded? I'm a doctor, and if there's anything I can do—"

"No, thanks, Doc. I got a bullet in the lung. Medics said I'll be good as new as soon as I learn to adjust. Lots of people live just as well on one lung, don't they?" he asked, losing some of his former bravado.

After I had quickly reassured him that this was true, he proceeded to tell us something of his experiences. "Mrs. Andros isn't home?"

"No, she and my sister...um, former sister-in-law are in England."

"That wouldn't be Alissa, would it?" Lieutenant Mannelli asked brightly.

"Yes, as a matter of fact, it is, but how did you know that?"

"Oh, John talked about her a lot. Had a sort of crush on her, I guess."

"You're joking!" Richard exclaimed.

"No. He was sure fond of Alissa. Used to tell the guys all about her. As a matter of fact, he always carried a picture of her," he said, rummaging through his pockets. He then produced a snapshot of Alissa wearing, of all things, her belly dancing outfit, her arms outstretched poised to begin.

"How in the world did he get this? It looks like it was taken in Uncle Theo's club, and John wasn't even there," I said.

"Yes, it was taken in his uncle's club. He told me how, through some friends, he had managed to bribe one of the waiters to take a picture of Alissa. He also said something about having been three of these, but when your uncle caught on to what was happening, he confiscated the film. Fortunately, he didn't fire the waiter who explained that he wasn't taking the pictures for himself but for Theo's own nephew. Seems your uncle ended up sending one to John, saying he was going to keep one for himself but never explained what he intended doing with the third one. Boy, I sure would have liked to meet your Uncle Theo. He sounded like quite a character," he said, laughing.

"He certainly was. One of the best," Richard, who was refilling our glasses, confirmed.

"You seem to know an awful lot about our family considering you can't have known my brother for more than two months."

"Oh, I've known John for longer than that. We were in the CCC together. Matter of fact, we decided to leave together and fight in Spain right from the start."

"You mean John had been thinking about going to Spain for a couple of months?"

"Sure!"

"Somehow we always thought it was just another of his impulsive acts."

"No, your brother really got hot under the collar whenever he heard what was going on over there. He was like that you know," the lieutenant said, smiling as he helped himself to another sandwich that Marcie had so thoughtfully provided for us.

I guess I hadn't known that about John along with a lot of other things. The only fact that I knew at that moment was that I wholeheartedly wished he were here right now so I could hug him and tell him how proud of him I was. I also wished that Mother were present to hear someone else who shared her unflagging pride in John.

As Marcie finally relinquished the photo of Alissa that she had been admiring all this time, I tried to return it to the lieutenant.

"No, no, that's yours. Actually, one of the reasons I came was to give you some of your brother's things."

As he started emptying his pockets, I withdrew my earlier wish for Mother's presence. Seeing those familiar objects was almost as painful as seeing John's poor battered body would have been. John was buried somewhere outside Madrid. After numerous family consultations, we finally decided not to try and have his body shipped home. Instead, with Mr. Saronna's help, we found someone in the government willing to see that all the arrangements were properly taken care of from that end to give him a decent burial. Needless to say, a rather substantial cash outlay which was whitewashed by the name "donation" further helped. We were also told that young girls from the village would care for the grave and see that fresh flowers were provided although I didn't put too much faith in that promise even if the sum "donated" could have provided perpetual care for a whole cemetery.

As I lovingly lifted John's watch from the coffee table, I turned it over and again read the inscription which Mother had had engraved on it when she presented it to him for his eighteenth birthday: "To John in whom I shall never lose faith. Love, Mother." Well, Mother's faith in John had finally been justified.

I then looked at his battered wallet which appeared to be overly stuffed. While the amount of money which he had was inconsequential, he also had two letters crammed inside. Seeing my hesitation as I went to open the first, which was addressed to him, Marcie and Richard encouraged me. The paper was of excellent quality and very lightly scented. As I again looked at the writing, I recognized Alissa's delicate flowery script.

"Why that's Alissa's handwriting!" Marcie shrieked in my ear. "How did she manage to get it delivered?"

"I don't know. In the letter he had mailed to us on the day he left for Spain, John said that he'd write again when he arrived and tell us where to write to him...but as you know, Marcie, we didn't hear anything else until the telegram came informing us that he'd been killed in action," Richard explained.

Examining the envelope, I noticed that it was simply addressed to John Andros, American Volunteers, Spain.

"Do you know how John managed to receive this?" I asked the lieutenant.

"As a matter of fact, I was with him when he got it. It was the darndest thing really. The sergeant in charge of supplies was opening some cartons that had just been shipped over from the US. Some rich dames had had some kind of benefit or something and had purchased supplies which they packed themselves. Boy, I sure would have liked to see them society dames packing crates for us! Anyway, the sarge came running over to your brother, waving this letter here. None of us, you know, had gotten any mail from home, and there was your brother bragging that he'd just gotten a letter from some gorgeous society chick. That's when he showed us Alissa's picture 'cause we didn't believe him. Told us she used to be married to his brother. I'll tell you after seeing her picture, we sure wanted to see what the girl he'd left her for must have looked like. You could have knocked me over with a feather when John said she's a dog. And doesn't she have some sort of strange habit?"

"That's right," Marcie agreed. "She sits on your thighs."

"You mean she sits on your lap?"

"No, no, on your thighs," Marcie said, demonstrating, much to Lieutenant Mannelli's delight.

"What's the letter say?" Richard inquired.

"You might as well read it aloud," Marcie suggested.

December 30, 1936

> Dearest John,
> I don't know if you'll ever receive this, but I couldn't let an opportunity go by without trying.
> I was just informed by Edward of you having decided to fight in Spain. While I am totally surprised by your decision, I am also equally proud. It was a very courageous and unselfish thing to do.
> Since I know you well enough to realize that you are probably concerned about how your news affected your mother, please be assured that she took it very well and can't stop bragging about her brave soldier son!
> When I agreed to sponsor that benefit dinner dance for Spain, I never thought that you

might be on the receiving end. I should have realized that something was up when you appeared so knowledgeable about the conflict. It was the first that I had ever known you to take such a profound interest in international news. Needless to say, I'm now doubly delighted that the benefit was such a success.

Having gained my vast military packing experience during WWI, I decided to lend a hand in shipping out our supplies. Bet you don't remember my invaluable contribution to that war when I packed peach pits. Anyway, while packing some crates, I decided to include this letter. Considering that I know nothing about where you are, it's probably a million to one shot that you'll ever receive it, but you can't blame me for trying.

If it's at all possible to get mail through, please do let me know what supplies are needed both on a personal level and a group one.

While I know that you'll do your best, please remember that you have a family over here who loves you dearly and is praying for you. You having volunteered to fight is brave enough, so please don't try to be a hero by taking unnecessary risks. To those who love you, you already are a hero, and we want you to come home in one piece so we can tell you in person just how we feel about you.

Take care of yourself, and remember that we're all rooting for you. God bless you and keep you safe.

With love,
Alissa

"Wasn't that a sweet thing to do? That's just like Alissa to think of such a thing," Marcie cooed.

"What's the other letter?" Richard asked.

"It's addressed to the Andros Family. Do you think I should open it without Mother being present?"

"Might as well," Richard conceded.

February 1, 1937

> Hi, folks,
>
> Arrived in Spain safe and sound. Sorry to have let you know about my decision at the last minute, but I thought it would be better for everyone this way. Since I couldn't be dissuaded, I didn't want Mother getting all upset ahead of time.
>
> Things aren't too bad here although the weather's really cold. Alissa was right in thinking that supplies would be needed.
>
> Speaking of Alissa, the damnedest thing happened. Here I was bedded down for the night in my foxhole when this crazy sergeant comes running over waving this letter in the air as if it's the white flag. Crazy fool got so excited he forgot to duck and almost had his head blown off.
>
> There he was unpacking some socks and winter gear when he comes across this letter at the bottom of the carton addressed to yours truly.
>
> Let me tell you, a word from home in these mudholes is like a ray of sunshine. Leave it to Alissa to find a way to get in touch. You can tell her for me that she's the pinup queen of the Abraham Lincoln Battalion. She's got her own fan club without even knowing it!
>
> Hope everyone over there is well and happy, especially Mother. I was really worried about her 'til I got Alissa's letter telling me she's okay. Boy, does that take a load off my mind!

I've got a real great bunch of guys here. Even my best buddy, Frederick Mannelli, is in the foxhole right next to me. He's a swell guy, and I hope to get to introduce him to you some day. We were in the CCC together and decided that if we had to put up with military discipline anyway, we might as well get in on some real military action. Oh, I'm not knocking the CCC, mind you. It's a fine organization, and they're doing some real worthwhile work, but it's not my cup of tea, if you know what I mean. If I've got to dig holes, I'd rather it were a foxhole than a hole to plant a tree in or a drainage ditch.

Funny thing, never thought I'd find my niche in life. I'd tried so many things and always either failed or gotten bored. Well, let me tell you, this is one job I'm not going to fail at, and as for getting bored—not a chance!

The Spanish people have been swell. There are even women fighting on the lines. Some of them are real dolls. There's this one chick, Consuela, whom I've really taken a fancy to. She reminds me a little of Alissa. Tell Mother to watch out, or she just might have a little senorita in the family someday.

Well, folks, I've got to go. Take good care of yourselves, and remember me sometimes. Still don't know where to tell you to write since foxholes don't have addresses, and we're still pretty disorganized. Matter of fact, I don't even know how I'm going to get this out to you.

Remember, do take care of yourselves, and don't worry about me. I'm going to come home a hero!

Love,
John

My brother hadn't come home, but there was no doubt in any of our minds that he was truly a hero.

Thinking about John, I couldn't help but think about the other young Americans fighting for Spain. I doubt if at any other time in our nation's history would so many young men have been willing to turn their backs on their families in order to aid a people whose language most of them couldn't even speak.

While there can be no doubt that these young men were guided by a mutual hatred of Fascism, I was equally certain that baser motives were involved. This was Depression America with fifteen million unemployed. At least some, if not most, of the volunteers were undoubtedly included in that number. Millions of bored, idle young men, just like John, were roaming all over the country, trying to find a place for themselves. Many saw their chance for excitement and adventure in this noble cause. The lure of being a hero had always appealed to young men all the way back to the time of the Crusades and undoubtedly from time immemorial.

While many countries sent out volunteers to Spain, it was especially apropos that the United States should have been responsible for supplying so many brave soldiers. After all, what other country better understands the necessity of fighting for the people's right to govern themselves? We had fought our own battle to preserve these same rights just 160 years ago and again more recently in WWI.

While John's battle was over, it was just about to begin for millions of people all over the world. Hitler and Mussolini had simply used Spain as an appetizer to whet their greedy appetites.

The curtain was being lifted on Germany's quest for world domination, and millions of young men would find themselves buried in unmarked graves all over the world—just like my brother John.

Chapter 26

The British Isles

> Merry, merry England has kissed the lips of June;
> All the wings of fairyland were here beneath the moon,
> Like a flight of rose leaves fluttering in a mist
> Of opal and ruby and pearl and amethyst.
> —Alfred Noyes

During the summer, I was kept abreast of how Mother and Alissa were faring through the long letters that Alissa sent to us every month, which sounded more like travelogues.

July 30, 1937

>   Dearest Edward and Marcie,
>   Your mother and I are having a wonderful time in "Merry Olde England." Although how it got that name, I certainly don't know. In truth, "Picturesque Olde England" would have suited it much better since the country is ancient and beautiful, but the people rather dour (but I'll save all that for another time).
>   Your Uncle Teddy's town house in Mayfair is quite grand (even if the plumbing leaves something to be desired). He has been a real dear and is doing everything possible to make us comfortable.

While your uncle and I have done a great deal of sightseeing, you needn't worry about your mother who is being very sensible and taking it easy. Besides, as she rightly pointed out, she's seen it all before. Since your uncle has also, I'm sure he is being bored to death, but because it's all new to me, I'm being relentlessly selfish and enjoying every minute of it with nary a twinge of conscience.

Although I realize how dull it is to read about someone else's itinerary, I will write about it anyway since I enjoy relating it all so much. And remember, in this way, when I return to New York and try to monopolize the conversation with scintillating discussions of my travels, you can ruin all my fun by reminding me that you already know all about them!

The first thing your uncle insisted on doing was to take me to his favorite casinos so that I could register. It seems that there is a law that requires that all visitors should register in them in person forty-eight hours in advance before they can enter for the first time to play. Not being much of a gambler, I wasn't particularly concerned about this, but your uncle is determined that London benefit monetarily from my visit.

After this all, important requirement was taken care of. We hit the usual tourist stops in the first two days. I visited and was impressed by Buckingham Palace, Kensington Gardens, and Hyde Park's 360 acres which include Serpentine Lake, Rotten Row, Ladies' Mile, and its famous Speakers' Corner where people stand on boxes and orate on various subjects, most of them absolutely ridiculous. I actually heard a Jacobite still calling for the return of a Stuart to the throne

(I wonder if any royal Stuarts are still alive). There was even a member of the International Flat Earth Society who was rallying people to his cause, which is just what his society's name implies.

My visit to the Houses of Parliament was as boring as I feared it would be. Since your uncle was so insistent that I visit the Strangers' Gallery of the House of Commons, I didn't like to disappoint him so I acquiesced. It really was quite a shocker. Here were the supposed crème de la crème of British society acting like unruly school children. These usually staid and stuffy gentlemen actually heckle their fellow members' speeches with absolutely no regard for decorum. And they consider Americans rude and ill-bred! To top it all off, here I was listening to some long-winded speech which was just about inaudible because of the heckling when the session was abruptly declared to be ended. Realizing that something unusual had occurred but not understanding what, I appealed to your uncle to clarify matters. It seems that the speaker had inadvertently, in his enthusiasm, stepped across a line on the floor that marked the point at which he would have been within a sword's length of his adversaries on the opposite side of the chamber. When this happens, the session is automatically suspended! Oh well, I suppose babies must play, as we good old Americans say.

The Tower of London is an awesome place. You can actually feel the presence of the ghosts of the many, such as Anne Boleyn, who had perished here. As we were rowed through Traitors' Gate, I tried to pretend that I had been condemned to death and did such a good job that my mental state was already precarious before I had even stepped foot on the cold gray stone.

Even that dreaded building has some redeeming qualities. Besides housing a fascinating museum, it also contains the Jewel House. Here are displayed the Crown Jewels, St. Edward's Crown, and the Imperial Crown of State, which is set with 3,093 precious jewels.

Your mother and I visited Madame Tussauds. It's a favorite of hers and now also one of mine. We lunched at Fortnum and Mason's where models show you the latest fashions while you eat.

Marcie, the stores are just fabulous! We've also shopped in Harrods at Knightsbridge which has over two hundred departments. We attended auctions at Sotheby's and Christie's just for the fun of it as neither of us really liked what was offered. Worcester Royal is one of my favorites. Here they offer limited editions of fine bone china birds and animals. I actually saw them smashing the molds after the limited numbers had been made. While London's casinos weren't lucky enough to get any money out of me, in fact, I won. The stores got back my winnings plus something extra thrown in.

One particularly lovely evening which your mother joined us on was spent at the Glyndebourne Festival Opera. It was a very posh affair to which everyone goes to be seen. I suppose the only equal of it that we have is our Hollywood Premieres. It's the type of affair that you would never be déclassé enough to arrive in anything less than a Rolls-Royce (fortunately, Teddy had access to a white beauty!). The opera was shown in two parts with a very long interval in between. This allows everyone time to walk on the grounds and show themselves off. After all, some people, Teddy says, save up all year just to be able to make a good showing on this day. The grounds are lovely with cool lakes and pools which some people had brought baskets to picnic beside. We had dinner at the Savoy Grill which is said to be one of *the* places to dine and be seen. They are certainly a very exhibitionist race, these British!

On the days when your uncle can't get away, I explore the museums which are legion. While the Victoria and Albert was interesting, the British Museum with its first editions of Chaucer and Shakespeare was a sheer delight. I even saw the original Magna Carta that naughty King John was forced to sign.

The Sport of Kings has not been overlooked either. I've been to the Derby at Epsom and that funny hat fashion show (as I call it) at Ascot. This seems to be more a contest for the ladies than the horses. A prize should be given to the one (lady not horse) wearing the most ludicrous chapeau.

Just one more item of interest (at least to me) before I close. I actually attended the Druid pilgrimage to Stonehenge on June 24. Although this was quite a distance from London, I was so anxious not to miss it that Roderick, of all people, took me. While the stones themselves were a disappointment, the ceremony was another story. It was an eerie and awesome spectacle which I will tell you more about in person although I never will be able to convey my feelings since it was the powerful atmosphere which so impressed me, and this, of course, must be experienced firsthand.

Since I can't possibly relate everything to you that I've done in a letter (although I've certainly given it a good try!), I will, much to your relief, I'm sure, end now 'til next month.

Take care of yourselves and give our regards to Richard.

Love,
Alissa

August 31, 1937

Dearest Marcie and Edward,

Hope that you received the packages and cards which your mother and I sent for your birthday, Edward. Not knowing how long it takes for mail to travel from this end, we aren't sure if we mailed them early enough. How does it feel to be twenty-seven? Your mother and I can't even remember back that far!

We visited with Melinda and her brood the first week in August. She is doing very well with your aunt's farm, and her husband seems a likable chap. Her two children—Henry, age four, and Edwina, age one and a half—are adorable. Your mother was enjoying being around the little ones so much that she decided to stay on for a while. She might join your uncle and me next month when we plan to visit some friends in the Lake District.

As it turned out, I ended up heading west all by myself since both your uncle and Roderick had taken their holidays in July. Since your uncle's car was available for me to use, this wasn't really such a bad thing. Although driving on the left side of the road took some getting used to, I've finally gotten the hang of it, or at least I hope so.

Since I did get lost several times, my itinerary was erratic. Somehow I managed to reach Henry VIII's Hampton Court with its park full of deer, its ornamental gardens, orangery, maze, and cavernous Tudor kitchens.

I also visited Windsor Castle whose first inhabitant, I think, was Edward the Confessor. Here I viewed the Queen's Doll House which, if you remember (if you were old enough) was given to Queen Mary in 1924. It is a perfect fully working little palace with real electric lights, doors with locks and keys, working lifts, and running water. To me, the most interesting little room was the miniature library with over two hundred tiny books in it.

After several days, I finally found my way to Oxford, which is where I had originally been heading. After reading Elizabeth Goudge's charming novel, *Towers in the Mist*, I wouldn't have missed it for anything. As I stood on a hillside on the outskirts of the town, I felt as though I had been transported back in time over three hundred years ago to the days of Tudor England. Oxford is all that I hoped it would be and more. It is a breathtaking fairyland of spires and turrets. The twentieth century has not disturbed the peace and dignity of these scenic buildings and streets. I kept expecting a fanfare of trumpets announcing the arrival of "Good Queen Bess" or one of the famous "town and gown" battles to erupt as they had since the twelfth century when Oxford first became a meeting place for scholars. Indeed, some things never change in Oxford— Christ Church's Great Tom still tolls 101 strokes at 9:05 p.m. every evening, summoning its students home.

While just about all of the buildings are impressive, I especially loved Bodleian Library where a copy of every book published in England must be sent and Magdalen (pronounced Maudlin) College which is one of the richest and most magnificent of all.

Another famous school which I visited was Eton. It reminded me somewhat of Oxford. It was established in 1440 and is still the most popular public school in England. As a matter of fact, its popularity is such that a child's name must be placed on a waiting list as soon as he's born if his parents harbor any hope at all of him attending this prestigious old institution.

After nearly a week of sightseeing and traveling, I finally reached my heart's ambition—Cornwall, home of Arthurian legend. It is a majestic land of rocky coasts and sandy beaches with hundreds of coves and bays. As I explored its Atlantic coast, it was immediately apparent why this land was, for so long, a favorite of pirates and smugglers. I sat for hours just watching the high granite cliffs being battered by towering breakers. Although I spent days exploring sheltered coves, I found nary a piece of gold.

The highlights for me were, of course, Camelford (the possible Camelot) and Tintagel, which is the reputed birthplace of King Arthur. All that remains of that great castle are the bare outlines of walls and the moats and towers. Despite all of this, it's still a fascinating place with Atlantic wind sweeping through it and the constant thunder of the breakers in your ears.

While the scenery is superb all along the coast, at Land's End, you have an unrivaled view of all the seas that surround the British Isles where the granite cliffs come to an abrupt halt.

I shall let you off easily this time with a short (for me) letter since next month's should be a beauty. Besides, Teddy's friends' party, I am also off to Scotland!

Love as always,
Alissa

September 30, 1937

Hi!

While I certainly don't agree with that stupid old saying that "God is an Englishman," I am starting to suspect that heaven can be found on the British Isles.

Despite the fact that Cornwall is still and probably will always be my first love, I am also in love with Scotland. It is a land in which there are not enough superlatives in the whole English language to describe the grandeur of the scenery, so please bear with my inadequate attempts.

Since my love affair with Scotland began in the north, I will begin my descriptions there. Just between the Black Isle at Muir of Ord and Lairg, I almost used up all my film. The moors are a magnificent tapestry of pinks and purples. Fortunately, my guide had more foresight and purchased a great deal of extra film. It seems he's seen overenthusiastic tourists react the same way that I did.

In case you're wondering about my guide, he's a handsome twenty-six-year-old child who was recommended to me by your uncle's friends.

Oh yes, I did get to meet the Howells, and while interesting, I'm too excited about my explorations to go into them now. But do ask me about them when I return as I believe you will find the story very entertaining.

 Back to my guide, while his manner is somewhat abrupt, he is very competent. While not exactly a source of intellectual stimulation since he won't talk with you, he is certainly a source of visual stimulation. His rugged tanned skin contrasts beautifully with his icy blue eyes and very dark brown hair which shines with copper highlights in the sun. While he mostly dresses in colorful kilts, there is nothing at all unmasculine about his brawny well-muscled physique. Although we do a lot of climbing on foot in this rugged country, he always makes me precede him so that I never was able to answer that often asked question which has plagued the minds of scholars for centuries: "What does a Scotsman wear under his kilt?" And after becoming acquainted with Ian McShane's stern Calvinistic countenance, I can understand why no one's ever asked them.

 To continue, from John o' Groats on the very tip of Scotland, I crossed over to the Orkney Isles, more Arthurian legend. Some historians claim that Morgan le Fay was married to Lot of Orkney while others claim her sister Morgause was. These islands are so ravaged during the winter by heavy gales that they are virtually bare of trees.

 I also visited the Shetland Isles. These are the northernmost limits of Britain. They are so far north that the sun never really sets on them during midsummer and the aurora borealis can be seen flickering in the northern sky. It's a magical eerie place where seabirds soar around the towering isolated cliffs.

Upon returning to the mainland, we headed west where beautiful wildflowers bloom between Lochinver and Kyle of Lochalsh. I became so distracted with trying to catch glimpses of Scotland's fauna that my guide was soon mumbling in disgust. No matter how much he grumbled, nothing deterred me from my pursuit of glimpses of herds of red deer, foxes, pine martens, and even Scotland's most elusive mammal—the wild cat.

The fantastic scenery seems to be infinite. Ben Nevis's 4,406 feet of majesty are not to be missed along with Loch Ness although I didn't sight the monster.

Edinburgh, the capital, is the most beautiful city in Scotland. It's a cultured city of breathtaking skylines and marvelous architecture. It was beloved by St. Margaret, Mary Queen of Scots, Prince Charles Edward Stuart, and John Knox, to name a few. Poets and writers such as Robert Louis Stevenson and Sir Walter Scott were all inspired by it.

As you enter the main gate of Edinburgh Castle, statues of Sir William Wallace on the right and King Robert Bruce on the left greet you. As you might remember, they were heroes of Scotland's wars of independence on the thirteenth and fourteenth centuries. I remember the stories of Robert the Bruce and the Black Douglas which I used to read as a youngster.

At the castle, I saw the Honors of Scotland which consist of the scepter, sword, and crown. King James V had ordered the crown remodeled in 1540. It is made entirely of Scottish gold and decorated with ninety-four pearls, ten diamonds, and thirty-three other precious stones.

Since the royal family was not in residence at the Palace of Holyrood, we were allowed to explore it. Mary Queen of Scots resided here for six years, and Bonnie Prince Charlie is said to have given a ball here. (I'm glad to know that that unfortunate young man did something other than fight!) The tapestries and furniture were magnificent. These royal families certainly know how to live!

This is finally the last of my travelogues. After this, it's back to Melinda's and your mother. It will not be easy removing my head from the Highland clouds it is enshrouded in.

I will soon be wrapping up my visit and returning home. While I have thoroughly enjoyed myself, the lure of Joyeuse Garde is for me the most irresistible of all, and I long for home and Tippy.

Take care, and we will probably be home before you know it.

Fondly,
Alissa

Chapter 27

There's No Place like Home!

> Counting the waves as they roll by,
>   I lean against the mast.
> Goodbye my lovely fatherland!
>   My ship is sailing fast.
>
> —Heinrich Heine

Marcie and I had driven into Queenstown on the first Sunday in October. It was a brisk day, and Marcie, who was anxious for a change in routine, suggested we drive over and pay Richard a visit. We were also hoping that perhaps he had received some word from Mother. After all, Mother and Alissa had been separated for about two months, and with Alissa's travels, she really couldn't be expected to keep in close touch with Mother who was notorious for hating to write. While I really wasn't very hopeful that she had written to Richard, likewise, I wasn't too concerned over her silence.

Visiting Richard was a glum affair, and so we actually did it more out of a sense of duty than for any real pleasure. We all recognized the fact that the emporium was on its last leg and must soon be given up to one of the popular chains. Richard had received a handsome monetary offer from one of them with the opportunity of managing that branch thrown in. With jobs so difficult to come by, I felt that this was a very considerate move on the company's part since I was sure they had many qualified men of their own whom they could have placed.

"Do you think you'll accept their offer, Richard?"

"I really haven't much choice, do I? We can't go on operating in the red much longer. The money that they offered will help pay the bills, and if invested wisely, it should see to Mother's needs for a while."

"Will you enjoy managing a chain store? I guess they'll train you since it's probably not the same as managing your own place."

"It certainly isn't the same. For over ten years, I've been my own boss. Now I'll have to answer to someone else for every move I make," he answered bitterly.

"Is there something else you could do? You always have your music."

"Yes, Marcie, I have my music for all the good it will do me. No, I don't know what else I can do. I hate the retail business. The only reason I stayed in it was because I promised Father, but now with the selling of the emporium, I don't—"

The front doorbell interrupted Richard who got up to answer it, obviously in some relief at not having to continue such a painful conversation. Hearing Richard's exclamation of surprise and some kind of disturbance, Marcie and I raced to the door.

"Mother! Alissa! No wonder Richard was surprised. Why didn't you let us know you were coming home? We'd have been there to meet you."

Just then, I noticed the irate cabbie who was trying to make himself heard above the din. It seemed that everyone had forgotten to pay him in the chaos.

"Edward, you help me take your mother's bags upstairs, and, Richard, you can make your mother comfortable on the sofa. She should really rest in bed, but I know she'll never stand for that," Alissa said, taking charge.

"I certainly won't!" Mother quickly agreed.

It was only then that I took a good look at Mother. She had lost more weight and definitely looked gray and exhausted. Seeing Alissa's anxious face as she also watched Mother, I hurriedly grabbed Mother's bags and followed Alissa upstairs.

"What happened?"

"Edward, your mother had another heart attack. It happened while I was in Scotland. Although Melinda could have reached me at various points on my itinerary, your mother stubbornly made her promise not to inform anyone."

"How serious was it?"

"Pretty serious. Here," she said, rummaging through her tote bag, "I have copies of the doctor's reports and test results."

They didn't take much studying to realize that it certainly was serious and that a lot of permanent damage had been done.

"She shouldn't have been moved," I protested.

"Everyone agrees with you except your mother. Edward, she realizes she hasn't much time. You know how much she loves England, but she still wanted to see her children and be with them," Alissa, who was openly crying by now, explained.

Holding her in my arms and comforting her, the toll of Mother's illness on Alissa was evident. She looked completely drained.

"If only I hadn't gone to Scotland!"

"You can't berate yourself. Maybe you would have been with her, but you certainly couldn't have prevented the attack. Look, the best thing we can do for Mother is to go downstairs as if nothing has happened. I know you can amuse us with stories of your travels," I said with a forced smile. "I'll go downstairs now, and you fix your makeup and hurry down too."

It was very difficult to go downstairs and not grab my little black bag and start examining Mother. While I would eventually do just that, I didn't want to appear overly concerned with what I had just heard. Anxiety was the worst thing for heart attack patients. As Mother looked worriedly at me as she tried to gauge my reaction to what she knew Alissa must have told me, I smiled reassuringly at her and was rewarded by her answering smile.

Marcie, who never missed a trick where I was concerned, looked at me questioningly, but I simply shook my head at her and mouthed the word *later*.

As Alissa entered the room, I heard her gasp of astonishment and looked up and followed her eyes.

"Marcie, you little sneak, when did that happen?" she asked, pointing to my beautiful wife's equally beautiful rounded stomach.

"Marcie! How could I not have noticed?" Mother asked incredulously.

"Well, I guess it's easy to miss. Even though I'm five months pregnant, I'm not very big."

"Just wait. Pretty soon, you'll forget what your feet look like," Mother laughingly consoled her.

"Five months! Do you mean that you knew before we left?"

"Yes, but I was afraid that if I mentioned it, you'd use it as an excuse not to go."

"You needn't have worried on that account. The trip was too important to both Eleanor and myself, but you would have given us a reason to look forward to returning." Alissa laughed as she hugged Marcie.

"Since you're so happy about it, how would you like to be the godmother? We've already asked Richard to be godfather, and he accepted."

"I'd love it! I can't wait to start planning the christening. You will let me help?"

"Do they have any choice?" Richard asked resignedly.

"How are Uncle Teddy and his family?" Richard asked Mother.

"Oh, well enough, I suppose. Alissa dear, you tell them everything. The trip knocked me out more than I thought it would."

Seeing Alissa's troubled look as she got up to fuss over Mother, I shook my head at her and motioned her back to her chair.

"While Marcie gets us some refreshments, I'll tuck Mother in upstairs."

"No, you won't! I want to hear Alissa tell you her impressions of England. She had me laughing on the ship all the way over."

"All the more reason for you to rest since you've already heard it all," Alissa argued.

"Oh, all right! But don't you dare leave for home before coming up to say goodbye even if I'm sleeping."

"Alissa can stay to dinner," Marcie offered.

"Splendid idea! Will you?"

"All right, Eleanor. Although I'd have thought you'd be tired of my company by now."

"How can I be with your traipsing all over Great Britain? Besides, you've been looking forward to some good American cooking…or so you've been saying. Have Alissa tell you about how much she enjoyed English food." Mother chuckled mischievously as I led her upstairs.

"All right, Edward," Richard said when I returned, "what's wrong with Mother?"

After I had explained the news to them and answered any questions which they had, I decided to phone our family doctor.

"Dr. Crowley said that he will pay Mother a visit tomorrow morning. Meanwhile, he also added that we're not supposed to sit around looking like the faces of doom."

"If you'll excuse me, I think I'll go to my room. Could you call me for dinner?"

"Sure, Richard."

Seeing the stricken looks on Marcie's and Alissa's faces, I tried to distract them. "Alissa, your letters were full of beautiful descriptions, but you said little about the people. How is Uncle Teddy?"

"Not very well, I'm afraid. Oh, his health seems good enough although he drinks and smokes too much, but it's his mental state that worries me.

"Your aunt's death seems to have hit him very hard. Of course, I expected that it would, but he's changed so much! I don't mean to sound critical. He treated us very well, but I'm afraid that the old lighthearted Teddy was buried with Henrietta. She was so much more than a wife to him. She was also a mother who coddled him disgracefully and his best friend whom he could confide in no matter what kind of scrape he had gotten himself into."

"He told you all of that?"

"No, you know as well as I how reticent the British are about revealing their own feelings. It was Roderick when he accompanied me to Stonehenge who spoke of it."

"Roderick!" Marcie exclaimed.

"Yes, he's turned out better than expected. He's as strikingly handsome as I thought he'd probably turn out to be, but more importantly, he's developed compassion and sensitivity—two traits I thought would always elude him."

"He's not married, is he?"

"No, he's definitely a playboy. He's always escorting some new beauty around town, but even with them, he must show some consideration because I could tell that he was genuinely liked by both the men and women whom we met."

"That's a pleasant surprise. How was he with you?"

"Charming! At first, I think that he was actually trying to form a match between his father and me, but after a few sharp words from us both, he finally gave up."

Noticing our astonishment, she laughed. "I know all about what you're thinking. You're remembering Roderick's hostility to me on his visit here. He apologized for that, and we've become good friends. I really like him. Too bad he's so young…"

"You can't be serious!"

"Of course, I'm not." She laughed, but I wasn't convinced.

"Tell us about Melinda. Has she changed much?"

"No, Marcie, she's still basically the same. She's a very sweet and perceptive young woman. The only thing that did surprise me was how easily she's taken over your aunt's role. Just like Henrietta, she insists on having a hand in every aspect of the farm much to her helpers' and her husband's chagrin. She works the machinery, cares for the animals, and personally tends to a large number of duties even though there's really enough help for it not to be necessary."

"Well, I don't suppose it was necessary for Aunt Henrietta to have been milking that cow either," I mused.

"What's her husband like?"

"He's a big affable fellow—the slow but steady type. Roderick says he drives him crazy. Instead of finding newer and more efficient ways of running the farm, Dick, Melinda's husband, just plods on like a bullock in a rut."

"Does Roderick visit them often?"

"No, only on Christmas and the children's birthdays. He's little Henry's godfather."

"Whom do the children look like?"

"I think that Henry resembles his grandmother, your aunt, and to me, little Edwina bears a striking resemblance to your mother although that could be only because their coloring is the same."

"Do you think Melinda's happy running the farm, or is she, like Richard, following a career out of obligation?"

"I think she's genuinely happy. Considering her love of learning, I was surprised too, but she seems content. Whether she will continue to be so in later years, only time will tell."

"Does Uncle Teddy spend much time there?"

"No, not at all. He finds it too painful without your aunt and prefers spending all his time in London. He has his job, and all his spare time is spent at that timeworn English institution, the club."

"Did you visit it?"

"Are you kidding? It is a bastion of male solidarity. To bring a female to visit would be nothing short of blasphemy. No, Roderick also told me about your uncle's club. He feels that your uncle spends too much time drinking and brooding and that he has to be lured away from his club which, in your uncle's mind, seems to represent the security of the womb. Now that he doesn't have your aunt for that purpose, he seems to have transferred those feelings to his club where they pamper and cater to him as much as your aunt did."

"Who takes care of him at home?"

"Edward, British men of your uncle's class always have what they call their 'man.' This is what they get when they're too old for nannies. He performs all the same functions for the spoiled man that nanny performed for the spoiled little boy. It's positively unhealthy! Especially in bachelors and widowers. They provide for every physical need from drawing baths to undressing them when they're 'in their cups' as they say."

"I take it that British men don't appeal to you."

"It isn't just the men, it's the whole society. You mentioned that my letters contained mostly scenery—well, that's why. I was very impressed by the scenery but much less by the people. It's a land of contradictions. For instance, they passionately love animals and yet consider it a great sport to watch a pack of hounds rip a fox to shreds. They hate the French and yet insist that their daughters attend French finishing schools and take pride in how well they speak the language."

"What were Uncle Teddy's friends like? I've always been under the impression that the British are snobs. Did you find that to be true? Well, I guess even if it is, you might not have seen it since I suppose rudeness to a guest would be considered 'bad form.'"

"They were a very snobby group. They live in the most ostentatious way possible and yet consider anyone else's doing so as vulgar. The house I stayed in had a staff of eleven whose main functions in life are to see the every need of a family of three."

"Eleven servants. That's almost four servants per person. All I can think of are a butler, cook, and maid."

"There's also the parlormaid, gardener, groom, nanny, valet, lady's maid, houseboy, and chauffeur. And this was considered roughing it since their regular staff is much larger, but this was their small summerhouse that we were staying in."

"What was the house like?"

"It was a beautiful Regency house surrounded by an elaborate Italian garden. It had two tennis courts, a swimming pool, and fully equipped riding stables. We discussed travel, and the British are so insular that even when they travel abroad, they bring all the comforts of home with them. They follow their schedules exactly like those of home and even eat their own food which they tote along. There's no sampling of 'foreign' ways for them. As they so blatantly point out, 'But, my deah, anything not British would only be inferior.' They never use superlatives in their speech, and the highest praise they can give something is to say that 'it's rather nice.'"

"They must have some good qualities," I laughingly protested.

"Yes, they're unfailingly polite—to each other. I actually saw two men bump into each other and spend at least ten minutes arguing but not blaming each other, as we would have done, but over each other taking the blame himself as they kept repeating 'My fault! My fault!' so many times that if it hadn't been 'bad form,' I'd have screamed. All joking aside though, on a one-to-one basis, most of them are dears like your relations, but when taken in large doses, I found them difficult to swallow.

"And their addiction to tea! There's 5:00 a.m.—yes, that's right, 5:00 a.m.—morning tea that's brought to your room, breakfast tea, elevenses, lunch, after lunch, supper, after supper, and 11:00 p.m. tea. If you refuse it, you're considered a barbarian because no truly civilized person ever tires of tea.

"Why I'll never forget the first time tea was served to me when I arrived at the Howells. Here we were a well-dressed, affluent, jaded group of seven when all of a sudden, someone shouts 'Tea!' as two servants entered carrying trays. Before I knew it, the cry was picked up by the others: 'Oh, tea! How wonderful!' and 'Thank goodness, the tea is here! Isn't it marvelous!' This fuss was accompanied by looks of pure ecstasy as they rolled their eyes heavenward as if all their prayers had been answered. All this fuss over some flavored water. It was unbelievable!

"It's a national panacea. Tea is offered for everything from a broken leg to a broken heart. No matter what happens, 'a nice cup of tea' is supposed to make it better. Your mother seemed to be having an even harder time than me in accepting all of this nonsense."

"Mother!"

"Yes, she kept looking at me and saying, 'Aren't they silly!' They feel pretty much the same about Americans. I even overheard one of the other guests remark in horrified tones when he heard that I was divorced: 'Not another American divorcée! They should be banned from the country. No good comes from them being here, no good at all!' I guess they're still smarting from the Mrs. Simpson problem from last year."

"To give up the throne for the woman you love! It was so-o romantic," Marcie cooed.

"Did you dress formally for dinner every evening?"

"Yes. Do you know that the maid lays your clothes out for you before dinner? She just goes through your wardrobe and picks out what *she* thinks you should wear. I suppose British people don't mind because it's an extension of having a nanny, but I wanted no part of it. The worst thing was that the maid actually felt hurt if I disregarded her choice!"

"Did you find their speech difficult to comprehend?"

"Not Teddy's friends, but the language in general can present some problems for Americans. For example, what we call a private school, they call a public school. What we call grammar school, they call infant or junior school, and what they call grammar school, we would call an academic high school. There were various other times when we seemed to speak at cross-purposes, not knowing that our usages are different."

"Eleanor said to ask you about the food," Marcie reminded.

"Actually, it wasn't as bad as I feared. Just rather dull roasted meat with boiled vegetables and gravy in one variation or another. Dessert was various things with custard poured over it. They seem to be constantly smothering their food, whether to hide it or try to flavor it, I really can't say."

"I've always heard that all they talk about are cricket, dogs, horses, and the weather."

"For the most part, that's true since these are pretty safe topics. Right now, however, they are concerned, like myself, over Hitler."

"Are you *still* worried about him?"

"Yes, Edward, more than ever, and there's Japan's aggression in China too. You must see where all this is heading."

"I prefer not to dwell on those things. We have enough problems. They're thousands of miles away and don't affect us."

More foolish words had never been spoken. Events of the next few years would force dreamers like myself to face the grim realities. What happened thousands of miles away *can* affect us—and with the most catastrophic results.

Chapter 28

The Circle of Life

> Forgive my grief for one removed,
>   Thy creature whom I found so fair.
>   I trust he lives in thee, and there,
> I find him worthier to be loved.
> —Tennyson, 1938

Mother's death occurred two weeks before the birth of her first grandchild. It was blessedly painless with death coming in the middle of the night of January 28, 1938, claiming the life of Eleanor Andros, age sixty-seven.

Richard discovered her body when he went to bring her her morning tea. We had been watching her grow frailer over the months, and she had suffered another attack during the holidays. With each attack, her activities were being curtailed more and more so that she was allowed to do very little. This added to her irritability and discontent, which also placed an additional strain on her heart. As she often complained, there wasn't much sense in staying alive if you had to mimic a zombie in order to do so.

Although I had a day nurse assigned to Mother during the hours when Richard was at work, a great deal of her care was still left in his hands. This was no small burden, and Mother did little to make it easier for him. Even though I couldn't see it at the time, on the whole, Mother's death was a blessing for the both of them. She had led an active and full life, and I hoped that her death would enable Richard to do the same. With both of our parents gone, there were no further excuses for Richard to hold on to either the store or that old-fashioned rambling house.

Knowing how Mother trusted and admired Alissa's good taste, we all agreed that she should be asked to supervise the funeral arrangements.

While at one time, I had worried that Marcie, who was Mother's real daughter-in-law, might feel slighted by her obvious preference for Alissa, I needn't have worried. It was Marcie herself who pointed out that while there might be ex-husbands and ex-wives, she had never heard of an ex-in-law. Since Alissa had been Mother's first daughter-in-law, Marcie could certainly understand Mother's feelings, especially since she also adored Alissa.

It wasn't as though Mother mistreated or ignored Marcie. On the contrary, she treated her like she did me and my brothers. It was only Alissa whom she seemed to have an especially close bond with.

Perhaps it's true what they say about the thin line between love and hate. Mother had never been indifferent toward Alissa like she had been toward Marcie in the days when Marcie was just a cute little kid with whom her son hung out. Mother had always had strong feelings toward Alissa—even if they were of hatred. Maybe that's why she did a 180-degree turnabout, and her feelings changed to a very strong love for the former object of her antipathy.

Whatever it was, we all agreed that with John dead, Alissa was definitely Mother's favorite and should, therefore, have the final say when it came to arrangements.

Our faith in Alissa was justified. When we all sat down to discuss the choices to be made, it seemed that none of us had any notion as to what Mother would have preferred. We didn't even know what her favorite color was or which flowers she favored. Alissa, on the other hand, had all this information at her fingertips.

"Did Mother discuss these things with you?"

"Of course not, but after knowing her for over a decade, somewhere along the line, I picked up the facts that powder blue is her favorite color and camellias her favorite flowers."

"We've known her all our lives, and we didn't know that," I answered.

"I guess that's why talking to strangers is preferable to talking to your own family, who seldom listen to what you're saying. When your Mother spoke to me, I listened, and I guess, subconsciously, I filed the information away because I enjoyed pleasing her. Looking back over the years, I have often given her powder blue articles of clothing and have sent her camellias."

"Yes, that's true," Richard admitted. "But I always thought that they were probably favorites of yours."

"Do you also know your own mother's favorite color and flowers?" Marcie asked.

"As a matter of fact, I do. Orchid is her favorite color and azaleas her favorite flowers."

Looking back over the years, I had also often received gifts of my favorite things from Alissa without me ever consciously mentioning them to her and so had Marcie and the rest of us. It was just one more way in which Alissa was so special to us.

*****

My daughter Tiffany was born on February 10, 1938. She was a very difficult breach birth, and after almost thirty-eight hours of excruciating labor, I would have agreed to any name Marcie wanted for our daughter, even Herman.

Actually, her name came from the many gift boxes which were delivered from that prestigious establishment after the baby's safe delivery. Alissa doted on her new godchild and had ordered a silver cup, silver teddy bear bank, silver teething ring, and the traditional silver spoon.

In addition to all the aforementioned, Alissa had purchased a christening outfit of the purest silk and the most delicate Valenciennes lace. This was still not enough; she also opened a safe deposit box in Tiffany's name and deposited $1,000 worth of pure silver in it, which she predicted would rise in value over the years.

There was something about new motherhood that would make women lose their sense of humor. When I jokingly suggested that if we were ever bankrupt, we could use Tiffany for collateral, I was disapprovingly ushered out of the nursery. Less than one week old, and she was already richer than her old man and having him strong-armed from her presence!

Although at her birth, I hadn't thought much of her looks, she rapidly improved, much to my relief. Whereas she had been a red wrinkled tadpole of a thing, by the day of her christening, two months later, she was a real beauty. She was dark-haired and gamin-faced, just like her mother. Her large liquid brown eyes were looking at you as though she possessed the wisdom of Solomon, again making her father feel as though he were a first-class oaf. I was the court jester whose only function was to amuse Her Royal Highness Princess Tiffany, and I loved every minute of it.

The christening was held in the same church where Marcie and I had been married in Pine River Falls. Unfortunately, I couldn't say the princess was on her best behavior. As the priest anointed her, she let out a most unroyal howl and screamed through the rest of the ceremony, much to Richard's embarrassment and Alissa's amusement.

The reception at Joyeuse Garde was a very small one since we were still officially in mourning for Mother. Only the immediate members of the family plus our maid of honor and best man and the Saronnas were invited.

The only unexpected guests, at least to Marcie and me, were George and Catheleen Carwood. Although they didn't arrive together, they created the same uncomfortable feelings in the rest of us.

Catheleen, who was going to be eighteen in the summer, wasn't a bad-looking girl. While larger than I like women, she didn't have a bad figure and had nice shiny chestnut hair. The only really negative thing about her was her disconcerting habit that she had of walking around with her eyes so wide open that all the whites showed. When, as a doctor, I became concerned that she might have an eye problem, I questioned her about it.

"Catheleen, are you having some pain in your eyes or trouble seeing clearly?"

"Of course not! Why should you ask such a thing?" she inquired haughtily as she opened her eyes even wider, a feat which I would not have thought physically possible.

Just then, her father motioned me over to him and explained that Catheleen felt that this made her eyes look larger.

"Little does she know that it makes her look as though she's just stuck her finger in an electric socket," he laughingly explained.

As was usually the case, George Carwood received as much female attention as Tiffany did. All the women cooed and drooled as much over him as they did over the baby. The only female who wasn't impressed by this suburban Adonis was my daughter, I was proud to say. Her only reaction was to spit up all over his impeccably tailored suit when he roughly bounced her up and down on his shoulder too soon after she had been nursed.

Although the Saronnas left when Arthur, Dee Dee, and Catheleen entered, their arrival didn't seem to fluster Alissa at all.

Dee Dee, as usual, made a big impression on everyone—especially their thighs. She seemed to really enjoy herself as she squashed people, stared in their faces, and giggled. She also gave us our first opportunity to see her other famous characteristic. As the party progressed, she surreptitiously stuffed her handbag, pockets, Arthur's pockets, and Catheleen's handbag and pockets with pastries, candy, and other delicacies.

When Alissa noticed what was going on, she angrily pulled Arthur aside and told him that if he would make his wife cease her ridiculous behavior, Alissa would make certain that they received a large package of delicacies to take home with them before they left.

At this, Arthur simply shrugged and said, "It's not that we need the food or that she really wants it. Dee Dee can't help herself. She'll still pocket the stuff even if I tell her what you said. Guess it's a kind of kleptomania," he explained as he tried to replace a sticky cream puff that Dee Dee had stuffed in his back pocket. Seeing Alissa's fury as he went to replace the pastry on the tray, he quickly stuffed it in his mouth instead.

Just then, I was distracted by an outraged squeal from Marcie who was snatching up Tiffany as Dee Dee bent over the elaborate hand-carved cradle which the Saronnas had kindly lent us for the day.

"Why did you do that, Marcie?" I asked in embarrassment since several people had noticed what happened.

"I don't trust that dumb-dumb!"

"Come on, Marcie. You can't believe that Dee Dee would hurt the baby."

"Well, I know that the cradle is too small for that dumb-dumb to climb into and squash Tiffany's thighs, but there was nothing to stop her from sticking the baby's bottle in her pocketbook," she argued.

"What would she want with Tiffany's bottle?"

"Who knows? What does she want with soiled paper napkins and used frilly toothpicks?"

"Do you mean that she's taking them too?" I asked incredulously.

"That's right. Nothing's safe, so you'd better keep a good eye on our baby," she admonished as she clutched Tiffany so tightly to her bosom that she soon had the baby again screaming like a banshee.

After the party had ended and only Marcie, Tiffany, Alissa, George, and I were left, we urged Alissa to try and take a quick inventory to see exactly what was missing. The list was so ludicrous that we were soon rolling with laughter.

"Let's see. I can't really tell with the food since I don't know what was eaten, but there are some inedibles gone too. There are two empty champagne bottles, one corkscrew, one potted geranium, salt and pepper shakers, one light bulb, plus various decorative picks all missing. But that's not all. Marcie, you did well in keeping a close watch on the baby. Dee Dee also stole Tippy's water bowl and one of his toy mice!" she said, laughing hysterically.

"I don't remember seeing any cats in her house when we visited."

"That's because they don't have any pets, Edward," George Carwood admitted. "She probably plays with the damned things herself."

"Oh, that dumb-dumb!" Marcie said, hugging Tiffany and then examining her as if she feared that Dee Dee might have lopped off a toe or finger to take home.

"Where did she put all that stuff? Some of it was large enough to be conspicuous," I reflected.

"Who knows? From what I remember from when we were married, she always carried a large tote bag and had large pockets in her dresses and coats. Then too, she wears full skirts and has a lumpy figure already so who would notice a few more lumps?"

One good thing about having Dee Dee around was that she was always good for a laugh. It's fortunate she had kept away from Mother's funeral out of respect; who knows what might have happened?

*****

The fates had not yet decreed that they were finished with the Andros family. They still had another blow to deliver that year. It was early on the morning of May 3 that Arthur phoned us to break the news.

"Edward, something awful has happened. Joyeuse Garde was burned down some time after midnight."

"My god! Is Alissa all right?"

"As far as I know, she just suffered some smoke inhalation when she tried to rescue Tippy. You know what a frightened cat is like. She got him out, but the doctor says she's suffering from shock and has to be hospitalized for several days."

"Do they know how the fire started?"

"Yes, empty gasoline cans were found in the woods. It was definitely arson."

"My god!"

"Fortunately, if you remember, Alissa had insisted on a large firebreak being cut all around the house just in case there ever was a fire, so it didn't spread to the rest of the Pine Barrens."

After informing Marcie, we quickly set out for the hospital. Since we had no one to leave Tiffany with and since Marcie couldn't be persuaded to remain behind, we decided to take her with us. We'd simply take turns going to Alissa's room.

"Arson! I still can't believe it, Edward. Who could want to hurt Alissa?"

"Who knows, Marcie? It might not have even been anything personal. There's still a lot of unemployment and some people just resent someone else being able to live so grandly. Remember too, since Alissa started to see George Carwood, she and Joyeuse Garde have received an awful lot of publicity."

"It has to be something like that. No one who knows Alissa could possibly hate her. She's so good and kind and that beautiful house! What will Alissa do?"

"I guess she's insured although that never covers everything, and there's the problem of arson—"

"Oh, Edward, her books and research! Some of those books were rare first editions." Marcie sobbed.

"Damn! I had forgotten about Alissa's research. I guess I never really took it very seriously since it was just a hobby although, God knows, Alissa took it seriously enough. She's spent years on that stuff. Let's keep our fingers crossed that maybe it's not a total loss."

"Well, what exactly did Arthur say?"

"He said it had burned down."

After that, we drove the rest of the way to the hospital in silence. Upon entering the hospital lobby, we saw Mrs. Saronna and old Jim leaving.

"Mrs. Saronna, how's Alissa?"

"Marcie, Edward! I'm so glad you've come." She sobbed.

"Is she hurt badly? Arthur said it was just smoke inhalation," I anxiously explained.

"No, no, she's not hurt badly—at least not physically. It's her mind. She's taking it very hard. She's just lost too many things recently. First, your brother Arthur, then your other brother, your mother, and now her home. To Alissa, it was more than just a house, you know. It was the symbol of all her hopes and dreams. Maybe it's our fault. We sheltered her too much. We never wanted her to get hurt, and me, I filled her head with all that romantic stuff about knights and princesses and unicorns. I guess, like me, she found her fantasies preferable to reality. I don't know what happened between her and your brother. Don't know what went wrong. Everyone else who knows her seems to love her. Why not Arthur?

"You've met that wife of his. I don't know her, but she seems like a real lulu to me. And those kids of hers—they're real oddballs.

It breaks my heart to think that he didn't want Alissa's children, but he accepted that big stupid lump of a son of Dee Dee's and that dopey-looking girl who walks around with her eyes bulging out of her head," she demonstrated. "What's wrong with her eyes anyway?"

"Nothing. She thinks it gives her glamorously big eyes."

"Glamorous! She looks like she's in a constant state of shock. Poor Alissa! To lose out to them. I just don't understand it…"

Since I didn't either, Marcie and I proceeded to go upstairs to Alissa after agreeing to leave Tiffany with Mrs. Saronna.

Alissa was a pitiful sight. While she only had minor burns on her hands and arms, she was pretty badly scratched up from trying to subdue her terrified cat. The worst part, however, was the lost and bewildered look on her face.

"I still don't believe it." She cried. "Why? Who hates me so much? Father's determined to rebuild, but I won't let him. He doesn't understand that you can't rebuild a broken dream."

*****

It wasn't until two weeks after the fire that Arthur and I went to view the ruins.

Mr. Saronna had hired guards to keep out the curious and to prevent any looting. All salvageable property had already been removed, and thankfully, there was more than anyone had expected.

As I walked among the pathetic rubble, the remains of Alissa's former life, like her dreams, were mostly ashes. Charred books, furniture, clothing, and even a badly singed cat's toy lay strewn about. Pieces of rainbow-colored glass were scattered everywhere. As I picked up a piece of what had once been the famed unicorn window, I had a difficult time fighting back my own tears.

"We must never allow Alissa to see this, Arthur."

"She already has. The guards say that she comes here almost every morning as if she's searching for something."

My heart went out to my broken beautiful friend as I could picture her searching through the rubble for something which she could never again hope to find—her lost youth and dreams.

CHAPTER 29

Reminiscences

> There is a pleasure in the pathless woods,
> There is a rapture on the lonely shore,
> There is society, where none intrudes,
> By the deep sea, and music in its roar:
> I love not Man the less, but Nature more.
> —Byron, 1946

Alissa's fears of Nazi Germany's and Japan's aggression materialized in the next few years. On September 3, 1939, Great Britain declared war on Germany after that country's attack on Czechoslovakia, and the United States declared war on the Axis powers after Japan's sneak attack on Pearl Harbor on December 7, 1941. As so many had foreseen, the United States was, for the second time, plunged into world war. While no one fooled themselves this time that it would be the war to end all wars or to make the world safe for democracy, everyone agreed that it was being fought for something even more essential—survival. The German war machine like a great tidal wave was sweeping up everything in its path, and the United States could no longer sit back complacently on its laurels.

The Andros family, unlike so many others, was to have a civilian role. The bloodlust of the fates had been sated by the sacrifice of John's life in the Spanish Civil War.

Marcie and I were living in a small Connecticut town where I had taken over a local doctor's practice. Since there were only two of us in the whole town, the draft board decided that I could serve the country best by staying at home.

Richard and Arthur were well into their forties and ineligible for active service although, like everyone else, they did what they could to support the war effort on the home front.

In the military or not, everyone's life was affected by the war. Americans, who were used to unlimited supplies of goods, were now faced with rationing. Gas was rationed to three gallons a week, and food was on a point system with steak twelve points a pound, hamburger seven, cheddar cheese eight, and a can of peaches eighteen.

Unlike the Depression years, work was now plentiful as industry strove to meet the demands of the military. When Pearl Harbor was attacked, United States' manufacture of war materials was negligible. Only two years later, we were producing as much as Germany, Italy, and Japan combined. By 1943, we were producing 50 percent more than all the Axis powers. By the end of the war, civilians were responsible for producing 297,000 planes; 86,000 tanks; 6,500 naval vessels; 64,500 land craft; 54,000 cargo ships; 315,000 artillery pieces; over 4 million tons of artillery shells; and 17 million rifles.

Civilians performed a great many other services as well. They conducted scrap metal drives, bought war bonds, and gave blood. They served as aircraft spotters, members of draft and rationing boards, air raid wardens, and police blackouts. Besides being factory workers, women, such as Marcie, served as nurses and nurses' helpers who visited hospitalized troops where they distributed cigarettes and wrote letters. The younger and prettier girls served as USP hostesses where they comforted many frightened homesick soldiers. They even sacrificed their nylons to provide parachutes and instead used leg makeup. The East Coast tolerated nightly "dimouts" to diminish the sky glow that silhouetted Allied merchantmen and made them more vulnerable to attacks by Nazi U-boats. These were only a few of the services performed by the nine million volunteers of the Office of Civilian Defense.

Although it seemed to be a little remembered fact, we did have some casualties on mainland American soil. During an outing in the Oregon mountains, several members of a fishing party were killed when a child picked up a Japanese bomb which had been sent across the Pacific by means of paper balloons. While this was not the only bomb which made it across the ocean in this way, we thank God that these were the only known casualties.

Our relatives in England were not so lucky. Uncle Teddy was killed on Sunday, December 29, 1940. He was passing St. Paul's Cathedral when twenty-eight incendiary bombs, some of which bounced off its double dome, scored a direct hit on my uncle. What they could find of him was buried with Aunt Henrietta. Sandbags made up the difference in weight in his coffin for what was missing, which according to Roderick was a great deal.

Roderick, despite the odds, survived the war. He was a captain in the justifiably praised UXB force whose officers had an expected life span of six months. They were responsible for detonating the many unexploded bombs which fell on England. This explained their high mortality rate.

Melinda's husband, Dick, lost an arm in April of 1941 when the Germans defeated the British in North Africa. Instead of being bitter when he returned home, he was of invaluable help to his wife, who was a sort of foster mother to about a dozen London children who had been transported to the safety of the country for the duration. It was "Auntie" Melinda and "Uncle" Dick to whom they turned for comfort.

Alissa had moved to Maine after the fire at Joyeuse Garde. During the war, she, like Melinda, transformed her small farm into a sort of temporary orphanage. Although we didn't hear from her too often, her letters were full of praise for her little boarders.

It wasn't until 1946 that I again saw Alissa. This came about when I was attending a medical convention in Quebec. There had been at least two big medical breakthroughs made during the war. In 1941, penicillin was first used on humans, and in 1943, streptomycin was discovered. It wasn't, however, until after the war that small-town doctors finally had the time to delve into their possibilities. Thus, many conferences and conventions resulted.

Alissa owned a small farm of about twenty acres where she grew potatoes, blueberries, and apples. Not really needing the money, she did it more as a diversion than a necessity. Since the Census Bureau in Maine counts any person who owns three acres or more of land and earns at least $250 a year from the land, a farmer was Alissa's official classification. It was no wonder then that Maine boasted over forty-three thousand farmers although less than half of that number work a farm full time. Because of rocky soil, most people also moonlight as fishermen and lumberjacks. They had learned to be very adaptable people who would also serve as hunting and fishing guides whenever the occasion would warrant it.

When I first drove up to Alissa's house, it appeared to be a rather nondescript place. While comfortable enough, it was hard to imagine that someone who had once lived in the splendor of Joyeuse Garde could be happy in such rustic surroundings. As I drove around to the back of the simple two-story saltbox house, I laughed aloud in relief as I spotted a brand-new white Rolls-Royce parked in the driveway. While a seemingly incongruous element, that elegant stately car was more like the old Alissa whom I knew and loved.

Just then, Alissa ran out the back door accompanied by two kittens and a beautiful full-grown calico. At forty-eight years old, Alissa was still a lovely woman. Except for tiny lines etched around her mouth and eyes, she really hadn't changed very much in the almost seven years since I had last seen her. The tight jeans and denim shirt which she was wearing showed that she still had a slender youthful figure. If anything, she was thinner than ever, and her huge green eyes seemed to take up her whole face. Pushing back a few loose strands of hair which had escaped the French knot she wore, Alissa nearly knocked me off my feet as she enthusiastically greeted me.

"Edward, I can't believe it's really you!"

"My god, Alissa, the years haven't even touched you. You're still the most beautiful woman I know!"

"Barring one." She laughed. "I had so hoped Marcie could have joined you."

"She really wanted to, but as her doctor, I advised against it. You see, she's eight months pregnant."

"Pregnant again! My, my, you certainly were busy during the war," she teased, alluding to our daughter Melissa who had been named after Alissa and Melinda in 1941, and our youngest, Veronica, born in 1943 who had been named after the actress, Veronica Lake.

"Hope it's a boy this time," I said, blushing like a schoolboy caught in some indiscretion instead of an old married man.

"There's no problem with this pregnancy?" she asked, looking worried.

"No, no, but Veronica's birth had been an ordeal. Unfortunately, she took after me and weighed ten pounds and nine ounces. That was quite a burden for my petite wife. Instead of her deliveries getting easier, they seem to be more difficult, and I'm determined that this will be the last. I was willing to stop after Tiffany. It's Marcie who's hard to convince."

"But if it's going to endanger her health…surely, Edward, as a doctor you could do something."

"Yes, I intend to." Changing the subject, I commented on the farm. "This is certainly a different setting than what I'm used to seeing you in."

"Yes, but you knew I was living on a small farm."

"I know, but hearing about it and seeing you on it are two different things. The only thing that I've seen so far that assures me I'm talking to the right woman is that," I said, pointing to the Rolls.

"Yes, it is gorgeous, isn't it? It certainly doesn't fit in with my new lifestyle, but what the heck. I've never changed where beautiful automobiles are concerned," she explained, leading me inside.

The interior was tastefully and comfortably furnished. Colorful chintzes brightened up the dark wood paneling, which seemed to dominate all the rooms. Having led me into a screened porch in the front of the house, I gratefully sank into a thickly stuffed rocking chair and accepted a tall frosty glass of apple cider, which Alissa explained had come from her orchards.

"As a matter of fact, after you rest, I'm going to stuff you with native Maine food. I've planned a special dinner for you. I hope you still like to eat," she said with a twinkle in her eyes.

*****

After a two-hour nap, I more than did justice to Alissa's dinner. There were clam chowder rich with cream and butter, succulent steamed lobsters, baked Maine potatoes, tender corn on the cob, and for dessert, blueberry cobbler with fresh whipped cream.

As I groaningly sat in front of a crackling fire in the living room, I tried to digest the second helping of cobbler, which I knew I shouldn't have eaten but couldn't resist while Alissa cleaned up and prepared more coffee.

Sipping the dark, rich beverage which had been so scarce during the war, I sat back contentedly, a kitten in my lap, and gazed in new appreciation at Alissa's home and at Alissa who had donned a gold-and-green quilted hostess gown for the evening.

"Tell me something about your war experiences. How did you enjoy having all those children with you? I don't really understand what you were doing with them. It wasn't like Melinda whose children had been evacuated from London because of the bombings."

"To answer your question, I loved having the children. I had six of them ranging in age from fourteen months to eight years old. They were the children of women whose husbands were overseas and who, themselves, were flocking to the cities which had 'defense' industries. Some of the children only stayed during the day since Maine had a rousing shipbuilding industry, and although we never beat Henry Kaiser's record of turning out freighters in twenty-two days, we still did very well. The women worked as riveters, welders, and just about anything else that they could find. Many a Depression husband left a practically destitute family to return to a well-set-up home."

"Do you think they appreciated it?"

"Some, I'm sure did, but American family life will never be the same. Too many women have, for the first time, tasted the nectar of financial independence. Then too, many men, whose families suffered because of their inability to find employment during the Depression, might not have strong enough egos to accept how well their wives did while they were gone. You know as well as I do that with so few things available to purchase during the war, most women put away nice little nest eggs and were just waiting for the end of rationing to try out their hard-earned purchasing power."

"Did you have the same children for the duration?"

"For the most part, I did. As a matter of fact, the mother of the fourteen-month-old took a job in Washington, DC, and remained there for the entire four years. Except for three brief visits during that time, I was the only 'mother' that little girl ever knew. It broke my heart to have to give her up. Next to losing Joyeuse Garde, I had never experienced a loss of that magnitude before."

Marcie had been concerned about just this sort of thing when she heard about Alissa's plan to take in children. I wondered how many other childless women's hearts had been broken by having to give up their wartime wards.

As if reading my mind, Alissa continued, "I don't suppose anyone will ever know all the broken hearts which resulted from the war. Families torn apart, not only through deaths but also by 'Dear John' and 'Dear Jane' letters. Why, in this town alone, I know of at least a dozen broken homes. Then there are the children, like my dear little Annabelle, who were torn from the foster mothers who loved and cared for them by natural mothers who were virtual strangers. These are all the casualties which are never recorded."

"Speaking of broken romances, an old friend of yours is always asking about you. You do remember someone named George Carwood?"

"George! Did you know that he asked me to marry him?"

"No, but I thought he might have. Why didn't you marry 'God's gift to women'?" I facetiously asked. "Marcie was certainly impressed by him."

"Yes, George truly was impressive. He spent so much time creating an impression that it was difficult to know what the real man was like. Actually, if you bothered to delve beneath the plastic exterior, he was a very nice man."

"If he was so nice, why didn't you marry him?"

"Obviously, because I didn't love him, and to tell you the truth, I think he was relieved. The only reason he really asked me was because he was about to lose his most successful hostess. We seemed to complement each other, and after all, he could have done worse."

"Yes, he could have gotten another Dee Dee Dumb-Dumb."

"Speaking of Dee Dee, I trust she and Arthur are doing well?"

"Yes, with one major change. They no longer waste time sleeping in front of the radio."

"Really! What do they do now?"

"They sleep in front of the television."

"I'm glad the war hasn't changed some people too much." Alissa laughed.

"What do you do for amusement around here? Aren't there any men in your life?"

"No one special. There was a handsome French Canadian whom I was seeing."

"'Was seeing'? What happened?"

"He claimed to be a lumberjack, but I discovered he was a trapper. You know how I feel about that. I guess some one tipped him off to it, which was the reason for the lumberjack charade."

"Don't you find it boring up here all alone?"

"Sometimes I do. After all, I had started to lead a very active social life for a while after my divorce, but to be honest, pretty soon, even that palled. The only things that I really do miss are the evenings we used to spend together at your mother's house especially when your uncle's family visited. Why that was the happiest time of my life."

As we both sat silently reminiscing, I was filled with an overpowering sense of loss. Mother, John, Uncle Theo, Aunt Henrietta, Uncle Teddy, and even Joyeuse Garde were all gone. Never before had the truth of the old saying "You can never go home again" hit me so hard.

I, at least, was lucky. I had Marcie, Tiffany, Melissa, Veronica, and the new baby to go home to. I had a future to look forward to. What about Alissa? While the farm was charming, she was miles away from the people who loved her. The thought of her spending long, lonely winter nights in the twenty-degree below-zero temperatures and the two-story high snowdrifts that this part of the country was known for was a depressing thought.

She was still a beautiful woman, but she was forty-eight years old, and everyone knows how quickly time goes by.

*****

As I left two days later to return to Connecticut, I had an almost overwhelming desire to tie Alissa up and forcibly drag her back with me.

Again, with the uncanny way that she had of reading my mind, she said, "Don't worry about me, Edward. I'm fine. Really, I am. And now with gasoline and tires available again, I'm sure we'll see more of each other. Wait! I have another gift I'd like you to take to Marcie."

"Another one? The car is already crammed with presents."

"This one's special. The winter nights are long, and I've been working on it for several winters. I hope you like it."

As I unrolled what proved to be a large petit point wall hanging, I couldn't help but gasp as I recognized a reproduction of Joyeuse Garde's uniquely beautiful unicorn stained glass window.

Driving away, I was undecided as to my feelings. Did this mean that Alissa still remembered and held on to her old hopes and dreams, or was she discarding the last vestiges of them or perhaps even passing them on to us? Only time would tell.

CHAPTER 30

Better Times

> For I dipped into the future, far as human
>   eye could see,
> Saw the vision of the world, and all the wonder
>   that would be.
>   —Tennyson, 1950

The '50s were a decennium of diversity. It was the age of Little League, the mambo, and the drive-in. Most of all, however, it was the age of the atom bomb. Ever since the bombing of Hiroshima, everyone was aware of the deadly force that had been unleashed on the world. What made the situation even more perilous was that soon after the Allied victory, the Soviet Union refused to abide by its agreement with the Allies and proceeded to take over half of Europe.

By 1950, Russia had three times as many combat planes as the US, four times the troops, and thirty tank divisions to our one, but most of all, Russia also had the bomb. Experts estimated that if Russia bombed US major cities, ten to fifteen billion people would die in a single day. As the Nobel Prize-winning chemist Harold C. Urey stated, "There is only one thing worse than one nation having the atomic bomb—that's two nations having it."

Because of the public's apprehension, atomic bomb shelters with concrete walls and shelves for canned goods sprang up in the backyards all over the US. While the actual value of these habitats was in question, other products whose worthlessness was all too obvious to anyone who was not in a state of panic were foisted off on a jittery public.

Everyone was offering amateur advice on what to do in the event of an atomic attack. One man advised shaving cats and dogs to prevent their fur from becoming radioactive. Another proposed carrying a drawstring bag around at all times which could be pulled on during an attack. Exactly what protection the bag would provide was never elaborated on. A booming business in aluminum pajamas, lead girdles, and lead-foil brassieres also sprang up. One innovative patent medicine mixer produced "U-235 Atomic Shock Cure," which it was prevented from marketing when the Public Health Service found its active ingredients to be nothing more than table salt, bicarbonate of soda, and water.

The bomb scare became even more pronounced after the US tested its first hydrogen bomb. During that test, Enewetak, an atoll in the Marshall Islands in the Pacific, was destroyed. News of the tremendous devastation that it caused was soon spread by passengers on various ships in the vicinity who had observed the explosion.

Despite these weighty concerns, on the whole, I felt that the '50s were more a time of newly discovered affluence and just plain fun. The '50s had its share of popular fads just some of which were 3D movies, paint by numbers, Hula-Hoops, and the Davy Crockett cult which had every child and even some adults sporting coonskin hats. There was also the popular college fad of students cramming themselves into everything from phone booths to Volkswagens.

If a color could be said to be associated with a decade, it's safe to say that green was the favorite '50s color. With the discovery of chlorophyll, green popped up in some of the most absurd places. Since the promotors of chlorophyll promised that it would make you smell fresh as a daisy, there were chlorinated toothpastes, gums, cough drops, deodorants, breath tablets, and even dog food! All this in spite of the fact that *The Journal of the American Medical Association* tried to point out to enthusiastic consumers that goats, who live on natural chlorophyll while grazing, still stink.

There were also some bizarre fads. In 1952, an amateur hypnotist put a Colorado housewife in a trance whereupon she was said to have become the spirit of Bridey Murphy, a nineteenth-century Irish girl. This incident caught the public imagination to such an extent that the spirit of Bridey Murphy was used in nightclub acts and people dressed as her to attend private parties. A best-selling book and even a drink known as the Reincarnation Cocktail, which looked something like a frozen daiquiri surrounded by cherries and topped by an orange slice and lighted candle, were just a few of the gimmicks that resulted. While most people just had fun with the whole Bridey Murphy story, one tragedy did result when a nineteen-year-old Oklahoman boy committed suicide because "I am curious about the Bridey Murphy story, so I am going to investigate the theory in person."

There were also fads in women's and men's clothing and hairdos. Stylish women of the '50s were dressed in hooded tube dresses, sack dresses, short shorts, and crinolines, which many husbands and parents like myself were worried about on windy days. I could still see my daughters billowing down the street, looking like large open umbrellas from below the waist. Pop-It Beads were the popular working girls' jewelry. Short poodle haircuts were considered de rigueur by the arbiters of high fashion.

Men managed to look equally, if not even more, silly. The color pink was suddenly transferred from babies' nurseries and ladies' boudoirs to men's shops. A fashionable gentleman could purchase everything from pink ties and dressing gowns to pink shirts, socks, and underwear. Stringy Colonel ties, pleated rogue pants, and executive Bermuda shorts were all part of male haute couture of the '50s. Two of the more absurd hairstyles of the day were the ducktail and Apache although only the young and daring wore them.

Around this time, we also noticed a distinct language change which certainly did nothing to bridge the generation gap. "Hot" became "cool." "Real gone" meant "the most." What was once "in" now became "out," and "way, way out" was the most "in" you could possibly get.

Many adult males became commuters as more and more families flocked to the suburbs in order to provide the "good life" for their families. With the postwar baby boom, it became increasingly important to find new and better schools. People spent more money than ever before in adorning their homes and such one-time luxuries as lawn ornaments, patio furniture, and barbecues were all abundantly evident as one drove through suburbia.

With so much money being spent on home improvements, the man of the house usually spent a good part of what should have been his leisure hours on do-it-yourself maintenance. It was not unusual to see whole families turned out on every street as they mowed lawns, washed cars, gardened, painted, and spent weekends making certain that their house's appearance kept up with the Joneses'.

This also had a seamier side. On my rounds as a doctor, I often knew of entire families who were shunned by their neighbors because their homes were not up to par. Regardless of the reason for this supposed dereliction of duty, be it sickness, poverty, or a lazy or tight-fisted head of the family, it was the whole clan from the wife to the youngest child who suffered the censure of their peers for inhabiting the neighborhood eyesore.

Besides providing attractive houses and good schools for their offspring, these newly affluent parents strove particularly hard to produce a very privileged generation of youngsters. Parents provided everything from dance, music, and baton twirling lessons to encyclopedias for the advancement of their children.

The suburbs, unfortunately, also became famous or rather infamous for its consumption of alcohol. As more families left their old ties and settled in new neighborhoods, the cocktail party became the number one form of entertainment. This enabled strangers to make new friends and discuss all things with that most popular subject—their kids.

Most young people after 1955 were listening to tunes by such performers as Elvis Presley, The Everly Brothers, Paul Anka, Frankie Avalon, and Little Richard. The age of rock and roll had arrived, and most adults bemoaned the fact that music would never be quite the same again.

There were also a group of nonconformists who became known as the Beat Generation. These rebels or beatniks, as they were better known, were resisting their parents' standards and the advantages which were so proudly being offered to them. The young women dressed in black leotards and black turtleneck sweaters and skirts. They had very long, preferably straight, hair and white pasty faces. While they wore no lipstick, they used so much dark eye shadow that they resembled raccoons. They experimented with "pot," lived in "pads," and listened to their own poetry, which was recited in coffeehouses. They even had their own folk heroes such as Jack Kerouac who wrote *On The Road*, Allen Ginsberg, and Kenneth Rexroth.

There was one Gregory Corso whom I especially disapproved of. He was the enfant terrible of the beatniks. At sixteen, he was arrested with two friends for actually attempting to take over New York City by means of a complex series of robberies which were coordinated with walkie-talkies.

Broadway was also doing a roaring business. Marcie and I went into Manhattan to see such delights as *My Fair Lady*, *The King and I*, *Flower Drum Song*, and *The Music Man*. My three oldest daughters insisted on accompanying us to see *Bye Bye Birdie* and *West Side Story*, which ended up being more enjoyable for them anyway.

With paper again in abundance, cheap paperbacks and comics, especially horror comics, became very popular. Detective story writers such as Mickey Spillane were having a heyday. People were being shocked by the new novel *Peyton Place* while the devout were reading such future classics as *The Robe*, *The Cardinal*, and *The Silver Chalice*, Marcie's particular favorite. I preferred *The Caine Mutiny*, *The Catcher in the Rye*, and *From Here to Eternity*.

For people like Arthur and Dee Dee, the '50s had a particular charm in that it was also the age of that electronic opiate—television. There was something for everyone in that electronic box. There were Westerns such as *Gunsmoke*, comedies such as *I Love Lucy*, and variety shows such as *The Ed Sullivan Show*. A new form of entertainment which became known as the situation comedy also emerged. They invariably portrayed an idealized family headed by a bumbling father. My favorites were *Father Knows Best* and *Ozzie and Harriet*. No Saturday evening was complete without the comic antics of Sid Caesar and Imogene Coca on *Your Show of Shows*. The children also had their favorites with *Lassie*; *Rin Tin Tin*; *Kukla, Fran, and Ollie*; and the *Mickey Mouse Club* heading the list.

With all these things going for us, I thought that the average suburban family was a close-knit and happy one. Parents were proud of what they were able to provide for their families, and who could blame them? The Depression years and their poverty were still too vivid of a memory. Now the lean Depression days were over, and everyone was jumping in with both feet to reap the results of their labors. While there weren't as many rags to riches stories, like the Saronnas, which the turn of the century had provided, the middle class had finally come into its own.

The Andros family also enjoyed a hard-earned period of peace and prosperity which was only blighted by the deaths of Josephine and Gabrial Saronna. They had been killed with their chauffeur in 1951 when driving up to Maine to visit Alissa. It was a terrible accident in which all three died instantly. Since Alissa decided to have the funeral in her parish church in New England, Arthur, Richard, and I went to Maine for the service. It was a very big blow for Alissa who was now devoid of all living relations. I had never before realized the void that the deaths of an unmarried, childless, only child's parents would leave. Alissa was in a state of shock, and she kept repeating, "While I couldn't have asked for longer lives for them [they were seventy-seven and eighty-one], I just wish they could have been happier, especially my poor mother." Since Big Al's disposition was generally well known, I could only agree with her.

Since Alissa's parents died in May, I was able to send her goddaughter, Tiffany, to spend the summer with her the very next month. This began a custom which was to last till Tiffany went away to college.

At twelve years old, Tiffany was a slender, petite, dark-haired, and dark-eyed miniature of her mother. The only differences were in their personalities. While Marcie was outgoing and vivacious, Tiffany was a serious quiet little girl who adored Alissa. They shared passions for animals and ice cream. It wasn't an unusual sight to see them seated in front of the TV crying over the latest episode of *Lassie* while devouring huge bowls of Alissa's homemade ice cream.

It always amused Marcie and myself that our children were such a mixed bag, and nowhere was this more evident than in the differences between Tiffany and our second daughter, Melissa. Being the namesake of her Aunt Melinda, I shouldn't have been surprised by her shock of bright-red hair. She was tall and big-boned like my mother had been with lovely large blue eyes and long shapely legs (another legacy of Melinda). It was no small wonder that she wanted to be a model like her idol Suzy Parker. She was outgoing, spoiled, and very demanding. In many ways, she reminded me of my brother John and was obviously our black sheep. She even ran away to Greenwich Village where she spent several months living as a beatnik. At the age of eighteen, she moved into Manhattan where she pursued a modeling career but more often worked as a movie usherette or waitress. If any family problems arose, unfortunately, Melissa was usually the cause.

My third daughter, Veronica, was something of a martinet. This child's bad luck was to take after me. She was large and ungainly with mousy brown hair, but more fortunately, like Tiffany and Marcie, she had large brown eyes. The fact that she had teaching aspirations was always apparent to us. She spent hours in front of the TV watching *Ding Dong School* and patterning herself after Ms. Frances. For a while, she annoyed the whole family by speaking in the same slow measured drawl. She also went around pasting gold stars on the forehead of anyone she considered "good" and would encouragingly say "very good" whenever we made any statement that was not erroneous, no matter how blatantly obvious it was. Since she had the patience of a saint and the hide of a rhinoceros, she never got angry or felt insulted at our protestations that she was driving us crazy.

In 1946, my fourth daughter, Miranda, had been born. Her name was easily explained by the fact that we lived near Stratford-upon-Avon and always attended the Shakespeare Festivals. Marcie and I had enjoyed seeing *The Tempest* the week before her birth. Since all my children had Marcie's huge eyes, Miranda's cornflower blue ones were knockouts. She was a tiny, slender towheaded waif whose coloring was similar to my mother's and Edwina's although Miranda was fairer than either. She was a gentle and sweet child who had inherited Richard's musical talent. She could sit at the piano for hours and delighted everyone, who was fortunate enough to be entertained by her with her brilliant renditions of both classical and popular music.

It wasn't until May 6, 1950, the same day that Liz Taylor married Nicky Hilton, by the way, that my son was finally born. Since Marcie's labor had caused complications which would prevent us having any more children, it was a lucky thing. Marcie insisted that the child be called Ted. In this, she reasoned, we would be honoring three people at the same time. Uncle Teddy was obviously one of them, and since Ted was a popular nickname for both Edward and Theophilus, Uncle Theo and I also had a namesake.

What could a man say about his only son? No words were adequate to express my feelings. While I adored my lovely daughters, this male child was more a part of me than they, by reason of their very natures, could ever be. I would be able to understand his problems, physical changes, and thoughts in ways in which I was totally bewildered by my daughters. Their very femininity mystified me, and I could only watch in awe as their bodies and personalities altered before me over the years. While Marcie appeared to understand and tolerate their drastic mood changes, I was not only hurt and confused but often infuriated by their seemingly unprecedented and illogical behavior.

My son, I felt certain, would be an entirely different experience. Hopefully, we would share the same interests, and even if we didn't, whatever he chose would never be as alien to me as his sisters' dolls had been.

The immortality of both myself and my family name were now assured, and I was a deliriously happy man. I now had my son and heir. What other words could be more satisfying to any man than those?

CHAPTER 31

Unicorn Dreams

> I have desired to go
>   Where springs not fail,
> To fields where flies no sharp and sided hail,
>   And a few lilies blow.
>   —Gerard Manley Hopkins, 1960

A telegram could instantly convey a feeling of terror. Although they just, as often, announced good news, no one would ever forget the one that proved to be a harbinger of death. Thus, the sight of that narrow yellow envelope had the power to make the blood run cold.

    I would never forget that morning of January 11, 1960. It was a winter morning just like any other. No, thinking back, it was actually better than the ones we had been having. The East Coast had several days before it was hit by a major snowstorm, which had left the city paralyzed. To make matters even worse, temperatures, which plunged below 15 °F, had made the cleanup operations virtually impossible. Telephone and electricity lines were snapping in the frigid air, and abnormal fuel consumption made heating oil, gas, and coal in short supply.

    This particular morning, as we gathered in the kitchen eating breakfast, the radio announcer was predicting temperatures above freezing for the day. Already, we could hear the dripping sounds as our house began to thaw out. The sun was shining; our telephone and electric power had been restored the previous evening, and as the saying goes, "God was in his heaven and all was right with the world!"—or so we foolishly thought.

"Edward, I wonder how Melissa is managing in Manhattan?"

"Stop fussing, Marcie. She's probably doing better than us. If you're really so worried, why don't you phone her now that service is restored?"

"Yes, Mother, you know that if you don't, you'll just spend the whole day worrying," Miranda agreed.

"Tiffany, do you think I'll have to go to school today?"

"Probably, Ted. The roads are fairly well cleared. I'm going to work, and if you hurry, I can drop you off."

Tiffany was now twenty-two years old and a licensed medical practitioner. Even though she hadn't chosen my field of medicine, I was nevertheless very proud of her. You see, she was a veterinarian. Despite the long waiting lists and stringent entrance requirements, Tiffany had trained with the best and graduated in the top ten of her class.

Just then, Marcie returned looking worried. "That's funny, Edward. No one answers at Melissa's apartment."

"So? Maybe she left for work early," I suggested.

"What is she working at this week, Mother?"

"I'm not sure, Ted, but the last time I spoke with her, last Monday, she was working part-time in Bloomingdale's."

"Do you know which department?"

"I think cosmetics, but what difference does that make? It's only eight o'clock. The stores don't open till ten, and she's only a few minutes away."

"Marcie, please calm down. Melissa's been taking care of herself for a long time. I'm sure she's just fine."

"Why don't you call Veronica? Maybe she's heard from Melissa," Miranda suggested.

Our seventeen-year-old daughter Veronica had graduated high school at sixteen and was already in her first year at Columbia's Teaching College. Where I ever got such brilliant children from never failed to astonish me.

As Marcie again left the kitchen to try and phone Veronica, I complacently sat back and fondly watched my two youngest eating pancakes. Fourteen-year-old Miranda was as fair as ever. She hadn't changed over the years. She was still as gentle, sweet, and shy as a tame doe. She was the peacemaker in the family, and although she didn't seem to have the intellectual capacity of Ted, Veronica, or Tiffany, it was to Miranda that everyone brought their problems. While this might seem like a terrible burden for such slender young shoulders, her air of compassion and serenity made her the perfect choice. Even though she was still absorbed in her music and, according to her teachers, showed a great deal of promise, she always found time for the other members of her family.

I had wanted to send her to Juilliard, and her teachers felt certain that she would qualify, but when Miranda actually became desolated at the thought of leaving home, we abandoned the idea. There were times when my gentle daughter frightened me with her obsessive attachment to her home and family. She often worried me by her resemblance to Emily Bronte who actually pined away and became ill when forced to leave her beloved homeland moors for long periods of time.

As she caught me looking at her, she melted my heart with her dulcet smile. I tried to convince myself that I was being a fool. Some young man would someday also be mesmerized by her large cornflower blue eyes, flaxen hair, and loving disposition, and all too soon, she would happily fly the nest.

Fortunately, I was distracted from these maudlin thoughts by my son Ted's impatient request for me to pass the maple syrup, which I had unconsciously been holding on to all this time.

Ted was my pride and joy. He was all that I had hoped for in a son. Although only ten years old, he was already in the seventh grade and, despite having been skipped, was ahead of most of his classmates. Learning seemed to come easily to him, and his memory was amazing. He was the one to turn to when anyone misplaced anything. He could usually remember where you had mislaid the item, and if he hadn't seen you with it, could prod your own memory with his logical and orderly questions.

In many ways, surprisingly enough, he reminded me of Arthur even though Arthur's lack of memory was a constant source of trouble and sometimes even laughter to everyone. Ted was slender, dark, and, from what I could see, would never be taller than medium height. He was an easygoing young fellow and was generally liked by everyone including his teachers and classmates. Despite the fact that he was popular, he still preferred being alone in order to work with his microscope and chemistry set.

"Edward, would you please stop daydreaming! You haven't heard a word I've said."

Not only hadn't I heard Marcie, I hadn't even been aware that she had reentered the room. "Of course, I heard you," I prevaricated. "What did Veronica say about Melissa?"

"If you'd been listening, you would know that Veronica hasn't heard from Melissa all week," Marcie frantically explained.

Before I could think of a calming reply, the doorbell rang, and I hastened to open it. Fully expecting to see a cold and destitute Melissa on our doorstep once again, I was just preparing a scathing tirade on her inconsideration when I was shocked to observe that our caller wasn't Melissa but a Western Union messenger. As I signed for the telegram and fumbled for a tip, I could hear Marcie's lamentations in the background.

"It's Melissa. I just know it. Something dreadful happened." She sobbed.

"Would you at least wait until I read this," I said, tearing at the envelope. "Calm down, Marcie. You're upsetting Ted and Miranda. There, you see? It has nothing to do with Melissa. It's from some attorney named Jeffrey Fuller asking me to phone him at 207-689-3578 after 10:00 a.m."

"Jeffrey Fuller. Do you know who he is?"

"No, Marcie, I've never heard of him."

"You don't suppose anyone could be suing you for malpractice?" she worried.

"I doubt it. If they were, I suppose they'd use a local attorney. I'll find out when I phone him. It's only 8:30 a.m. now, so why don't we just continue about our business?"

"Father," Tiffany queried, "did you say that the area code on that number was 207?"

"That's right. Is it familiar to you?"

"Of course. Don't you recognize it? It's the same as Aunt Alissa's."

"Oh my god! Something's happened to Alissa!"

"Marcie, please don't start that again. Try phoning her."

While Marcie dialed, I tried to mask my own concern. We hadn't heard from Alissa since Christmas, and she had sounded strangely distracted. Although I chalked it up to a bad connection, I had been worried about her and meant to phone her after the New Year, but as usual, I had gotten sidetracked. None of us had seen her since Tiffany had visited her four years previously.

Alissa was sixty-two years old and alone but, as far as I knew, in good health except for the severe headaches which she still suffered from. This was unusual since most women stop getting migraines around the time of menopause. While I had tried to get Alissa to admit herself into the hospital for tests, she had simply shrugged aside my suggestion by jokingly saying that her headaches had remained loyally with her for over forty years, and she'd miss them if they went away.

"Did you get through?"

"No, there's no answer."

"Well, that doesn't mean anything. The lines could be down. She is quite a distance from town, and repair crews probably take a while to get to isolated areas," I counseled.

"No," Ted contradicted, "if the lines were down, you'd get a busy signal or nothing at all." Sometimes he was too smart.

"If the lines are down, how will you reach this Jeffrey Fuller?" Miranda asked.

"Enough!" I exploded. "I will take care of everything. Tiffany, you will be late for work if you don't hurry, and, Ted and Miranda, if you don't move, you will be late for school."

As they all half-heartedly scurried around, I tried to appear unconcerned as I repeatedly read the morning paper's headline.

After the children had left, I tried to distract Marcie by asking about my appointments for the day. With the postwar baby boom, our little village had grown enormously, and I had taken on a young associate. We were now living in a very large old colonial house, one wing of which had been converted into offices, x-ray, and examining rooms. Since Marcie worked as my nurse-receptionist, I hoped that once we began our daily routine, she would calm down.

"Well, nurse," I joked, "my appointments?"

"You don't have any. Don't you remember that the phones have been down for the past few days?"

"I must still have appointments."

"Oh, all right. I'll get the book and check."

As she hurried off, the doorbell rang again. This time, it was my associate Robert Cunningham followed by a bedraggled Melissa.

"Greetings! Look what I found in your driveway." He laughed, pushing Melissa in front of him.

"Where have you been? Damn it, Melissa! Your mother has been worried sick. She's been trying to phone you all morning."

Just as she was about to explain, I impatiently cut her off by yelling, "Not now, Melissa. Go inside to the office and reassure your mother. I'm not interested in listening to your latest failure right now. I have other things on my mind."

"Very well," she said, giving me a withering look and marching off.

"Weren't you a little hard on her?" Robert asked, helping himself to some coffee and spearing one of Miranda's leftover pancakes. Since Robert was a bachelor and always ravenous, I had learned to overlook his unprofessional disregard for germs.

As I explained my problem, he looked concerned and understanding something I really didn't trust since he was known for having cultivated Connecticut's most charming bedside manner.

Finally ten o'clock arrived, and my call to Maine went through.

"Mr. Jeffrey Fuller? This is Dr. Edward Andros. I received your telegram this morning instructing me to phone you."

"Yes, Dr. Andros. I represent Mrs. Alissa Andros. I believe she was at one time your sister-in-law?"

"That's right. Has something happened to Alissa? Is she ill?"

"I'm afraid I have some bad news for you. Mrs. Alissa Andros is dead."

As I felt the room spin around me, I was too stunned to reply.

"Dr. Andros, are you still there?"

"Yes," I said hoarsely.

"I know this is a great shock to you, and I wish that there was some easier way to break the news, but I guess as a doctor, you understand that nothing softens this sort of blow."

"Yes, I do know… How did it happen?"

"We're still not certain. Her body was discovered late yesterday in the woods several miles from her home. Although the doctor's unofficial verdict is death from exposure, there will have to be an autopsy."

"Oh god," I groaned.

"Yes, it is awful, but there's really no choice. This is one of the reasons I'm calling. As a doctor, if you wish to be present, the coroner has agreed to hold off the autopsy until you arrive."

"No," I gasped.

"Well, I guess I can understand that. Mrs. Andros left clear instructions as to funeral arrangements in her will. I also have to tell you that you and your family are beneficiaries in her will. Do you think that you could possibly come up here? I realize that as a doctor, this might be difficult, but it's a complicated will, and I thought you might like to attend the funeral service."

"Yes, of course, I'll try to get a flight today."

"Fine. If you let me know what time you expect to arrive, I will have someone meet you at the airport."

"Thank you. I'll be in touch."

After breaking the terrible news to my family, I arranged for Robert to take over my practice and for Melissa to take care of Ted and Miranda while we were away.

Tiffany insisted on accompanying us, and so Melissa drove the three of us to the airport. After the initial hysterics, we were all grim-faced and numb as we each invariably recalled our own memories and stirred up our own guilts.

It was a short flight, and we insisted on being driven straight to Mr. Fuller's office where the coroner would be waiting with the autopsy results.

There was no doubt that Alissa's death was due to exposure. She had frozen to death. The autopsy, however, also revealed the fact that Alissa was in the advanced stages of brain cancer. According to her doctor, even he had been unaware of this since she had refused to go for tests, and so the possibility of suicide was also ruled out.

The question of what she was doing out in the woods in the middle of a severe snowstorm was impossible to be certain of. Since this form of cancer leads to disorientation and even hallucinations, it was more than possible that some strange impulse of poor Alissa's disease-ridden brain had caused her to leave the safety of her home that day.

Mr. Fuller had made arrangements for us to stay at the inn until the funeral, and so we sadly left his office after agreeing unanimously with the coroner's verdict of death by mischance.

Since Alissa had requested not to be laid out and for a simple graveside service to be conducted immediately, we gathered early the next morning at the cemetery where the Saronnas had been buried. There had been no time to order the usual elaborate floral arrangements, and my heart broke as I looked at the paltry offerings which we clutched. Knowing Alissa's great love of flowers, they seemed very inadequate, and I silently vowed that she would have all the appropriate floral tributes in the next few days.

We were so consumed by grief that I doubt if any of us even heard the words of the twenty-third Psalm which was being read, "Yea though I walk through the valley of the shadow of death I will fear no evil; for thou art with me, thy rod and thy staff they comfort me."

I was so overwhelmed by my own grief that I did little to comfort Tiffany and Marcie who were by now sobbing openly.

After the funeral, we headed like sleepwalkers back to the inn where we would rest until one o'clock when we would again meet at Mr. Fuller's office for the reading of the will.

Mr. Fuller had been correct in that Alissa's will was very detailed. She had left generous bequests to just about everyone that she had ever known, but the full extent of her wealth only became evident when the bequests to my family were read. To Marcie and each of my children, she had left $100,000. In addition, various furs and jewels were distributed among the women and a beautiful antique musical pocketwatch, which had belonged to Mr. Saronna, to be left to me in trust for Ted. Also to me, Mr. Fuller handed a thick envelope which he asked me to open. In it was a sizeable amount of money with a note from Alissa explaining that it was the sum I had paid back to her a little at a time, despite her protests, for putting me through medical school.

Tiffany was also handed a letter which took her quite a while to read. It seemed that she was left the house and farm which were hers to do with as she pleased. The astonishing part was that the letter also asked Tiffany if she would establish and head what was to be known as the Alissa Andros Memorial Foundation.

Seeing Tiffany's face light up and then hearing her burst into tears as she accepted, I realized that she seemed to know what this was all about.

"Aunt Alissa and I discussed it. It's very involved. Could we go into the details later?" she asked a relieved Mr. Fuller.

"I'm really pleased about this, and I know Mrs. Andros would be overjoyed. Of course, I know all about the foundation, but I do want to go over all the details with you at a later date. It will be a million dollar undertaking, you know."

"Million dollar!" we gasped in unison.

"Oh yes. Despite the simple way she lived, Alissa Andros was a very wealthy woman. Well, here are the keys to the house, Ms. Andros, and…oh yes, I almost forgot. There's a special gift for you which Mrs. Andros told me can be found in the center drawer of her desk. It's for your whole family, Mr. Andros, and if I do say so myself, it is really a gift of love."

With these perplexing words in our ears, we set out for Alissa's in the car I had rented that afternoon.

Entering for the first time the house of someone who had died was an eerie and tragic experience. As I unlocked the door, I could tangibly feel Alissa's presence. Glancing at Marcie and Tiffany, I could see that they were affected in the same way. Feeling something brush against my leg, I almost hit the ceiling before I realized that it was one of Alissa's cats. No doubt one of them was descended from Tippy who had died at the ripe old age of twenty. Seeing that their food and water bowls were full, I was glad that someone had arranged for their care.

Since both Marcie and Tiffany were again starting to cry as they lovingly caressed Alissa's belongings, I suggested that we look in her desk as Mr. Fuller had instructed. Unlocking the drawer, I pulled out a nine-by-twelve-inch package bound in heavy paper and flannel. As I slowly unwrapped it, we stared in wide-eyed astonishment at a beautiful Moroccan bound book. It was covered in fine red leather and tooled in twenty-four karat gold. On the cover was the picture of a pure white unicorn rampant whose horn I would later learn was made out of genuine ivory from the tusk of a narwhal. The book was simply entitled *The Unicorn*. Opening it up, I recognized Alissa's delicate writing as I read the inscription, "To the Andros Family, when the world is too much with you, take the time to contemplate a unicorn."

As I glanced reverently through its high-quality parchment pages, I was delighted by the beautiful illustrations and decorative Gothic printing. The book was fashioned after the old medieval illuminated manuscripts and touched on every possible aspect of unicorn lore. Alissa's detailed research was evident in every page. As Mr. Fuller had stated, it certainly was a labor of love. This was definitely the worthy legacy of a very unique woman.

While we were absorbed in the book, we were rudely brought back to reality by the ringing of the doorbell. Opening the door, I spotted a sheriff's car and three men waiting to enter.

"Hello. I'm Sheriff Hawthorne. I wonder if we could step in for a minute."

"Of course. I'm Dr. Edward Andros, and this is my wife, Marcie, and my daughter Tiffany. Is there some problem?"

"No, no. Just thought I'd stop by to extend my condolences. Mrs. Andros was a fine woman... Oh yeah, these two are Mr. Nathen Cromwell and his son Jeb. They're the ones who found the bod...uh, I mean Mrs. Andros," he said, reddening.

"Pleased to meet you. Mr. Cromwell, could you tell us about finding Alissa?"

"Well, guess you know all the important facts already," he said warily.

"Come on, Nate. Just tell the folks how you came to find her," the sheriff urged.

"W-well, Jeb and I were out trapping when Jeb here trips over this here mound of snow. Since he's kind of clumsy, I didn't pay it no mind till Jeb started yelling for me to take a look. Well, you could have knocked me over with a feather when we realized it was a woman. Real hard to tell at first. You see, besides all the snow, she was dressed in all white. If old Jeb here hadn't tripped over her, we'd never have spotted the old girl. Ain't that right, Jeb?"

"Yeah, Pa."

"You see, she had on white pants and boots and a white parka with the hood up. At first glance, I thought old Jeb had found a big white animal." He laughed uneasily.

Seeing our distressed looks, he cleared his throat and went on. "Well, we knew she was dead right away, so we improvised a sort of stretcher and carried her back to our place and called the sheriff. Guess you know the rest."

"Thank you," I said simply from want of anything else to say.

"Hey, Doc, what do you think the old girl was doing out in the woods anyway?" Jeb asked.

"I don't know for sure. The autopsy revealed brain cancer, and this could have caused some kind of delusions."

"Well, it's a shame. Sorry about it, you know."

"Thanks for coming over. It was good of you," I said, ushering them out the door.

Just as they were about to leave, Jeb turned around and asked, "Hey, Doc, did they ever find out what that strange white fur was that the old lady had clutched in her hands?"

"Now, Jeb, you know the sheriff said not to worry these folks about that. All the same, it sure was strange. I've been a trapper for over thirty years, and I never saw the likes of it before."

Looking embarrassed, the sheriff explained that all the lab tests had failed to analyze the fur, but sooner or later, they'd find out what it was.

"Almost like a horse's hair," he elaborated, "but real soft. Like fur but different than the parka. It's probably some new synthetic stuff. Boys in the lab are sending it out to a larger lab tomorrow. We'll find out what it is. Don't worry, we'll keep you folks informed. Good night."

After Marcie and Tiffany were asleep, I got out of bed and wandered around, my head filled with loving thoughts of Alissa. Walking into Alissa's study, I noticed an envelope on the floor which must have accidentally fallen out of the desk drawer. As I picked it up, a photograph fell out. It was the missing third photo of Alissa in her belly dancing costume. Looking at the postmark, I saw that it had been mailed on January 3, 1940, from London, only five days after Uncle Teddy's death. It seemed that Roderick had come across the picture when going through his father's things and felt that it would comfort Alissa to know that Uncle Teddy had kept it for so many years. Well, that was one mystery solved.

There was still the mystery of Alissa's death. Seated at her desk, one of the many pages of notes, which were piled on it, caught my eye. On it was written, "In the seventeenth century, Dr. Olfert Dapper claimed to have sighted unicorns in the woods of northern Maine and on the Canadian border."

Epilogue

> That nothing walks with aimless feet;
>   That not one life shall be destroyed,
>   Or cast as rubbish to the void,
> When God hath made the pie complete.
> —Tennyson, 1980

The Alissa Andros Animal Clinic and Shelter is the result of the multimillion-dollar memorial foundation. It is a lovely sprawling complex which is renowned for its advanced medical and research procedures.

It seems that Tiffany and her Aunt Alissa had often discussed the details of the clinic down to the most minute aspect. They had even drawn up rough diagrams and blueprints for it. While Tiffany enjoyed all of this, she never really believed that it would become a reality. More likely, it would be as elusive of a dream as…the capture of a unicorn…*a unicorn dream.*

Tiffany revels in her running of the clinic, and despite all this entails, she also is responsible for handpicking the personnel. She appears to have a natural instinct where this is concerned and relies heavily on her instincts along with the scholastic records of her applicants. As she has often explained, compassion and a genuine love for animals are the two major prerequisites in being considered for a position at either the clinic or the shelter.

They never turn away an animal because of the owner's inability to pay and have a sliding scale for fees. Fortunately, their work is so highly regarded that large contributions from animal lovers all over the country keep pouring in.

They also have another way of making money. Alissa also left the foundation a surprise gift. While exploring the farm, we came across a large well-maintained barn which was locked. Upon finally discovering the right key, we were amazed to find that it was filled with treasures of its own. It contained row after row of beautifully maintained antique automobiles. It seems that both Alissa and the Saronnas had certain automobiles to which they had formed deep attachments. Among the many are the 1898 locomotor which Gabrial Saronna had possessed at the time of Alissa's birth. There are also, to my delight, Alissa's 1927 Niagara blue Roadster (my particular favorite) and two Bentleys, one from 1928 which had belonged to the Saronnas and the other to Alissa in 1936. I am also happy to see Alissa's 1946 white Rolls-Royce among the treasures. These automobiles have been responsible for raising not only funds but also publicity for the foundation.

Tiffany is married to one of the veterinarians at the clinic, and although they have no children, with over two hundred cats and dogs in the shelter plus the various sick and injured animals inhabiting the clinic, they don't seem to miss them.

I suppose it was inevitable that I would also lose Ted to the clinic. He had made annual visits to it since its establishment in 1965. *Time* magazine did an article on him, and he has received many humanitarian awards along with Tiffany for his advanced research and introduction of new surgical techniques. He is certainly a son to be proud of.

He is married to a charming young woman who supervises the shelter. They have two daughters and one son and another on the way. No one can say that he has time for nothing but his work!

Melissa has attained some success as a model. You might even have seen her on the glossy covers of various magazines. Her private life is less successful. She has been married and divorced three times.

Her first marriage was to my associate Robert Cunningham in 1963. When this ended, she not only broke up a marriage but also his medical career in conservative Connecticut due to her scandalous behavior. She did leave him with the custody of their only child, a daughter named Amanda, who is as headstrong, saucy, and beautiful as her mother.

Veronica has a PhD in education. She never got married and is a huge success in her field. For the last few years, I have enjoyed receiving letters and postcards from her from all over Europe where she is doing research for a book on comparative educational techniques.

My gentle Miranda never did marry and seems content playing her piano and looking after her old father since the death of my beloved wife, Marcie, six years ago. She died peacefully in her sleep when her gentle heart gave out. It is a subject still too painful for me to dwell on.

I am an old man now and will be happy to go when my time comes. I have just about outlived my usefulness anyway, and most of my contemporaries are gone.

Thanks to Alissa again, I need have no fears for Miranda's future. Tiffany, Ted, and the others are all looking forward to having Miranda join them in Maine where her gentleness and compassion will be great assets in running the shelter.

Richard is still alive at eighty-two years of age. He is independent and very crotchety. He continues to inhabit the old Andros abode and seems to take great pleasure in bossing around his housekeeper and nurse.

Arthur and Dee Dee weren't so lucky. They both died in their sleep in front of the TV in 1968 when their heater sprung a gas leak. At least it was a peaceful death, and they were partaking their favorite pastime.

Catheleen Carwood cared for her father George until his death in 1965. She afterward married one of the executives of her great uncle's sewing machine company. With Arthur's death, I failed to hear any more about her.

Her brother Patrick was, for a while, a cause célèbre. It seems that he was caught trying to set fire to the Victory Sewing Machine Company and was responsible for various other fires in the area. When someone questioned him about the fire at Joyeuse Garde, over thirty years before, he merely laughed hysterically as he was dragged off to Pilgrim State Hospital for psychiatric care.

Sitting here, looking over again Alissa's beautiful book *The Unicorn*, my heart aches for the days that were. I miss Alissa almost as much as I do Marcie, but these thoughts become too painful to be borne, so I think of other things.

That fur which Alissa was found clutching has always puzzled me, and it seems everyone else as well. I like to think that perhaps Alissa, like Dr. Olfert Dapper, found her unicorn in the woods of Maine. While to some, this might sound ridiculous, stranger things have been known to happen… And after all, the older I become, the more convinced I am that the passage of time tends to transform the rare and extraordinary into the commonplace.

About the Author

Amber Stryker is a die-hard New Yorker having been born in Manhattan, raised in Queens, and presently lives on the South Shore of Long Island in Western Suffolk County. She and her late husband of forty-eight years devoted much of their leisure time to saving abandoned and abused cats. The cats plus Long Island are often featured in her writing.

Ms. Stryker, who has degrees in both English and literature, published a cat newsletter that had a large following for over twenty years. She was awarded the Harmony Editors' Award for Excellence. She is the author of her new book *Unicorn Dreams*, an amusing family saga that spans three generations. She is currently working on completing a historic romance that takes place during the reign of Edward II of England. Regardless of the genre she is writing, Ms. Stryker approaches them all with thorough research, intelligence, and humor.

CPSIA information can be obtained
at www.ICGtesting.com
Printed in the USA
JSHW022114260323
39499JS00001B/29